Ecstasy and Terror

Ecstasy and Terror

From the Greeks to
Game of Thrones

DANIEL MENDELSOHN

nyrb **New York Review Books** New York

This is a New York Review Book

published by The New York Review of Books

435 Hudson Street, New York, NY 10014

www.nyrb.com

Library of Congress Cataloging-in-Publication Data
Names: Mendelsohn, Daniel Adam, 1960– author. | Levin, Anna, 1961–
Title: Ecstasy and terror : from the Greeks to Game of Thrones / by
   Daniel Mendelsohn.
Description: New York : New York Review Books, [2019]
Identifiers: LCCN 2019012373 (print) | LCCN 2019981315 (ebook) |
   ISBN 9781681374055 (alk. paper) | ISBN 9781681374093 (ebook)
Subjects: LCSH: Literature, Modern—Classical influences. |
   Civilization, Western—Classical influences. | Classical literature—
   Influence. | Civilization, Classical—Influence. | Civilization,
   Ancient, in popular culture. | Mendelsohn, Daniel. | Critics—United
   States—Biography. | Film critics—United States—Biography.
Classification: LCC PN883 M46 2019 (print) | LCC PN883 (ebook) |
   DDC 801/.95—dc23
LC record available at https://lccn.loc.gov/2019012373
LC ebook record available at https://lccn.loc.gov/2019981315

ISBN 978-1-68137-405-5
Available as an electronic book; ISBN 978-1-68137-409-3

Printed in the United States of America on acid-free paper

10 9 8 7 6 5 4 3 2 1

For Lily Knezevich

Contents

Preface

IN THE AUTUMN OF 1990, when I was thirty years old and halfway through my doctoral thesis on Greek tragedy, I started submitting book and film reviews to various magazines and newspapers; a few of these were accepted, and within a year I'd decided to leave academia and try my hand at being a full-time writer.

On hearing of my plans, my father, a taciturn mathematician who I knew had abandoned his own PhD thesis many years earlier, urged me with uncommon heat to finish my degree. "Just in case the writing thing doesn't work out!" he grumbled. Mostly to placate him and my mother—I'd already stretched my parents' patience, to say nothing of their resources, by studying Greek as an undergraduate and then pursuing the graduate degree—I agreed to stay the course. I finished my thesis (about the role of women in two obscure and rather lumpy plays by Euripides) in 1994 and took the degree. A week after the graduation ceremony I moved to a one-room apartment in New York City and started freelancing full-time.

This bit of autobiography should help explain both the style and content of much of my writing over the past three decades. Back in the mid-1990s, when I was first settling into my writing life, I was eager to write about genres and subjects (movies, theater, music videos, opera, television; family history, parenthood, sexuality) that I would never have been able to delve into as an academic classicist.

This I began to do. But early on in my freelancing career I was often asked by editors who were aware that I'd done a degree in classics to review, say, a new translation of the *Iliad*, or a big-budget TV adaptation of the *Odyssey*, or a modern-dress production of *Medea*. I ended up finding real pleasure in these assignments, largely because they allowed me to write about the classics in a way that was, finally, congenial to me. My graduate school years had coincided with a period in academic scholarship remembered today for its risibly dense jargon and rebarbative theoretical posturing. In writing for the mainstream press about the ancient cultures that I'd studied, I could think and talk about the Greeks and Romans in a way that for me was more natural, more conversational—putting my training in the service of getting readers to love and appreciate the works that I myself loved and appreciated. And yet, when writing about movies, or TV series, or current fiction, I often found myself invoking the classics as models for thinking about contemporary culture. That cross-pollination between the classics and popular culture has characterized most of my writing.

The desire to present the ancient Greeks and Romans and their culture in a way that meaningfully connects the past to the present informs many of the pieces in the first part of this collection. One examines the furor over the burial of Tamerlan Tsarnaev, one of the Boston Marathon bombers, in the light of Sophocles's *Antigone*—still the most relevant of Western texts about certain pressing moral questions, not least the dignity in death to which even our enemies are entitled. In another, the fiftieth anniversary of the assassination of John Fitzgerald Kennedy allows me to ponder the enduring fascination of that culturally traumatic historical event, which, I argue, lingers in the national consciousness precisely because it so uncannily replays important elements from myth. A recent essay occasioned by a new translation of the *Aeneid* finds that Virgil's epic turns out to have surprising contemporary resonance, anticipating as it does the great historical horrors of the twentieth century: mass extermination, refugee crises, the fragmentation of personality that results from trauma.

And yet the mirror of the past is sometimes a distorting one: the likeness that we often want to see between ourselves and the Greeks and Romans can be deceptive. In some of these "Ancient" essays, I focus on the ways in which our interpretations and adaptations of the classical can ultimately say more about us than they do about the ancients. As I argue in a review of a recent book about the Parthenon, our eagerness to see that famous ruin as the iconic classical building prevents us from appreciating how avant-garde it was when it was built; a new translation of Sappho provides an occasion to think about why that poet with her intense, eroticized subjectivity has meant so much to us today—although what she means to us turns out to be quite different from what she may have meant to the Greeks. This section of the collection ends with my essay on the modern Greek poet Constantine Cavafy. A twentieth-century writer who repeatedly turned to Archaic, Classical, Hellenistic, and Byzantine Greek history and literature for his inspiration, Cavafy created a body of work that pays homage to the ancient Hellenic history while discouraging any facile parallels with the present: a model of how to simultaneously reanimate and refashion the past through writing.

Most of the twenty essays collected here are not about the classics per se—although inevitably, and I hope interestingly, some of them betray the influence of my classical background. (Hence a review of a pair of recent movies about artificial intelligence, *Ex Machina* and *Her*, begins—necessarily, as I see it—with a consideration of the robots that appear in Homer's *Iliad* and what they imply about how we think about the relationship between automation and humanity.) Just over half of the critical essays here survey writers and writing of the recent past, along with films and television: from Evelyn Waugh to John Williams (whose *Augustus*, a fictional evocation of the Roman emperor, is his finest treatment of themes that go back to his posthumously best-selling *Stoner*) to Henry Roth and the philhellenic British travel writer Patrick Leigh Fermor. Here once again, what often interests me is not only the book I happen to be reviewing but what our reaction to the work or its author says about us: how the fervent critical embrace of Hanya Yanagihara's *A Little Life*, with its baroque aestheticization of physical and emotional trauma, mirrors (and could only arise in) a culture obsessed with victimhood, or how the intensely solipsistic worldview of Karl Ove Knausgård's novels reflects—while bringing to impressive artistic heights—the ethos of the blog.

Certain themes and subjects recur in many of these pieces, both ancient and modern. How could they not? However many genres a critic may write about, however varied the subjects may be, the writing itself always reflects personal predilections, tastes, interests. Some of these are intellectual. My essay on the representation of women and power in *Game of Thrones* is a direct descendant of my dissertation on "brides of death" in Euripides's dramas; the questions I first explored in the thesis, about how male writers represent extremes of female suffering, is one that has surfaced in many pieces I've written over the years, on authors from Euripides to Tennessee Williams and Michael Cunningham. Sometimes the recurrent themes are more clearly personal. My interest in Sappho and how we may or may not be getting her sexuality wrong, or in the complex ways in which Cavafy's poetry balances his interest in history with his homosexual yearnings, is obviously connected to the fact that I am gay myself.

This brings me to the title of this collection, borrowed from my essay on Euripides's *Bacchae*. It is no accident that the emotions to which that title refers, and which recur through so many of the works discussed in the following pages—from the ecstatic longings of Sappho and Cavafy to the abject terror that interests me in *Bacchae* or *Game of Thrones* or *A Little Life*—are the extreme ones characteristic of the two genres that first captured my imagination when I was a teenager: opera, Greek tragedy. For me as with so many closeted adolescents of my generation, there was a kind of comfort to be derived from finding, in drama and art, extreme representations of the emotions we dared not express in public: the ecstasy of desire, the terror of being found out. The thrill of encountering such high emotion, whether in drama or literature, novels or television series, and the resultant craving, once the flush of excited recognition was past, to understand the artistic mechanics by which that emotion had been produced on stage or on the page—to figure out how the feeling "I" intersects with the work—were, I imagine, the beginnings of the critical impulse.

This autobiographical consideration leads me to the third and final section here. *Ecstasy and Terror* is the first collection I've published that includes examples of my personal writing, as distinct from my critical writing—a distinction that, however, I'm beginning to find invidious. Just as my criticism necessarily reflects my personal interests, my autobiographical writing has always been inflected by the fact that I am a critic. In each of my book-length memoirs—*The Elusive Embrace, The Lost, An Odyssey*—the personal narrative is entwined with a reading of some ancient text: Sappho and Catullus, Genesis, Homer's epics. So it should come as no surprise that this volume concludes with ostensibly personal narratives in which my critical interests make an appearance: the Greeks, powerful female figures, historical trauma, homosexuality, autobiographical writing. In the longest of the pieces collected here, for instance, I recall my youthful epistolary relationship with the historical novelist Mary Renault, whose work I analyze even as I describe our long-distance friendship: she did much to encourage both my love of Greek culture—which, in my adolescent mind, was complicatedly connected to my growing awareness of my homosexuality—and my desire to be a writer. The final piece here, commissioned by *The New Yorker* during a recent controversy about the place of criticism in contemporary culture, expands a reminiscence of what that magazine's critics meant to me when I first read them as a teenager into a larger statement about what I think criticism should be. That "manifesto" can be read as a retrospective statement about what the other essays here have strived to accomplish.

All but two of the pieces here were written for periodicals, and such editing as has been done for this volume served merely to smooth out certain roughnesses or approximations that are inevitably the result of writing to a deadline. (The exceptions are the essays on *Bacchae* and on Cavafy, which were written as introductions to new translations, the latter to my own translation of the Alexandrian poet. Both appear here in the form they took when republished in *The New York Review of Books*.) Those datelines are meant as a reminder that every piece of criticism—every piece of writing, really—arises out of a certain moment in its author's life, a certain way of thinking about a subject. The author overseeing the selection of essays for a collection like this one, which stretches across half a career's worth of writing, is not necessarily the same person who first wrote some of those essays. These collections may be thought of as maps of an intellectual journey—one that, like Odysseus's, takes years to complete. For me—to quote Cavafy's most famous poem, "Ithaca"—the road has been "a long one, filled with adventures, filled with discoveries." I hope the same is true for the reader of these pages.

I. Ancients

Girl, Interrupted

ONE DAY NOT LONG AFTER New Year's 2012, an antiquities collector approached an eminent Oxford scholar for his opinion about some brownish, tattered scraps of writing. The collector's identity has never been revealed, but the scholar was Dirk Obbink, a MacArthur-winning classicist whose specialty is the study of texts written on papyrus—the material, made of plant fibers, that was the paper of the ancient world. When pieced together, the scraps that the collector showed Obbink formed a fragment about seven inches long and four inches wide: a little larger than a woman's hand. Densely covered with lines of black Greek characters, they had been extracted from a piece of desiccated cartonnage, a papier-mâché-like plaster that the Egyptians and Greeks used for everything from mummy cases to book bindings. After acquiring the cartonnage at a Christie's auction, the collector soaked it in a warm-water solution to free up the precious bits of papyrus.

Judging from the style of the handwriting, Obbink estimated that it dated to around 200 AD. But as he looked at the curious pattern of the lines—repeated sequences of three long lines followed by a short fourth—he saw that the text, a poem whose beginning had disappeared but of which five stanzas were still intact, had to be older.

Much older: about a thousand years more ancient than the papyrus itself. The dialect, diction, and meter of these Greek verses were all typical of the work of Sappho, the seventh-century-BC lyric genius whose sometimes playful, sometimes anguished songs about her susceptibility to the graces of younger women bequeathed us the adjectives "sapphic" and "lesbian" (from the island of Lesbos, where she lived). The four-line stanzas were part of a schema that she is said to have invented, called the "sapphic stanza." To clinch the identification, two names mentioned in the poem were ones that several ancient sources attribute to Sappho's brothers. The text is now known as the "Brothers Poem."

Remarkably enough, this was the second major Sappho find in a decade: another nearly complete poem, about the deprivations of old age, came to light in 2004. The new additions to the extant corpus of antiquity's greatest female artist were reported in papers around the world, leaving scholars gratified and a bit dazzled. "Papyrological finds," as one classicist put it, "ordinarily do not make international headlines."

But then Sappho is no ordinary poet. For the better part of three millennia, she has been the subject of furious controversies—about her work, her family life, and, above all, her sexuality. In antiquity, literary critics praised her "sublime" style, even as comic playwrights ridiculed her allegedly loose morals. Legend has it that the early church burned her works. ("A sex-crazed whore who sings of her own wantonness," one theologian wrote, just as a scribe was meticulously copying out the lines that Obbink deciphered.) A millennium passed, and Byzantine grammarians were regretting that so little of her poetry had survived. Seven centuries later, Victorian scholars were doing their best to explain away her erotic predilections, while their literary contemporaries, the Decadents and the Aesthetes, seized on her verses for inspiration. Even today, experts can't agree on whether the poems were performed in private or in public, by soloists or by choruses, or, indeed, whether they were meant to celebrate or to subvert the conventions of love and marriage. The last is a particularly loaded issue, given that for many readers and scholars, Sappho has been a feminist heroine or a gay role model, or both. "As far as I knew, there was only me and a woman called Sappho," the critic Judith Butler once remarked.

Now the first English version of Sappho's works to include the recent finds has appeared: *Sappho: A New Translation of the Complete Works*, with translations by Diane J. Rayor and a thoroughgoing introduction by André Lardinois, a Sappho specialist who teaches in the Netherlands. (Publication of the book was delayed by several months to accommodate the "Brothers Poem.") It will come as no surprise to those who have followed the Sappho wars that the new poems have created new controversies.

The greatest problem for Sappho studies is that there's so little Sappho to study. It would be hard to think of another poet whose status is so disproportionate to the size of her surviving body of work.

We don't even know how much of her poetry Sappho actually wrote down. The ancients referred to her works as *melê*, "songs." Composed to be sung to the accompaniment of a lyre—this is what "lyric" poetry meant for the Greeks—they may well have been passed down from memory by her admirers and other poets before being committed at last to paper. (Or whatever. One fragment, in which the poet calls on Aphrodite, the goddess of love, to come into a charming shrine "where cold water ripples through apple branches, the whole place shadowed in roses," was scribbled onto a broken clay pot.) Like other great poets of the time, she would have been a musician and a performer as well as a lyricist. She was credited with having invented a certain kind of lyre and the plectrum.

Four centuries after her death, scholars at the Library of Alexandria catalogued nine "books"—papyrus scrolls—of Sappho's poems, organized primarily by meter. Book 1, for instance, gathered all the poems that had been composed in the sapphic stanza—the verse form Obbink recognized in the "Brothers Poem." This book alone reportedly contained thirteen hundred and twenty lines of verse; the contents of all nine volumes may have amounted to some ten thousand lines. So much of Sappho was circulating in antiquity that one Greek author, writing three centuries after her death, confidently predicted that "the white columns of Sappho's lovely song endure / and will endure, speaking out loud . . . as long as ships sail from the Nile."

By the Middle Ages, nearly everything had disappeared. As with much of classical literature, texts of her work existed in relatively few copies, all painstakingly transcribed by hand; as the centuries passed, fire, flood, neglect, and bookworms—to say nothing of disapproving Church Fathers—took their devastating toll. Market forces were also at work. Over time, fewer readers—and fewer scribes—understood Aeolic, the dialect in which Sappho composed, and so demand for new copies diminished. A twelfth-century Byzantine scholar who had hoped to write about her grumbled that "both Sappho and her works, the lyrics and the songs, have been trashed by time."

Until a hundred years ago or so, when papyrus fragments of her poems started turning up, all that remained of those "white columns of Sappho's song" was a handful of lines quoted in the works of later Greek and Roman authors. Some of these writers were interested in Lesbos's most famous daughter for reasons that can strike us as comically arcane: the only poem that has survived in its entirety—a playful hymn to Aphrodite in which the poet calls upon the goddess to be her "comrade in arms" in an erotic escapade —was saved for posterity because the author of a first-century-BC treatise called "On the Arrangement of Words" admired her handling of vowels. At present, scholars have catalogued around two hundred and fifty fragments, of which fewer than seventy contain complete lines. A great many consist of just a few words; some, of a single word.

The common theme of most ancient responses to Sappho's work is rapturous admiration for her exquisite style or for her searing content, or both. An anecdote from a later classical author about the Athenian legislator Solon, a contemporary of Sappho's and one of the Seven Sages of Greece, is typical:

> Solon of Athens, son of Execestides, after hearing his nephew singing a song of Sappho's over the wine, liked the song so much that he told the boy to teach it to him. When someone asked him why he was so eager, he replied, "so that I may learn it and then die."

Plato, whose attitude toward literature was, to say the least, vexed— he thought most poetry had no place in the ideal state—is said to have called her the "Tenth Muse." The scholars at the Library of Alexandria enshrined her in their canon of nine lyric geniuses—the only woman to be included. At least two towns on Lesbos vied for the distinction of being her birthplace; Aristotle reports that she "was honored although she was a woman."

All this buzz is both titillating and frustrating, stoking our appetite for a body of work that we're unable to read, much less assess critically: imagine what the name Homer would mean to Western civilization if all we had of the *Iliad* and the *Odyssey* was their reputations and ninety lines of each poem. The Greeks, in fact, seem to have thought of Sappho as the female counterpart of Homer: he was known as "the Poet," and they referred to her as "the Poetess." Many scholars now see her poetry as an attempt to appropriate and "feminize" the diction and subject matter of heroic epic. (For instance, the appeal to Aphrodite to be her "comrade in arms"—in love.)

The good news is that the surviving fragments of Sappho bear out the ancient verdict. One fine example is her best-known verse, known to classicists as Fragment 31, which consists of four sapphic stanzas. (They appear below in my own translation.) These were singled out by the author of a first-century-AD literary treatise called "On the Sublime" for the way in which they "select and juxtapose the most striking, intense symptoms of erotic passion." Here the speaker expresses her envy of the men who, presumably in the course of certain kinds of social occasions, have a chance to talk to the girl she yearns for:

He seems to me an equal of the gods—
whoever gets to sit across from you
and listen to the sound of your sweet speech
so close to him,

to your beguiling laughter: O it makes my
panicked heart go fluttering in my chest,

for the moment I catch sight of you there's no
speech left in me,

but tongue gags—: all at once a faint
fever courses down beneath the skin,
eyes no longer capable of sight, a thrumming
in the ears,

and sweat drips down my body, and the shakes
lay siege to me all over, and I'm greener
than grass, I'm just a little short of dying,
I seem to me;

but all must be endured, since even a pauper…

Even without its final lines (which, maddeningly, the author of the treatise didn't go on to quote), it's a remarkable work. Slyly, the speaker avoids physical description of the girl, instead evoking her beauty by detailing the effect it has on the beholder; the whole poem is a kind of reaction shot. The verses subtly enact the symptoms they describe: as the poet's faculties fail one by one in the overpowering presence of her beloved, the outside world—the girl, the man she's talking to—dissolves and disappears from the poem, too, leaving the speaker in a kind of interior echo chamber. The arc from "he seems to me" in the first line to the solipsistic "I seem to me" at the end says it all.

Even the tiniest scraps can be potent, as Rayor's plainspoken and comprehensive translation makes clear. (Until now, the most noteworthy English version to include translations of virtually every fragment was *If Not, Winter*, published by the poet and classicist Anne Carson in 2002.) To flip through these truncated texts is a strangely moving experience, one that has been compared to "reading a note in a bottle":

You came, I yearned for you,
and you cooled my senses that burned with desire

or

love shook my senses
like wind crashing on mountain oaks

or

Maidenhood, my maidenhood, where have you gone
leaving me behind?
Never again will I come to you, never again

or

Once again Love, that loosener of limbs,
bittersweet and inescapable, crawling thing,
seizes me.

It's in that last verse that the notion of desire as "bittersweet" appears for the first time in Western literature.

The very incompleteness of the verses can heighten the starkness of the emotions—a fact that a number of contemporary classicists and translators have made much of. For Stanley Lombardo, whose *Complete Poems and Fragments: Sappho* (2002) offers a selection of about a quarter of the fragments, the truncated remains are like "beautiful, isolated limbs." Thomas Habinek, a classicist at the University of Southern California, has nicely summed up this rather postmodern aspect of Sappho's appeal: "The fragmentary preservation of poems of yearning and separation serves as a reminder of the inevitable incompleteness of human knowledge and affection."

In Sappho's biography, as in her work, gaps predominate. A few facts can be inferred by triangulating various sources: the poems themselves, ancient reference works, citations in later classical writers who had access to information that has since been lost. The *Suda*, a tenth-century Byzantine encyclopedia of ancient culture, which is the basis of much of our information, asserts that Sappho "flourished" between 612 and 608 BC; from this, scholars have concluded that she was born around 640. She was likely past middle age when she died, since in at least one poem she complains about her graying hair and cranky knees.

Although her birthplace cannot be verified, Sappho seems to have lived mostly in Mytilene, the capital of Lesbos. Just across the strip of water that separates Lesbos from the mainland of Asia Minor (present-day Turkey) was the opulent city of Sardis, the capital of Lydia. Some classicists have argued that the proximity of Lesbos to this lush Eastern trading hub helps to explain Sappho's taste for visual gorgeousness and sensual luxury: the "myrrh, cassia, and frankincense," the "bracelets, fragrant / purple robes, iridescent trinkets, / countless silver cups, and ivory" that waft and glitter in her lines, often in striking counterpoint to their raw emotionality.

Mytilene was constantly seething with political and social dramas occasioned by rivalries and shifting alliances among aristocratic clans. Sappho belonged to one of these—there's a fragment in which she chastises a friend "of bad character" for siding with a rival clan— and a famous literary contemporary, a poet called Alcaeus, belonged to another. Alcaeus often refers to the island's political turbulence in his poems, and it's possible that at some point Sappho and her family fled, or were exiled, to southern Italy: Cicero refers in one of his speeches to a statue of the poet that had been erected in the town hall of Syracuse, in Sicily. The Victorian critic John Addington Symonds saw the unstable political milieu of Sappho's homeland as entwined with the heady erotic climate of her poems. Lesbos, he wrote in an 1872 essay on the poet, was "the island of overmastering passions."

Some things seem relatively certain, then. But when it comes to Sappho's personal life—the aspect of her biography that scholars and readers are most eager to know about—the ancient record is confused. What did she look like? A dialogue by Plato, written in the fourth century BC, refers to her as "beautiful"; a later author insisted that she was "very ugly, being short and swarthy." Who were her family? The *Suda* (which gives eight possible names for Sappho's father) asserts that she had a daughter and a mother both named Kleïs, a gaggle of brothers, and a wealthy husband named Kerkylas from the island of Andros. But some of these seemingly precious facts merely show that the encyclopedia—which, as old as it is, was compiled fifteen centuries after Sappho lived—could be prone to comic misunderstandings. "Kerkylas," for instance, looks a lot like *kerkos*, Greek slang for "penis," and "Andros" is very close to the word for "man"; and so the encyclopedia turns out to have been unwittingly recycling a tired old joke about oversexed Sappho, who was married to "Dick of Man."

Many other alleged facts of Sappho's biography similarly dissolve on close scrutiny. Was Sappho really a mother? There is indeed a fragment that mentions a girl named Kleïs, "whose form resembles golden blossoms," but the word that some people have translated as "daughter" can also mean "child," or even "slave." (Because Greek children were often named for their grandparents, it's easy to see how the already wobbly assumption that Kleïs must have been a daughter in turn led to the assertion that Sappho had a mother with the same name.) Who were the members of her circle? The *Suda* refers by name to three female "students" and three female companions—Atthis, Telesippa, and Megara—with whom she had "disgraceful friendships." But much of this is no more than can be reasonably extrapolated from the poems, since the extant verses mention nearly all those names. The compilers of the *Suda*, like scholars today, may have been making educated guesses.

Even Sappho's sexuality, which for general audiences is the most famous thing about her, has been controversial from the start. However exalted her reputation among the ancient literati, in Greek popular culture of the Classical period and afterward Sappho was known primarily as an oversexed predator—of men. This, in fact, was the ancient cliché about "lesbians": when we hear the word today we think of love between women, but when the ancient

Greeks heard it they thought of fellatio. In classical Greek, the verb *lesbiazein*—"to act like someone from Lesbos"—meant "to perform oral sex," an activity for which inhabitants of the island were thought to have a particular penchant. Comic playwrights and authors of light verse portrayed Sappho as just another daughter of Lesbos, only too happy to fall into bed with her younger male rivals.

For centuries, the most popular story about her love life was one about a hopeless passion for a handsome young boatman called Phaon, which allegedly led her to jump off a cliff. That tale has been embroidered, dramatized, and novelized over the centuries by writers from Ovid—who in one poem has Sappho abjectly renouncing her gay past—to Erica Jong, in her novel *Sappho's Leap* (2003). As fanciful as it is, it's easy to see how this melodrama of heterosexual passion could have been inspired by her verse, which so often describes the anguish of unrequited love. ("You have forgotten me / or you love someone else more.") The added element of suicide suggests that those who wove this improbable story wanted us to take away a moral: unfettered expressions of great passion will have dire consequences.

As time went on, the fantasies about Sappho's private life became more extreme. Midway through the first century AD, the Roman philosopher Seneca, tutor to Nero, was complaining about a Greek scholar who had devoted an entire treatise to the question of whether Sappho was a prostitute. Some ancient writers assumed that there had to have been two Sapphos: one the great poet, the other the notorious slut. There is an entry for each in the *Suda*.

The uncertainties plaguing the biography of literature's most famous lesbian explain why classicists who study Sappho like to cite the entry for her in Monique Wittig and Sande Zeig's *Lesbian Peo-*

ples: Material for a Dictionary (1979). To honor Sappho's central position in the history of female homosexuality, the two editors devoted an entire page to her. The page is blank.

The controversies about Sappho's sexuality have never been far from the center of scholarship about her. Starting in the early nineteenth century, when classics was becoming a formal discipline, scholars who were embarrassed by what they found in the fragments worked hard to whitewash Sappho's reputation. The title of one early work of German scholarship is *Sappho Liberated from a Prevalent Prejudice*: in it, the author acknowledged that what Sappho felt for her female friends was "love" but hastened to insist that it was in no way "objectionable, vulgarly sensual, and illegal," and that her poems of love were neither "monstrous nor abominable."

The eagerness to come up with "innocent" explanations for the poet's attachment to young women persisted through the late nineteenth century and into the twentieth. The most tenacious theory held that Sappho was the head of a girls' boarding school, a matron whose interest in her pupils was purely pedagogical. (One scholar claimed to have found evidence that classes were taught on how to apply makeup.) Another theory made her into an august priestess who led "an association of young women who devoted themselves to the cult of the goddess."

Most classicists today have no problem with the idea of a gay Sappho. But some have been challenging the interpretation of her work that seems most natural to twenty-first-century readers: that the poems are deeply personal expressions of private homoerotic passion. Pointing to the relentlessly public and communitarian character of ancient Greek society, with its clan allegiances, its endless rounds of athletic games and artistic competitions, its jammed calendar of civic and religious festivals, they wonder whether "personal" poetry, as we understand the term, even existed for someone like Sappho. As Lardinois, the co-author of the new English edition, has written, "Can we be sure that these are really her own feelings? . . . What is 'personality' in such a group-oriented society as archaic Greece?"

Indeed, the vision of Sappho as a solitary figure pouring out her heart in the women's quarters of a nobleman's mansion is a sentimental anachronism—a projection, like so much of our thinking about her, of our own habits and institutions onto the past. In Lawrence Alma-Tadema's painting *Sappho and Alcaeus*, the poetess and four diaphanously clad, flower-wreathed acolytes relax in a charming little performance space, enraptured as the male bard sings and plays, as if he were a Beat poet in a Telegraph Hill café. But Lardinois and others have argued that many, if not most, of Sappho's poems were written to be performed by choruses on public occasions. In some lyrics, the speaker uses the first-person plural "we"; in others, the form of "you" that she uses is the plural, suggesting that she's addressing a group—presumably the chorus, who danced as she sang. (Even when Sappho uses the first-person singular, it doesn't mean she was singing solo: in Greek tragedy the chorus, which numbered fifteen singers, regularly uses "I.")

This communal voice, which to us seems jarring in lyrics of deep, even erotic feeling—imagine that Shakespeare's sonnets had been written as choral hymns—is one that some translators today simply ignore, in keeping with the modern interest in individual psychology. But if the proper translation of the sexy little Fragment 38 is not "you scorch me" but "you scorch us," which is what the Greek actually says, how, exactly, should we interpret it?

To answer that question, classicists lately have been imagining the purposes to which public performance of erotic poems might have been put. Ancient references to the poet's "companions" and "students" have led one expert to argue that Sappho was the leader of a female collective, whose role was "instruction leading to marriage." Rather than expressions of individual yearning for a young woman, the poems were, in Lardinois's view, "public forms of praise of the general attractiveness of the girl," celebrating her readiness for wedlock and integration into the larger society. The late Harvard classicist Charles Segal made even larger claims. As he saw it, the strongly rhythmic erotic lyrics were "incantatory" in nature; he believed that public performance of poems like Fragment 31 would have served to socialize desire itself for the entire city—to lift sexual yearning "out of the realm of the formless and terrible, bring it into the light of form, make it visible to the individual poet and, by extension, to his or her society."

Even purely literary issues—for instance, the tendency to think of Sappho as the inventor of "the lyric I," a single, emotionally naked speaker who becomes a stand-in for the reader—are affected by these new theories. After all, if the "I" who speaks in Sappho's work is a persona (a "poetic construct rather than a real-life figure," as Lardinois put it), how much does her biography actually matter?

Between the paucity of actual poems and the woeful unreliability of the biographical tradition, these debates are unlikely to be resolved anytime soon. Indeed, the study of Sappho is beset by a curious circularity. For the better part of a millennium—between the compilation of the *Suda* and the late nineteenth century—the same bits of poetry and the same biographical gossip were endlessly recycled, the poetic fragments providing the sources for biographies that were then used as the basis for new interpretations of those same fragments. This is why the "new Sappho" has been so galvanizing for classicists: every now and then, the circle expands, letting in a little more light.

Dirk Obbink's revelation in 2012 was, in fact, only the latest in a series of papyrological discoveries that have dramatically enhanced our understanding of Sappho and her work. Until the late nineteenth century, when the papyri started turning up, there were only the ancient quotations. Since then, the amount of Sappho that we have has more than doubled.

In 1897, two young Oxford archaeologists started excavating a site in Egypt that had been the municipal dump of a town called Oxyrhynchus—"City of the Sharp-Nosed Fish." In ancient times, it had been home to a large Greek-speaking population. However lowly its original purpose, the dump soon yielded treasures. Papyrus manuscripts dating to the first few centuries AD, containing both Greek and Roman texts, began to surface. Some were fragments of works long known, such as the *Iliad*, but even these were of great value, since the Oxyrhynchus papyri were often far older than what had been, until that point, the oldest surviving copies. Others revealed works previously unknown. Among the latter were several exciting new fragments of Sappho, some substantial. From the tattered papyri, the voice came through as distinctive as ever:

Some men say cavalry, some men say infantry,
some men say the navy's the loveliest thing
on this black earth, but I say it's what-
ever you love

Over the decades that followed, more of the papyri were deciphered and published. But by 1955, when the British classicist Denys Page published *Sappho and Alcaeus*, a definitive study of the two poets from Lesbos, it seemed that even this rich new vein had been exhausted. "There is not at present," Page declared, "any reason to expect that we shall ever possess much more of the poetry of Sappho and Alcaeus than we do today, and this seems a suitable time to begin the difficult and doubtful task of interpreting."

Sappho herself, it seems fair to say, would have raised an eyebrow at Page's confidence in his judgment. Human fortune, she writes, is as variable as the weather at sea, where "fair winds swiftly follow harsh gales." And indeed, this verse was unknown to Page, since it comes from the papyrus fragment that Obbink brought to light: the "Brothers Poem."

For specialists, the most exciting feature of the "Brothers Poem" is that it seems to corroborate the closest thing we have to a contemporary reference to Sappho's personal life: an oblique mention of her in Herodotus's *Histories*, written about a century and a half after her death. During a long discussion of Egyptian society, Herodotus mentions one of Sappho's brothers, a rather dashing character named Charaxus. A swashbuckling merchant sailor, he supposedly spent a fortune to buy the freedom of a favorite courtesan in Egypt—an act, Herodotus reports, for which Sappho "severely chided" her sibling in verse. Ovid and other later classical authors also refer to some kind of tension between Sappho and this brother, but, in the absence of a surviving poem on the subject by Sappho herself, generations of scholars were unable to verify even the brother's name. So it's easy to imagine Obbink's excitement as he worked his way through the first lines of the poem:

but you're always nattering on that Charaxus must come,
his ship full-laden. That much, I reckon, Zeus knows . . .

The pious thing to do, the speaker says, is to pray to the gods for this brother's return, since human happiness depends on divine good will. The poem closes with the hope that another, younger brother will grow up honorably and save his family from heartache—presumably, the anxiety caused by their wayward elder sibling. At last, that particular biographical tidbit could be confirmed.

For nonclassicists, the "Brothers Poem" may be less enthralling than the other recent Sappho find, the poem that surfaced in 2004, about old age—a bittersweet work indeed. After the University of Cologne acquired some papyri, scholars found that one of the texts overlapped with a poem already known: Fragment 58, one of the Oxyrhynchus papyri. The fragment consisted mostly of the ends of a handful of lines; the new Cologne papyrus filled in the blanks, leaving only a few words missing. Finally, the lines made sense.

As with much Archaic Greek poetry, the newly restored Fragment 58—the "Old Age Poem," as it is now called—illustrates its theme with an example from myth. Sappho alludes to the story of Eos, the dawn goddess, who wished for, and was granted, eternal life for her mortal lover, Tithonus, but forgot to ask for eternal youth:

[I bring] the beautiful gifts of the violet Muses, girls,
and [I love] that song lover, the sweet-toned lyre.
My skin was [delicate] before, but now old age
[claims it]; my hair turned from black [to white].
My spirit has grown heavy; knees buckle
that once could dance light as fawns.
I often groan, but what can I do?
Impossible for humans not to age.
For they say that rosy-armed Dawn in love
went to the ends of the earth holding Tithonos,
beautiful and young, but in time gray old age
seized even him with an immortal wife.

Here as elsewhere in the new translation, Diane J. Rayor captures
the distinctively plainspoken quality of Sappho's Greek, which, for
all the poet's naked emotionality and love of luxury, is never overwrought or baroque. Every translation is a series of sacrifices; in
Rayor's case, emphasis on plainness of expression sometimes comes
at the cost of certain formal elements—not least, meter. The late
classicist M. L. West, who published a translation in *The Times Literary Supplement*, took pains to emulate the long line of Sappho's
original:

But me—my skin which once was soft is withered now
by age, my hair has turned to white which once was black . . .

Still, given how disastrously cloying many attempts to recreate Sappho's verse as "song" have proved to be, you're grateful for Rayor's
directness. Her notes on the translations are particularly useful,

especially when she alerts readers to choices that are left "silent" in other English versions. The last extant line of Fragment 31, for instance, presents a notorious problem: it could mean something like "all must be endured" or, on the other hand, "all must be dared." Rayor prefers "endured," and tells you why she thinks it's the better reading.

Rayor makes one very interesting choice in translating the "Old Age Poem." The Cologne manuscript dates to the third century BC, which makes it the oldest and therefore presumably the most reliable manuscript of Sappho that we currently possess. In that text, the poem ends after the sixth couplet, with its glum reference to Tithonus being seized by gray old age. But Rayor has decided to include some additional lines that appear only in the fragmentary Oxyrhynchus papyrus. These give the poem a far more upbeat ending:

> Yet I love the finer things . . . this and passion
> for the light of life have granted me brilliance and beauty.

The manuscript containing those lines was copied out five hundred years after the newly discovered version—half a millennium further away from the moment when the Poetess first sang this song.

And so the new Sappho raises as many questions as it answers. Did different versions of a single poem coexist in antiquity, and, if so, did ancient audiences know or care? Who in the "Brothers Poem" has been chattering on about Sappho's brother Charaxus, and why? Where, exactly, does the "Old Age Poem" end? Was it a melancholy testament to the mortifying effects of age or a triumphant assertion of the power of beauty, of the "finer things"—of poetry itself—to redeem the ravages of time? Even as we strain to hear this remarkable woman's sweet speech, the thrumming in our ears grows louder.

—*The New Yorker*, March 16, 2015

Deep Frieze

WHAT WILL ARCHAEOLOGISTS twenty-five centuries from now make of the ruins of One World Trade Center, currently nearing completion in downtown Manhattan? Some scholars in the year 4514, familiar with ancient accounts describing the diminutive structure as a "skyscraper," will no doubt speculate about the significance of its height—although they will be forced to admit that 1,368, the number of "feet" from base to roof, was a figure with no known significance in the culture of the ancient builders. Others, drawing on fragmentary scriptural texts ("wikis") that refer to a now-missing aerial spire, will propose an ingenious theory that the original height of the building was 1,776 of those antique units of measure: a symbolic reference to a date known to have had considerable ideological importance for the builders. (Still others will dismiss this notion as vulgarly literal-minded.)

Meanwhile, experts in epigraphy and prosopography will pore over inscriptions bearing the names of the ordinary people who lived, loved, and worked here ("Condé Nast," "Michael Kors"). The presence of mysterious symbols—in particular, an apple with a bite taken out of it—will raise the vexed question of whether the site was sacred or secular. A few researchers will argue that the two immense rectangular pits near the site of the ruin, once fitted with pipes and, as most historians in the forty-sixth century agree, used as public baths, were the footprints of earlier, "archaic" structures known to have existed on the site, although they will not be able to explain why the outlines of those ruins were preserved. Try as all these scholars may, the unifying theory that connects the number 1,776, the names, the symbols, and the traces of earlier structures will remain elusive.

When we look at the Parthenon today, what we see is one of the most famous ruins in the world, a structure that has been iconic since the moment it was completed. Its majesty has been celebrated from Plutarch in the first century AD ("no less stately in size than exquisite in form") to the Ottoman diarist Evliya Çelebi in the seventeenth ("We have seen all the mosques of the world, but we have never seen the likes of this!"), its aesthetic perfections adulated by professionals as well as tourists. (Le Corbusier called it "the basis for all measurement in art.") Starting in ancient times, it has been reproduced in every medium and on every scale imaginable, from stone to paper, in tombs, stock exchanges, and courthouses, from ancient coins to a full-size replica in Nashville, Tennessee, to the blue-and-white image on millions of takeout coffee cups.

But what the Athenians who built the Parthenon saw, on the day in 438 BC when it was dedicated, was a memorial to a devastating attack. It, too, rose as a replacement for a predecessor incinerated by enemies; it, too, towered over a plaza where the footprint of an earlier structure had been left deliberately visible. And it, too, was indelibly associated, in the minds of the citizens who beheld it, with one terrible day in September.

On the 23rd of that month in 480 BC, near the climax of a decades-long conflict between the Persian Empire and a loose confederation of Greek city-states, a Persian force sacked Athens and the Acropolis. A great flat-topped rock that hunches up in the center of the city, the Acropolis ("the high place of the city") was home to the Athenians' holiest structures. There stood the shrine to Erechtheus, one of Athens's mythical founders and first kings, a sanctuary that featured the olive tree said to have been a gift from Athena, the city's patron deity, to her people; not far away was a temple to Athena herself, which housed a wooden image of the virgin goddess so old that it was believed to have fallen from Heaven. Along promenades and temple steps innumerable votive offerings sprouted: panoplies from defeated enemies, bronzes of heroes and gods, the life-size stone youths and maidens known as *kouroi* and *korai*, smiling their secret smiles.

All this the Persians burned. Blood was shed, too: the invaders killed citizens and priests who had taken refuge in the holy places—a slaughter that, for the Greeks, represented an inconceivable violation of sacred law. Later, after the Persians were defeated and the rest of the Athenians returned to their ruined city, the smiling statues were carefully gathered and buried, as if they were people. You can still see the charring on some of them.

The attack and destruction scarred the Athenian consciousness in a way that is difficult for us, traumatized though we still are by September 11, to imagine. A generation passed before the Athenians could bring themselves to rebuild. (Jon D. Mikalson, a professor of classics at the University of Virginia, recently observed that, to get a full sense of the Athenian ordeal, you'd have to "imagine that on 9/11 the whole of D.C. and New York City was levelled and the whole country evacuated—and it took thirty years to rebuild.") What the Athenian and the American national traumas had in common was that the attack almost immediately became symbolic, a dramatization

43

of the political and moral differences between the victims and the perpetrators. One Greek term for the people who had destroyed their city was *barbaroi*, which is the root of our word "barbarians."

Since the mid-eighteenth century, when Greece and its ruins were being popularized by European intellectuals, writers, and artists, the Parthenon—the jewel in the crown of the rebuilt Acropolis, a gleaming marble temple to the goddess of wisdom—appeared designed to represent everything we have wanted both ancient Athens and our own liberal democracies to be: the pure expression of a rational, humanistic worldview. Now a book by an archaeologist at New York University claims that the passage of twenty-five centuries has hopelessly obscured the building's original meaning, and that the temple's most famous sculpture in fact represents something "unbearable to imagine on a building regarded as the 'icon of Western art.'" In *The Parthenon Enigma*, Joan Breton Connelly argues that "the biggest, most technically astonishing, ornately decorated, and aesthetically compelling temple ever known" was designed to commemorate a human sacrifice—a barbarous act of which the Greeks were not the victims but the perpetrators. Her controversial thesis is only the latest in a series of arguments about the Parthenon that have been going on since before it was even finished.

The first great controversy was political; as with so many construction projects, the brouhaha had to do with money. The Persian Wars were for Athens what World War I was to the United States: a global struggle from which an ambitious young nation emerged as a major world power. During the three decades between the sack of the

Acropolis, in the 470s, and its lavish reconstruction under the statesman Pericles starting in the 440s, Athens came to dominate the
Aegean and parts of the Greek mainland, eventually assuming control of a strategic alliance known to historians as the Delian League
(after the island of Delos, the site of its treasury). In everything but
name, the league was Athens's empire, and its "members" little more
than subject states. Shortly before rebuilding on the Acropolis
began, Pericles seized the treasury and moved it to Athens, ostensibly
for safekeeping. At the time, it was valued at eight thousand talents
—roughly $4.8 billion in today's money, by one estimate. Another
six hundred talents, or about $360 million, rolled in annually as
tribute from Athens's "allies."

To the Athenians, who prided themselves on their piety as well
as on their cultural superiority, one obvious place to sink this cash
was into the rebuilding of the blackened ruins on the Acropolis. In
its marriage of artistic ambition and economic practicality, this
immense project was somewhat like the Depression-era WPA. (Athens enjoyed full employment for nearly half a century after the work
began; Plutarch, in his *Life of Pericles*, wrote that the projects
"divided and distributed surplus money to pretty well every age-
group and type of person.") When Pericles's enemies tried to use the
astronomical costs of the Acropolis project as a political weapon
against him, the politician—who was the scion of an old-money,
Rockefeller-ish clan—said that he'd be perfectly happy to finance
the construction himself, provided that he be allowed to dedicate
the buildings in his own name. Eager for the glory that they knew
would cling to the project, the Athenians stopped grumbling.

The new temples were like none that had ever been built.
Although many people think of the Parthenon, in particular, as the

epitome of Greek architecture, it was typical of nothing at all, an anomaly in terms of material, size, and design: what we today see as the ultimate "classic" would have struck Athenian eyes the way Frank Gehry's Guggenheim Bilbao struck ours. It was the first temple in mainland Greece to be built entirely of marble—twenty-two thousand tons of it, quarried about ten miles away and hauled up the Acropolis by sledges, carts, and pulleys. It was also the largest. Most temples in the rather plain architectural style known as Doric have six columns across the front and thirteen down the sides; the Parthenon has eight columns in front and seventeen down the sides— an expanded scale that made possible an unprecedented amount of sculptural decoration. Marching along the entablature (the horizontal element that rests above the outer columns) were huge rectangular panels, called metopes, showing scenes from four famous mythic battles. Across the east front of the building (the side the entrance is on), the gods battle the rebellious race of Giants; on the west, Greeks triumph over Amazons, and on the north side they trounce the Trojans, while on the south men vanquish the half-human, half-horse centaurs. In both pediments (the triangular gables at either end), brightly painted statues were used to depict crucial moments in the life of Athena. On the east, above the front door, the goddess sprang full grown from the head of her father, Zeus, as other gods looked on, gesticulating with understandable astonishment; on the west, she battled her uncle Poseidon for possession of Athens. Merely to walk around the temple was to get a lesson in Greek and Athenian civic history.

Another radical departure from architectural tradition was the inclusion of an element typical of an entirely different and considerably more ornate architectural order, the Ionic. This element consisted of a continuous sculptured bas-relief frieze running around the entirety of a temple's rectangular, walled inner sanctum, or cella, the chamber in which the statue of the god was typically housed. The Parthenon's cella was unusual, too, consisting of two rooms rather than one: the larger did contain a cult statue, but the purpose of the smaller rear chamber remains unclear. Some scholars think it was where young virgins who served as temple acolytes were housed or worked. Others, noting ancient references to expensive dedications stored in that room, believe it served as a treasury of some kind—perhaps for part of the immense fortune that belonged to the Delian League.

The degree to which high art, religion, and international finance converged in the Parthenon is apparent in what was, in antiquity, the temple's most famous feature: a forty-foot-high gold-and-ivory statue of Athena Parthenos ("the Virgin"), which stood inside the main room of the cella. Depicting the goddess in armor, the severed head of Medusa on her chest, a shield at her side, a giant snake—the symbol of Athens's mythic kings—at her feet, and a six-foot-high winged victory in her right hand, this prodigy was the work of a close friend of Pericles, the sculptor Pheidias, the greatest artist of the day and, according to some sources, the artistic overseer and general designer of the entire Acropolis project. The gold plates used for the goddess's gown, worth around forty-four talents, or $26 million, were designed to be detachable, in the event that an over-whelming need for cash arose—the usual fate for ancient art made of metal. (Sure enough, within a century of the building's comple-tion, the precious garments had been liquidated by an Athenian leader to pay for mercenaries.)

Even more remarkable than the richness of the Parthenon's decor was a series of technical refinements that continue to excite the admiration of architects. The façade may have the memorable simplicity of a logo—those eight verticals surmounted by the shallow isosceles triangle—but there is nothing simple about it. For starters, there are almost no straight lines in the building: both the entablature atop the columns and the platform upon which the entire structure sits curve upward at the center; the metopes lean outward, while the panels that alternated with them lean inward, as do the north and south walls of the cella. The foundation of the entire structure tilts slightly upward toward the west end—the side that confronts you as you walk onto the Acropolis—giving it the slightly aggressive, elbow-in-your-face quality that still strikes you on first viewing. The columns of the outer colonnade, which appear to be perfectly straight, actually swell slightly at the center. This adjustment served, in part, to correct an optical illusion—pillars with perfectly straight sides appear to cave inward toward the middle—but the slight swelling also conveys the subliminal impression of muscular effort. The Greek archaeologist and architect who has overseen the Parthenon restoration for more than twenty years—since 1975, most of the structure has been, essentially, taken apart and put back together again—describes the effect of this slight swelling as "the deep breath taken by the athlete." The forty-four massive outer columns themselves all lean inward slightly; if extended, they would meet a mile and a half above the surface of the earth.

Arching, leaning, straining, swelling, breathing: the overall effect of the Parthenon's architectural subtleties is to give the building a special and slightly unsettling quality of being somehow alive. During the recent restoration, it was found that the vertical grooves, or flutes, carved into the building's columns represent the arcs not of a circle, as had previously been thought, but of an ellipse. This ostensibly minor technical feature accounts for a major effect: the uncanny play of light and shadow along the columned façade as the sun rises and sets, which, as one member of the restoration teams has put it, can make it seem that every day "the Parthenon is moving into the light."

Just about everyone who has ever struggled up the slippery marble steps of the Acropolis and gazed at this astonishing building seems to have wanted to lay claim to it. With its ideologically fraught sculptures, it began, as Connelly puts it in *The Parthenon Enigma*, as the city-state's "great billboard"; the various politicians, emperors, theologians, infidels, invaders, thieves, and liberators who have passed through Athens since then have all tried to scrawl their messages on it.

First, there were the Greeks themselves. Barely a century after construction ended, the orator Demosthenes, nostalgic for the hey-day of the Periclean democracy, referred to the building as a symbol of the Athenians' past greatness. Around the same time, Alexander the Great decorated the entablature with shields captured from his Asiatic enemies, along with a sardonic inscription lambasting the Spartans for not joining his campaign. Three hundred years later, the Roman emperor Nero splashed a Greek text, fashioned from bronze letters, on the east façade, honoring himself.

After a major fire in the third or fourth century AD devastated the interior and destroyed the roof, the billboard became available for other messages. Toward the end of the sixth century, by which time virgins other than Athena had come to be worshiped in Athens, the Parthenon became a church. Many of its pagan images were defaced, icons were erected, the west end replaced the east as the main entrance, and a curved apse bulged out the back. A hundred years later, it was the Orthodox Cathedral of the Virgin Atheniotissa, the "God-bearing Mother of Athens." After 1204, when the French and Venetian leaders of the Fourth Crusade passed through, the building began a new life as the Roman Catholic cathedral of Notre Dame d'Athènes, complete with a bell tower. In another three centuries, after the Ottoman Turks occupied the Greek mainland, Athena's temple and Mary's church was reborn as a mosque. The bell tower morphed easily into a minaret.

Despite these disasters, deprivations, and redecorations, by the early modern era the Parthenon was still largely intact. At this point it began a strange new career as a pawn in a conflict between Europe and the Ottomans. Late in the seventeenth century, during a clash whose name—the Sixth Ottoman–Venetian War—tells you a good deal about the whole wearying period, the Turks used the Parthenon as an ammunition depot, confident that the Venetians would never fire on so sacrosanct a monument to European culture. They were wrong. One of the seven hundred cannonballs that the Venetians fired at the Acropolis during the autumn of 1687—another bad September for Athens—found its mark. The immense explosion blew out the cella walls, toppled two dozen columns, and sent metopes, blocks of frieze, and pedimental sculptures flying. "How it dismayed His Excellency to destroy the beautiful temple that has existed three thousand years," a member of the household of the general who led the Venetian forces wrote, with great feeling if lopsided chronology. Three hundred Turkish women and children who'd taken refuge on the Acropolis were killed, although this fact tends to go underreported—just another of the ways in which the vagaries of the Parthenon's history can reflect the prejudices and predilections of its historians.

The Parthenon's relatively brief life as a total ruin has made it even more available as a blank screen on which to project our fantasies about the past. For instance, despite the fact that the building was a church and a mosque for far longer than it was ever a temple of Athena, relatively few scholars or archaeologists since 1832, when Greece won its independence from the Turks, have questioned that the correct way to "restore" the Acropolis was to strip away all evidence of those subsequent incarnations and return it to the Golden Age of Pericles. "All the remains of barbarity will be removed," one German architect declared, soon after Otto, a Bavarian princeling, was installed as king of the newly independent Greece. Not everyone agreed. One critic lambasted the wrong-headed "restoration" in terms that, to us, seem refreshingly modern:

> It is but a narrow view of the Akropolis of Athens to look on it simply as the place where the great works of the age of Perikles may be seen as models in a museum.... We can conceive of nothing more paltry, nothing more narrow, nothing more opposed to the true spirit of scholarship, than these attempts to wipe out the history of any age.

Much of the Parthenon itself had been removed by then. Beginning in 1801, Thomas Bruce, the seventh Earl of Elgin, a Scottish aristocrat who was the British ambassador to the Ottoman court, acting on the basis of a permit whose language has since been studied with Talmudic fervor, pried loose from the ruin much of the frieze, most of the remaining pediment statues, and fifteen of the metopes, and shipped them back to England. In 1816, short of money, he sold the lot to the British government, and since 1817 the sculptures have been displayed as part of the permanent collection of the British Museum.

The debate over the Elgin Marbles—you call them the Parthenon Marbles if you think the British should give them back—is without question the most famous of the many controversies that the Parthenon has excited since its construction. For some, Elgin was an aesthetic criminal. (He severed the sculptures from their proper architectural setting.) For others, he is a political criminal. (He was an arrogant imperialist appropriating native artworks.) For others he was a savior—a minority viewpoint today, when art-world sensitivities about provenance and patrimony have never been more acute. It's worth remembering that in his day the Acropolis was a ghastly and filthy ruin: thirty years later, a Bavarian soldier who was present at a ceremony honoring King Otto noted the presence of "broken pillars, marble blocks, large and small, cannonballs, shell fragments, human skulls and bones" littering the ground. By the time Elgin took the marbles, locals were in the habit of walking off with bits of the Acropolis buildings for reuse in their homes or to burn in lime kilns.

Even while Elgin's cargo was sailing, to denounce him was a badge of cultural and political bona fides in certain circles. Lord Byron devoted part of *Childe Harold* to vituperating him as "cold as the crags upon his native coast." Since then, the list of those who have been moved to pronounce on the rightful place of the marbles includes everyone from Canova to Cavafy ("Honesty is the best policy, and honesty in the case of the Elgin Marbles means restitution"), from Jacqueline Kennedy to Melina Mercouri ("They are the symbol and blood and the soul of the Greek people"), from the Clintons to Christopher Hitchens, who found time to write an indignant book on the subject. Even Vladimir Putin and Iran's Supreme Leader Ali Khamenei have weighed in. Both are in favor of restitution.

If the question raised by the debate over the Elgin Marbles is "Who does the Parthenon belong to?," the question that *The Parthenon Enigma* raises is "Who were the people who built it?" Joan Breton Connelly thinks the answer lies in the long frieze that ran around the inner sanctum: without a doubt, the most mystifying of the building's many sculptural decorations.

A little more than three feet high and five hundred and twenty-four feet long, the frieze represents an immense procession featuring more than six hundred participants—human, animal, and divine. Parade marshals impatiently beckon, cavalrymen get their frisky mounts under control, elderly dignitaries fuss with their robes, maidens carry ritual implements, musicians play pipes and lyres, comely youths stand around being comely, and sacrificial cows and sheep process mildly to their demise. For most admirers of the building over the centuries, this tour de force exemplifies the high-classical union of art and science, of aesthetic subtlety and technical finesse, that characterized the Parthenon as a whole. But for Connelly, a MacArthur-winning scholar whose previous works include an engaging study of the life of a Greek priestess, it reveals a far "darker" side of classical Greek culture—a more "primitive outlook than later cultures and classicists have been prepared to face."

No one disputes that the bas-relief represents a grand ceremonial parade. But what kind of parade? The first modern visitors to the

Parthenon were perplexed. A fifteenth-century antiquarian called Cyriac of Ancona thought it showed "the victories of Athens in the time of Pericles." Three centuries later, two English architects traveling in Greece and studying its ruins had a different idea. James ("Athenian") Stuart and Nicholas Revett, whose multivolume *Antiquities of Athens* did much to popularize Greek neoclassicism in the eighteenth century, argued that the frieze depicted a civic procession known as the Panathenaea (that is, the "all-Athens" parade), which was held every four years during Pericles' time in honor of the birth of Athena.

The proof of this seemed to be the scene depicted on the frieze's climactic panel, which rested above the temple's front door on the east side. This panel depicts five mortals—a man, a woman, and three younger people—enacting some kind of ritual while the twelve Olympian gods, lounging in chairs and chatting amiably, look on. The rite centers on the man, who is handing a large folded cloth to the youngest child—or, perhaps, taking the cloth from the child. Here, Stuart and Revett surmised, was a depiction of the culmination of the Panathenaea festival, which ancient sources describe: the presentation of a new woolen cloak, or *peplos*, as a dedication to the goddess. To our eye, the folded garment being handled by the man and the child lends a charmingly quotidian note to the lofty goings-on and august guests. If you didn't know better, you'd say that they were folding laundry.

From the start, there were doubts about the Panathenaea theory. For one thing, important features of the real-life festival were missing, even though the frieze hardly lacked for space. In particular, there was no sign of the huge cohort of foot soldiers—the backbone of the Athenian army, celebrated in every kind of civic discourse—

who were known to have marched in the parade. (In the frieze, it's cavalry that dominates.) A far more fundamental objection was stylistic. There is no precedent in any other extant Greek temple for a sculptural decoration representing a contemporary, or even historical, occasion; as an absolute rule, the subjects of temple decoration are always mythological. As A. W. Lawrence, an archaeologist who was the brother of Lawrence of Arabia, put it, "the flagrant breach with tradition requires explanation."

Explanations, needless to say, abounded. Like the sinking of the *Titanic*, the death of Marilyn Monroe, and the JFK assassination, the Parthenon frieze has inspired enthusiasts to detect significance where it may not be present. Some archaeologists ingeniously explained the preponderance of horses and horsemen by noting that Pericles was expanding the Athenian cavalry just as construction began. Certain art historians, meanwhile, commonsensically pointed out that horses and horsemen are simply more interesting to look at than hundreds of infantrymen's feet. Others have gotten around the complaint that there is no precedent for representing a historical event by arguing that the procession depicted in the Parthenon frieze wasn't an actual Panathenaic parade of Pericles' time but a mythical one—the very first such procession, instituted by Athens's mythic king Erechtheus. The theories, like the figures in the frieze, marched on.

One reason the debates have raged as loudly and long as they have is that there is no ancient authority on what they might mean: no ancient description of the frieze survives. When Greek and Roman writers who visited Athens were moved to mention architecture, they tended to rhapsodize about the Propylaea, the Acropolis's multilevel entrance building; if they mentioned the Parthenon, it was usually to focus their attention on the immense golden statue of Athena. "I have little doubt," wrote John Boardman, Britain's most distinguished historian of classical art, "that the problems of the Parthenon frieze—iconographic, religious, artistic—will continue to be regarded as an open sport for scholars until a fifth-century text is discovered which tells us the truth."

Twenty years ago, Connelly came across what she believed was precisely such a text. In her book, she recounts how, while she was visiting Oxford in the early 1990s, her attention was drawn to the fragments of a lost play by Euripides called *Erechtheus*. The fragments had come to light after the discovery of some papyrus sheets on which the play had been copied out: they had been reused in antiquity as wrappings for a mummy, and when the mummy was unwrapped, the sheets with their literary text came to light and were published. Euripides' play, first produced about a decade after the Parthenon was completed, dramatized a myth of supreme importance to the Athenians: the tale of the three daughters of the Athenian king Erechtheus, who volunteered to die after an oracle declared that only the sacrifice of a royal virgin would guarantee victory for Athens in its war against a neighboring city.

Until the papyri were discovered and deciphered, the play had been known primarily from a long excerpt that was quoted in a legal oration written a hundred years after Euripides' time. In the excerpt, the mother of the Athenian princesses, Queen Praxithea, extols the virtue of making sacrifices on behalf of the city—a virtue sadly lacking, according to the lawyer who gave the oration and saw fit to quote this bit of the play, in the accused. The fragments discovered in the mummy wrappings provided a big new chunk from the end of the play. In this climactic speech, Athena orders the Athenians to erect two tombs, one for King Erechtheus (who, though Athens was victorious, perished in the battle), and the other for his altruistic daughters, who volunteered to be human sacrifices and are all to be buried in "the same earth tomb."

For Connelly, the implication of the new fragment was electrifying. Scholars had long assumed that the Greek word that came to be used of the Acropolis's preeminent building, *parthenón*—"the maiden chamber"—referred either to Athena the Virgin, the dedicatee of the building, or, perhaps, to the female servants of the goddess who may have been housed in the temple's rear chamber, who would, as a matter of course, have been virgins. But after reading the *Erechtheus* fragments, a "stunned" Connelly became convinced that the five figures at the center of the Parthenon frieze were the Athenian royals in Euripides' play—Erechtheus, Praxithea, and their three daughters, depicted just before the awful sacrifice—and that the maidens of the "maiden chamber" were the sacrificial victims, the site of the Parthenon itself being the "earth tomb" mentioned in the play. Her idea has been rather sensationally garbled in some of the mainstream reviews of her book, bringing it the kind of notoriety that warms the hearts of publishers. "Was the Parthenon used as a site for virgin sacrifice?" *The Daily Beast* goggled.

Connelly's "sensational" theory is, in fact, nearly two decades old. She first aired it in a 1996 scholarly article that has, over time, failed to persuade art historians and archaeologists. In the new book, she takes her case directly to the people. Like other popularizing tomes by specialists who, in promoting controversial theses, have done what amounts to an end run around the academic establishment, this one has the defects of its virtues. The infectious enthusiasm, even emotionality, that the author displays toward her subject— "stunned" is not a word you often come across in discussions of Hellenistic literary papyri—cannot, in the end, compensate for questionable methods and wobbly evidence.

Connelly doesn't get into her hypothesis until halfway through the book. The first chapters are devoted to generously padded descriptions of Athenian topography, history, and mythology, intended to let the reader "see the monument through ancient eyes." Some of this is sneakily tendentious: if you get an awful lot about the streams and rivers of Athens in Chapter 1, it's not because Connelly is a tree-hugger: she believes that one of the pediment sculptures represents a certain river god who was Erechtheus's father-in-law. When she gets down to the frieze itself, she shows herself to be adept at the interpretative gymnastics at which frieze theorists have excelled from the start. To scholars who have argued that the smallest of the five key figures, a scantily clad child, is a boy—and therefore clearly not a daughter of Erechtheus—she responds, "Archaic and classical Greek artists were so unused to depicting the female nude that when confronted with this challenge, they relied on what they knew best: the male nude." To those who wonder why, in a scene supposedly depicting a human sacrifice, there happen to be 243 head of livestock clumping along on their way to slaughter, Connelly asserts that this scene represents a different moment in the myth from the one represented over the east door. And so on.

The effect of all this ingenuity is an inevitable sense of protesting-too-much: as intriguing as individual arguments may be, the mood of the whole is both hectoring and unpersuasive. Connelly's tendency to see Erechtheus and his myth behind every potted palm takes on the manic quality you associate with conspiracy theorists. "Sometimes," she writes apropos of some ritual objects in the central scene, "a stool is not just a stool"—a line that makes you wonder what the Greek for "uh-*huh*" was. A good example of the wishful methodology is her attempt to show that the Parthenon's rear chamber was the tomb of Erechtheus's daughters. First, she seizes on a single scholar's theory that the columns in that room, long since destroyed, were in a style known as "proto-Corinthian." From there she segues into a tale told by a Roman architect—writing five hundred years after the Parthenon was built—to the effect that the very first Corinthian column was inspired by an offering left at a...tomb. For Connelly, this can mean only one thing: "The Parthenon signals loud and clear that it is...a final resting place for the maidens who gave their lives to win Athenian triumph." Too much of the argumentation here is similarly impressionistic.

The greatest problem with *The Parthenon Enigma* is that the big "controversial" news it delivers—the "shocking" claim about the "dark side" of the Greeks that is the basis of its headline-grabbing appeal, complete with human sacrifice, missing texts, and mummy wrappings—isn't news at all. For one thing, the *Erechtheus* fragments had been published a quarter of a century by the time Connelly became aware of them; her "discovery" of material that had been well known to literary scholars for a generation would be an embarrassment to most scholars. As for the myth of Erechtheus and his daughters, which in her eyes demonstrates that the Athenians had a "far darker and more primitive outlook than later cultures and classicists have been prepared to face," the fact is that commentators have been facing and writing about it for millennia, with no apparent emotional trauma. And no wonder: for the Athenians themselves, tales of virgin self-sacrifice were old hat. Frequently dramatized in tragedies and referred to in patriotic speeches and legal arguments, they were clearly to be taken metaphorically. And far from being a startling discovery about "Athenian consciousness . . . that directly challenges our own self-identifications with it," mythic tales of self-sacrifice have been the focus of scholarly investigation and interpretation for decades. Many scholars now agree that, as treated in plays like *Erechtheus*, self-sacrificing gestures by young women were part of a rhetorical trope that was all too familiar as the Peloponnesian War ground into its second decade: the need for families and individuals to make sacrifices on behalf of the state.

Hence even if Connelly were right about the identity of the figures at the center of the frieze, there would still be no reason for the hype —except, of course, that it sells books. To insinuate that depictions of Erechtheus's daughters are evidence of a darkly barbaric culture of virgin sacrifice is a risible misrepresentation; it's like claiming that the famous old poster of a white-bearded Uncle Sam, pointing a bony finger and saying "*I WANT YOU!*," is evidence of a nationwide cult of elderly pedophiles. Sometimes a stool is just a stool. The fact that this scholar has spent years laboring over a book-length attempt to bolster what is, in the end, a pet theory ultimately tells you more about the Parthenon's strange allure than about the building itself.

If Connelly's idea is far-fetched and her methods inexcusable, her fixation is, at least to me, wholly forgivable. In the long line of Greeks, Romans, Byzantines, Ottomans, Crusaders, Venetians, Swedes, Frenchmen, Germans, Englishmen, and Americans who have found it hard to stop thinking about the monument, I occupy a tiny place. When I was in the sixth grade, already hooked on Greek myth and history, I made a cardboard model of the building as part of a project for a world history class; the numerically correct colonnades were rendered in toilet-paper rolls. By the time I was in junior high school, I was spending many nights and most weekends at a workbench in our basement laboring over a scale model of the building, three feet wide by six feet long, complete with a thirteen-inch-high plaster replica of Phidias's statue, for the decoration of which I learned how to apply real gold leaf. The basement workbench on which I labored is still known as "Athena's Table."

I never completed the project, but I did a good bit of the frieze—the part from the east front, with the gods lounging around—in gray-green modeling clay on a cardboard backing. What became of it, and of the golden Athena, I have no idea. *Plus ça change:* time passes, eras—in the lives of people as of civilizations—succeed one another, what once was treasured ends up in the lime kiln or the wastebasket. I suppose it was out of sentimentality for my own past, as much as for the Greeks, that a few years ago, when I saw, at a flea market in upstate New York, a plaster cast of the section of the frieze known as "W X"—the tenth block on the west side, which shows a pair of horsemen and their frisky mounts high-stepping toward the left—I bought it without hesitating. It hangs in my living room, above a small table. Sometimes, in the evening, I'll light a fat candle beneath it; the dancing shadows can make it look as if the horses and riders are moving. Where they are going, we may never be able to say for sure, but I know that they are beautiful.

—*The New Yorker*, April 14, 2014

Ecstasy and Terror

IN THE SPRING of 411 BC, the comic playwright Aristophanes presented to the citizens of Athens a new work, *Thesmophoriazousae*, lampooning the tragedian Euripides. The tongue-twisting title of the play means "Women Celebrating the Thesmophoria," a reference to an annual all-female rite held in honor of the fertility goddess Demeter. The ritual setting was crucial to the plot: in the play, the women of Athens, long irritated by Euripides' penchant for putting oversexed and murderous heroines (Phaedra, Medea) onstage, take advantage of the seclusion offered by the Demeter festival to plot their revenge. An anxious Euripides, having got wind of their scheme, persuades an elderly relative, Mnesilochus, to dress up as a woman, sneak into the rite, and spy on the proceedings. But the old man is found out, and as the play reaches its farcical climax, Euripides himself appears and attempts to rescue poor Mnesilochus. (As he does so, both men quote passages from various Euripidean dramas in which heroes fly to the rescue of helpless females.) The play ends in rejoicing, as Euripides vows never again to insult the women of Athens in his work.

Ancient biographers assert that not long after *Thesmophoriazousae* premiered, Euripides left the city of his birth for good, having accepted an invitation from the king of Macedon, a realm occupying the remote northern wilds of the Balkan peninsula, to adorn his court as a kind of writer in residence. There is little reason to believe that the playwright's abandonment of the most civilized city in Greece for a remote cultural backwater was in any way connected to the comic drubbing he had received at Aristophanes' hands; some scholars, for instance, believe that Euripides had become disgusted by Athens's political and moral descent during the Peloponnesian War.

But perhaps Aristophanes' comedy had planted a creative seed in the mind of the great tragedian. A couple of years after arriving in Macedon, Euripides died, in his mid-seventies; the following year, in 405 BC, his final work for the stage, *Bacchae* (Bacchantes) was produced in Athens. At the climax of that drama—which oscillates disturbingly between black humor and deepest horror, between the city and the untamed wilds beyond—a man possessed by curiosity about what certain women are doing during the celebration of an all-female rite dresses up as a woman in order to spy on them. But this time there is no rescue, no rejoicing. At least not for the characters: the play won Euripides a posthumous first prize at that year's annual dramatic competition, an accolade that had so often eluded the irreligious and daringly experimental playwright during his lifetime. Within the year his great rival, Sophocles, was also dead, and soon after tragedy itself seemed to peter out and die as well.

It's appropriate that *Bacchae*—an undisputed masterpiece, whose status as one of the greatest Greek tragedies is colored by our knowledge that it was among the last of the canonical works produced during the genre's heyday—may have begun as a bit of theatrical gamesmanship, a sophisticated tragic riposte to a comedian's tease. Few works in the history of the theater, and certainly no other work in the extant corpus of thirty-three Athenian tragedies (all that remain of the thousand or so that were performed during the fifth century BC), are as self-consciously preoccupied as this one is with the theater and its mechanisms: illusion and reality, belief and disbelief, costume and performance, laughter and terror.

And how not? It is the only surviving Greek play about Dionysus himself, the god of drama who is also the protagonist of this drama; the deity who lent his name to the festival for which all Greek tragedies were originally composed (the "City Dionysia") and to the theater where they were performed: the Theater of Dionysus, still visible today, nestled against the southern slope of the Acropolis, its location a powerful reminder of how central the theater was to the life of the city. Euripides' bold choice of subject, the decision to make the theater and its smilingly ambiguous god the subjects of his theater piece, allowed him, in his final play, to explore in a remarkably complex way the tensions and conflicts that had always animated his work: between civilization and nature, appearance and reality, sanity and madness, masculinity and femininity.

The plot of *Bacchae* recalls, in a highly literary form, an event from a dimly remembered Hellenic prehistory: the introduction of the worship of Dionysus from Asia into Greece. As dramatized by Euripides, the most overtly psychologizing of the three great tragedians, the bare anthropological fact becomes a charged personal drama. In his prologue speech, the young god—who, we should remember, presides not only over wine and theater but over ecstatic song and dance and "liberating" madness (as one of his epithets, *eleutherios*, "the Liberator," suggests)—announces that he has come from distant Asia to Thebes, the hometown of his late mother, Semele, for the express purpose of forcing the Greeks to accept his worship. But the Thebans have resisted thus far, and so the deity, intent on demonstrating his power and authority, has afflicted the women with his special brand of madness, sending them running into the hills outside of town. There they have become *bacchae*, female celebrants of Bacchus—Dionysus's other name—cavorting in the wild and consorting with wild animals, much to the consternation of the men who have remained home.

No man is more aggrieved by this lapse in civilized behavior than the young king of Thebes, Pentheus—Dionysus's first cousin, in fact, the son of Semele's sister, Agave, who happens to be one of the women running amok. Loudly advocating self-control, decrying what he is sure are the orgiastic practices of the new religion, determined to demonstrate his power and authority, this rigidly self-righteous young man makes his entrance announcing his intention to root out the cult. Ignoring the advice of seasoned elders who advise a more moderate path, he plans to round up the Bacchantes and to seize and punish their mysterious, strangely effeminate ringleader—who, unbeknownst to him, is Dionysus himself, masquerading as his own priest. This is just one of the play's many instances of sly doubling and "acting."

Eventually the king and the god come face-to-face. Both are willful, each convinced of his own righteousness: the one ostensibly representing civilization and its concerns (political authority, masculinity, morality, reason, the *polis*), the other representing nature and its concerns (the body, sexuality, inebriation, femininity, the wild spaces outside the city). The escalating conflict between the two propels this most dramatic of all Greek dramas to its awful end.

"Most dramatic," because the vehicle of Dionysus's climactic revenge on Pentheus is a kind of play-within-a-play, a mini-tragedy staged by Dionysus himself in which Pentheus becomes the unwitting protagonist. By this point, the arguments between the increasingly enraged Pentheus and the eerily nonchalant Dionysus have made clear to the sly immortal—and to the audience—a psychological truth of a sort we now take for granted: the repugnance the Theban king feels for the new god's rites and everything they represent is, in fact, fueled by a suppressed subconscious fascination. During the course of the play's most brilliantly charged exchange, the god uses this knowledge to seduce the mortal into becoming what he had claimed to find repellent: in order to spy on the women practicing their secret rites, Dionysus smoothly explains, Pentheus must dress as a woman. This he does. Our final glimpse of the once-arrogant king, who has by now succumbed to a hallucinatory madness (he claims to see "two suns, two cities of Thebes"), is of a grotesque drag show: a bearded man fussing over the folds of his skirt and worrying about his hairdo as he exits to his doom.

Or, rather, enters: for this overtly theatrical, "backstage" preparation—the costuming, the wigs, the makeup—precedes a kind of performance. When Pentheus arrives on the mountain, where his mother and the other women are celebrating the Bacchic rites, he conceals himself and spies on them—only to be discovered, exposed, and set upon by the Bacchantes, who, mistaking him in their demonic ecstasy for a lion (more double vision), tear him apart limb from limb in a grotesque parody of a Dionysiac rite known as *sparagmos*, the ritual dismemberment of a wild animal. It is a horribly apt punishment for the king who had so vehemently insisted on self-containment, on maintaining, as we would say today, "boundaries."

This grotesquely staged human sacrifice makes possible both a return to reality (in the play's famous coda, Pentheus's mother, one of the frenzied maenads who kills him, slowly comes down from her madness and recognizes what she has done) and, more important

67

to Dionysus, the establishment of his worship in Greece. In his final speech, the god prophesies that Pentheus's survivors will travel throughout Greece at the head of an Asiatic horde, knocking down the old gods' altars and setting up new ones, including one for this young god, whose power has been so violently manifested. The play's ending provides a colorful mythic explication for a historical fact: at some point in remote history, worship of Dionysus was added to that of the other gods.

But despite the ostensible closure, a nightmarish horror lingers. As in the most awful of anxiety nightmares, the spectator has become the main attraction, the audience member forced to be an actor, religious symbolism transformed into deadly violence.

A great part of the thrill of *Bacchae* is, then, its unusual self-reflectiveness: the "meta" quality of its reflections on how the theater works. All of us, when we attend the theater, are seeing double—seeing "two suns, two cities of Thebes." We know we are looking at a set, at an actor; but we allow ourselves to see the setting, the character.

The appeal of this extremely modern, or indeed postmodern, motif should not blind us to the play's other great themes. One, certainly, is gender—the subject that got Euripides into trouble in the first place in *Thesmophoriazousae*. In his final work, the playwright whose representations of extreme feminine emotionality had won him such notoriety decided to make two young males his leads. And yet it is their interactions with women, and their experiments with stereotypically feminine attitudes, roles, and gestures, that become the vehicle for the play's investigation of character, desire, and mind.

In Dionysus, Euripides created a character unique in the history of tragedy. Hovering between divine majesty and human weakness, magnificence and pettiness—and between male and female—the teasing, seductive, playful, epicene god is a great study in ambiguity. Above all, it is his effeminacy—the girlish curls and womanishly delicate complexion that draw Pentheus's attention, the odd passivity that stands in such contrast to Pentheus's aggressiveness—that fascinates both us and the other characters. As we know, it secretly attracts the insecure mortal; an attraction that becomes the vehicle of his destruction, as repressed desires so often do. The play's psychological insights alone would justify its status as a masterwork.

The nature and violence of Pentheus's destruction remind us of another great theme of the play, a very ancient one that preoccupied Euripides throughout his career, and one that his choice of Dionysus as the protagonist and of the Bacchantes themselves as the Chorus raises to a new level: religion. *Bacchae* is one of the great texts about what the philosopher William James would call, twenty-three centuries after Euripides, "the varieties of religious experience." The play shrewdly explores both the benevolent and the punishing faces of divinity: the ecstasy, beautifully conveyed in scenes depicting the Maenads at one with nature, suckling young animals and drinking milk that gushes from the earth, but also the terror, harrowingly evoked in that dreadful finale. Both elements are consummately summed up in the ambiguous Dionysus himself.

Not the least of the means by which Euripides conveys the swift shifts in mood associated with the mercurial god is the play's remarkable poetry. Commentators have long admired its extravagantly colored choral lyrics, whose unusual density, intricacy, and power stand in stark contrast to the plainspoken, quotidian language the playwright uses for his dialogue—a conventional contrast that here pointedly echoes this work's overarching tensions between the sacred and the secular, between the heightened consciousness of religious revelation and the coolly marmoreal contours of rationalism. The intellectualism makes itself felt in the terse, gnomic language of the characters' exchanges with each other. ("That makes no sense," a confused Pentheus sputters when faced with Dionysus's shape-shifting. "Sense is nonsense to a fool" comes the famous retort from the god.)

The ecstasy is exemplified by the chorus the Maenads sing at the fateful moment when Pentheus finally succumbs to Dionysus's teasing and agrees to dress up as a woman—his last moment onstage, in fact. This is the true climax of the play, and it is marked by verse in which the Chorus, eager to dance in triumph over their stubborn adversary, compares its joyful movements to those of a fawn that has escaped the hunter. These famous lines' swiftness and dappled coloration, the breathless alterations between light and dark, density and clarity, simile and metaphor, *comparandum* and *comparatum* convey the sense of swift movement through a shaded wood:

> *Shall I toss my head and skip through the open fields*
> *as a fawn slipped free of the hunt and the hunters,*
> *leaping their nets, outrunning their hounds?*
> *She runs like a gale runs over the plain*
> *near the river, each bound*
> *and plunge like a gust of joy, taking her*
> *dancing, deep through the forest*
> *where no one can find her, and the dark*
> *is free and its heart is the darkest green.*

Such lyrics, quoted here in Robin Robertson's limpid new translation, remind us why Euripides' songs were so highly prized in antiquity—and not just by his Athenian audience. The historian Plutarch relates that during the Peloponnesian War, Athenian prisoners of war laboring in the mines in Sicily would sing the playwright's lyrics in return for better treatment from their masters.

The strong presence of the Chorus in this play is, in fact, a self-conscious gesture on the playwright's part that unites *Bacchae*'s two dominant preoccupations: theater and religion. Euripides and his audiences were bound to be aware that tragedy had its origin in a Dionysiac rite that was accompanied by a particular kind of choral song called the dithyramb, which was sung by choruses of fifty men and boys in celebration of the bizarre birth of the god. (When the pregnant Semele was burned by Zeus's fire, the king of the gods sewed the unborn fetus into his thigh until it could grow to full term—a story derided by the atheistic Pentheus in the play, to his cost.) Aristotle, writing a century after tragedy's golden age, surmises in his *Poetics* that drama began when the leader of the dithyrambic chorus stood apart from the rest of the group and began to sing back to them—the origin of the oppositional stance, the dialogic structure, that allowed tragedy to embody conflict rather than merely describe it.

By the time Euripides was an old man, he (like us today, often) seemed to be increasingly embarrassed by the Chorus, relegating it to a perfunctory role in some of his later plays. But in his final work—inspired, as some scholars think, by the stark, numinous magnificence of the wild Macedonian surroundings where he sought refuge from the madness of Athenian politics—he restored the Chorus to its central position, making it as vital a character as it had been a hundred years earlier, when tragedy itself was in its infancy.

Like so much else about *Bacchae*, a work that is at once alarmingly primitive and enormously sophisticated, elemental and complex, the famously "archaizing" prominence of the Chorus adds to our sense that this is the ultimate, the compleat tragedy—a genre that, in its end, found its beginnings once again. Like the god it both celebrates and abhors, a god of both growth and decay, of beauty and terror, the play embodies ostensibly incompatible contradictions. All too conscious that it stood at the end of great tradition, it also seems aware of the possibility of perennial revival and rebirth—a possibility borne out by a line of translations and adaptations that goes back centuries. But then, *Bacchae* knows well that we must expect the improbable. As the Chorus sings in its final song, while the ruined body is being borne away and the survivors turn to the difficult business of living, "What we look for does not happen; / what we least expect is fashioned by the gods."

—From the Introduction to *Bacchae: A New Translation*, by Robin Robertson (Ecco, 2014)

Unburied

"BURY THIS TERRORIST on US soil and we will unbury him."

Three weeks after the Boston Marathon bombing, this was the slogan on one of the signs brandished by enraged protesters outside the Worcester, Massachusetts, funeral home that had agreed to receive the body of the accused bomber Tamerlan Tsarnaev—a cadaver seemingly so morally polluted that his own widow would not claim it, that no funeral director would touch it, that no cemetery would bury it. Even after Peter Stefan, a Worcester funeral director, had washed and shrouded the battered, bullet-ridden body for burial according to Muslim law, the cadaver became the object of a macabre game of civic and political football. Cemetery officials and community leaders in the Boston area were concerned that a local burial would spark civic unrest. ("It is not in the best interest of 'peace within the city' to execute a cemetery deed," the Cambridge city manager, Robert Healy, announced.) While the state's governor carefully sidestepped the issue, asserting that it was a family matter, other politicians seemed to sense an advantage in catering to the high popular feeling. "If the people of Massachusetts do not want that terrorist to be buried on our soil," declared Representative Edward J. Markey, a Democratic candidate for the US Senate, "then it should not be."

And so it went until May 9, when—due to the intervention of Martha Mullen, a Richmond, Virginia, woman who'd been following the story and a practicing Christian who cited Jesus's injunction to "love our enemies" as her inspiration—Tsarnaev's body was finally transported to a tiny Muslim cemetery in rural Virginia and interred there in an unmarked grave. Until then, the corpse had languished for weeks—not only unburied but, in a way, unburiable. In one of several updates it published on the grisly affair, *The New York Times* quoted Ray Madoff, a Boston law professor who specializes in "what she calls the law of the dead," about the case. "There is no precedent for this type of thing," Madoff told a reporter. "It is a legal no-man's-land."

A legal no-man's-land, perhaps, but familiar territory to anyone even casually acquainted with the Greek classics. From its epic dawn to its tragic high noon, Greek literature expressed tremendous cultural anxiety about what happens when the dead are left unburied. In part, the issue was a religious one: the souls of the dead were thought to be stranded, unable to reach the underworld without proper burial. (And without a proper tomb, or *sêma*—a "sign" or grave marker—a dead person could not hope for postmortem recognition, some sign that he or she had once lived and died.) The religious prohibition had civic consequences, since refusal to bury the dead was considered an affront to the gods and could bring ritual pollution on the community. The right of all sides to bury soldiers who had fallen in battle was a convention of war; burial truces were regularly granted during even the bitterest conflicts. In myth, even characters who act more like terrorists than like soldiers—for instance, the great warrior Ajax, who plots to assassinate his commanding officers but ends up dead himself—are deemed worthy of burial in the end. Which is to say, the body even of an enemy was sacrosanct.

This preoccupation with the implications of burial and nonburial haunts a number of the greatest works of Greek literature. The opening lines of the *Iliad*, the oldest extant work of Western poetry, refer with pointed revulsion to the possibility that the bodies of the warriors who died at Troy could become the "delicate pickings of birds and dogs." And indeed, you might say that getting the dead buried—even the reviled enemy dead—is the principle object of the epic's grand narrative arc. Fifteen thousand lines after that opening reference to unburied corpses, the poem closes, magnificently, with a scene of reconciliation between the grief-maddened Achilles— who has daily defiled the unburied body of his mortal enemy, the Trojan prince Hector, dragging it back and forth through the dirt before the walls of Troy—and Hector's aged father, Priam, the king of the doomed city. In a gesture of redemption for himself as much as for the Trojans, Achilles finally agrees to release the body for burial. The gigantic epic ends not (as some first-time readers expect) with the Wooden Horse, or the Fall of Troy, or an arrow in Achilles' heel, but with the all-important funeral of the greatest of the Greeks' enemies: a rite of burial that allows the Trojans to mourn their prince and, in a way, the audience to find closure after the unrelenting violence that has preceded. The work's final line is as plain, and as final, as the sound of dirt on the lid of a coffin. "This was the funeral of Hector, breaker of horses."

As for the *Odyssey*, it, too—for all its emphasis on its fantastical, proto-sci-fi adventures—reveals a telling preoccupation with this issue. The great adventure epic features an extended visit to the underworld, where, among other things, the flitting shades of the dead express anxiety about their own funerals (and where Odysseus learns how he himself will die, many years hence, "from the sea"). Precisely at the poem's midpoint, Odysseus dutifully halts his homeward journey—and the epic's narrative momentum—to bury, with full honors, the body of a young sailor who has died in a clumsy accident, as if to say that even the most hapless and pointless of deaths merits the dignity of ritual. And in the work's final, culminating book, Homer slips in the information, ostensibly *en passant* but of course crucial, that the bodies of the hated Suitors, the gluttonous competitors for the hand of Odysseus's faithful queen, Penelope—whose gory deaths we are, to some extent, invited to savor, given their gross outrages against Odysseus and his family— were duly permitted to be retrieved by their families for burial.

The subject continued to fascinate Greek writers and poets for centuries after Homer. It makes itself felt at the end of a play by Sophocles from around 450 BC: *Ajax*, his drama about the good soldier turned evil terrorist. At the end of this tragedy, a conflict arises over whether the body of the criminal (who by this point has committed suicide) should be buried. His enemies—Agamemnon and Menelaus, the leaders of the Greek expedition, whom Ajax had plotted to murder—insist that his body be cast forth unburied, like the body of an animal, "food for the birds." (Again.) Yet unexpectedly, there springs to his defense a man who also had been his enemy. That man is Odysseus, who in a climactic confrontation with the two Greek generals—who are his allies and commanding officers— persuades them that to pursue their hatred after death would be grotesque. In response to this generous suggestion, the swaggering Agamemnon worries that to relent would make him appear "soft"; but Odysseus, wily as he always is, argues that "softness" is nothing more than justice—nothing more than acting like a human being. Then he makes his final, stark point:

> *AGAMEMNON*: You will make us appear cowards this day.
> *ODYSSEUS*: Not so, but just men in the sight of all the Greeks.
> *AGAMEMNON*: So you would have me allow the burying of the dead?
> *ODYSSEUS*: Yes; for I too shall come to that need.

In this crudely masculine milieu, it's the practical benefits of burying the enemy dead that matter: who knows, after all, whether one day we ourselves will be someone's enemy, dead on the battlefield and in need of burial?

But it is another work by the same playwright that most famously poses the question of why we ought to bury our enemies and explores in unparalleled depth the moral and ethical implications of that question: *Antigone*, a tragedy first produced in Athens around 442 BC, perhaps a decade after *Ajax*. The entire plot of this play centers on the controversy over how a community that has survived a deadly attack will dispose of the body of the perpetrator of that attack—the body, as it happens, of a young man who had planned to bring destruction on the city that had been his home, who "sought to consume the city with fire . . . sought to taste blood."

The young man in question is Polyneices, a son of the late, spectacularly ill-fated king Oedipus; after a power struggle with his brother, Eteocles, Polyneices fled the city, eventually returning with an invading army (the "Seven Against Thebes") to make war on his homeland. At a climactic moment in the battle, the two brothers slay each other; the invasion is ultimately repelled and the city saved. In the opening lines of Sophocles' play, we learn that the body of Eteocles, the defender of the city, has been buried with full honors, but according to a decree promulgated by the new king, Creon (who is the young men's uncle), no one, under pain of death, may bury or mourn Polyneices, whose corpse is to be left "unwept, unsepulchered, a treasure to feast on for birds looking out for a dainty meal." (The particular horror, expressed from the *Iliad* on down, that we humans might become the food of the animals we normally eat, is noteworthy: a powerful symbol of a total inversion in the scheme of things, an unhealthy disorder of which the unburied body, the corpse that remains above rather than below ground, is a symptom.)

Like the Senate candidate from Massachusetts who defended his constituents' opposition to burying Tsarnaev's body, Sophocles' Creon cares a great deal about public opinion, as we later learn; but it's certainly possible to argue that his edict is grounded in a strong if idiosyncratic morality. When confronted about his rationale for enshrining in the city's law what is, after all, a religious abomination, the king declares that Polyneices' crime against the city has put the young man beyond morality—that while burial of the dead is a religious obligation, it is impossible to imagine that "the gods have care for this corpse," incredible to think that one might see "the gods honoring the wicked." As he sputters his final line in this debate, you sense that he is acting out of a genuine, if narrow, conviction that evil men do not merit human treatment. "It cannot be," Creon proclaims—a conviction echoed by Representative Markey, the present-day politician, who declared to reporters, apropos of burial of Tsarnaev's body in his home state, "It should not be."

Just as strong as Creon's convictions, however, are those of his niece Antigone: sister to both of the dead young men—Eteocles enshrined in his hero's tomb, Polyneices lying naked on the ground, his weapon-torn body exposed to the elements, to the ravenous birds. From the moment she appears on stage, outraged after having heard about the new edict, Antigone argues for the absolute imperative of burial—indeed, you might say, for the absolute itself. For her, burial of the dead is a universal institution that transcends culture and even time itself: the "unwavering, unwritten customs of the gods . . . not some trifle of now or yesterday, but for all eternity." (She mockingly asks whether these can be overruled by the mere "pronouncements" of Creon.) This conviction is what leads her to perform the galvanizing action of the play: under cover of night she goes to the desolate place where Polyneices' body lies out in the open and performs a token burial, scattering some dirt on it.

It is to this symbolic burial that a terrified soldier—one of the guards whom Creon had set around the body, to make sure no one would inter it—presumably refers later on when he anxiously reports to Creon that someone has performed the rite. Enraged, Creon orders the man to go back and "unbury" the body: to strip off the thin covering of dirt and expose the corpse once more to the elements. It is upon his return to the foul-smelling site that the soldier discovers Antigone, who at that moment is arriving, and who cries out in despair when she sees the denuded corpse. She is taken prisoner, has her great confrontation with her uncle (from which I quote above), and, in one of the diabolically symmetrical punishments so beloved of Greek tragedians, is herself buried alive as punishment for her crime of burying the dead—walled into a tomb of rock. (By not actually killing her, Creon, who has the master bureaucrat's deep feeling for the small procedural detail, hopes to avoid incurring ritual pollution.)

There she does die—imperious to the end, she hangs herself, rather than waste away as anybody's victim—but not before Creon has been persuaded of the folly of his policy. As often happens in tragedy, the persuasion takes its final form as a heap of dead bodies: not only Antigone's but those of Creon's son, the dead girl's fiancé, who has slain himself over the body of his beloved, and Creon's wife, too, who kills herself in despair at the news of their child's violent end. The king who had refused to recognize the claims of family is, in the end, made horribly aware of how important family is.

"The claims of family" is just one way to describe what Antigone represents. The titanic battle between her and Creon is, in fact, one of the most thrilling moral, intellectual, and philosophical confrontations ever dramatized; inevitably, it has been seen as representing any number of cultural conflicts. Certainly in the play there is the tension between the family and the community, but there is also that between the individual and the state, between religious and secular worldviews, between divine and human law, feminine and masculine concerns, the domestic and political realms.

Perhaps a broader rubric is applicable, too. For you could say that what preoccupies Antigone, who as we know is attracted to universals, is simply another "absolute": the absolute personhood of the dead man, stripped of all labels, all categories—at least those imposed by temporal concerns, by politics and war. For her, the defeated and disgraced Polyneices, naked and unburied, is just as much her brother as the triumphant and heroic Eteocles, splendidly entombed. In the end, what entitles Polyneices to burial has nothing to do with which side he was on. (The play is not at all shy about enumerating the horrors the dead man intended to perpetrate on the city, on his native land: the pillage, the burning, the killing, the enslavement of the survivors.) He deserves to be buried because he is an *anthropos*, a human being. This word occurs in one of the most famous choral songs in the tragedy, in which the chorus expresses a kind of astonished wonder at what *Homo sapiens* is capable of—accomplishments for which Sophocles uses the ambiguous adjective *deina*, which means both "terrible" and "wonderful." ("Awesome," we might say, in the original sense of that word.) "There are many awesome/wondrous/terrible things," the chorus sings after Creon is informed that someone has dared to contradict his edict and bury Polyneices' body, "but none is more awesome/wonderous/terrible than humankind."

This is why, after Antigone is apprehended and has her great confrontation with Creon—who keeps insisting on the fact that Eteocles was the champion of the city and Polyneices its foe, and that "a foe is never a friend"—such distinctions are moot for the young woman. The gods themselves, she implies, do not make such distinctions: "Hades requires these rites" for all human beings. The only salient distinction, in this matter, is the one that divides gods from men—which, if true, makes all humans equal.

As I followed the story of Tamerlan Tsarnaev's unburied body, I thought of all this—of the *Iliad* with its grand funereal finale, of the *Odyssey* strangely pivoting around so many burials, and of course of *Antigone*. I thought of canny politicians eyeing the public mood, and of the public to whom those politicians were pandering. I thought even more of the protesters who, understandably to be sure, wanted to make clear the distinction between victim and perpetrator, between friend and foe, by threatening to strip from the enemy what they saw as the prerogatives of the friend: humane treatment in death. The protesters who indeed wanted, like Creon, not only to deny those prerogatives to an enemy but to strip them away again should anyone else grant them: to "unbury the body." I thought of Martha Mullen, a Christian, who insisted that the Muslim Tsarnaev, accused of heinous atrocities against innocent citizens, be buried just as a loved one might deserve to be buried, because she honored the religious precept that demands that we see all humans as "brothers," whatever the evil they have done.

This final point is worth lingering over just now. The last of the many articles I've read about the strange odyssey of Tsarnaev's body was about the reactions of the residents of the small Virginia town where it was, finally, buried. "What do you do when a monster is buried just down the street?" the subhead asked. The sensationalist diction, the word "monster," I realized, is the problem—and brings you to the deep meaning of Mullen's gesture, and of Antigone's argument, too. There is, in the end, a great ethical wisdom in insisting that the criminal dead, that your bitterest enemy, be buried, too; for in doing so, you are insisting that the criminal, however heinous, is precisely not a "monster." Whatever else is true of the terrible crime that Tamerlan Tsarnaev is accused of having perpetrated, it was, all too clearly, the product of an entirely human psyche, horribly motivated by beliefs and passions that are very human indeed—*deina* in the worst possible sense. To call him a monster is to treat this enemy's mind precisely the way some would treat his unburied body; which is to say, to put it beyond the reach of human consideration—and therefore, paradoxically, to refuse to confront his "monstrosity" at all.

This is the point that obsessed Sophocles' Antigone: that to not bury her brother, to not treat the war criminal like a human being, would ultimately have been to forfeit her own humanity. The paradox of the play is that to preserve the life of her soul, she must abandon the life of her body. This is the cost of principle, and she knows it. "I owe a longer allegiance to the dead than to the living," she says at one point, with a moral clarity we might do well to emulate right now, "for in that world I shall abide forever."

—*The New Yorker*, Page-Turner, May 14, 2013

JFK, Tragedy, Myth

"MY FAVORITE POET was Aeschylus."

Thus Senator Robert F. Kennedy, speaking to a traumatized crowd in April 1968. Kennedy, who'd come to a poor black neighborhood in Indianapolis to give a routine campaign speech, had learned en route that Martin Luther King Jr. had been assassinated; it fell to the New York senator to announce the dreadful news. As he struggled to find appropriate language for the day's carnage— which would inevitably have recalled to his mind, and the minds of his audience, the assassination of his brother John five years earlier—it was to Aeschylus's *Oresteia* that Kennedy turned, the grand trilogy about the search for justice in a world filled with metastasizing violence. In the verse he quoted, the Chorus of city elders ponders the meaning of violence and suffering:

> *Even in our sleep, pain which cannot forget*
> *falls drop by drop upon the heart,*
> *until, in our own despair,*
> *against our will,*
> *comes wisdom*
> *through the awful grace of God.*

Kennedy concluded his remarks with an exhortation to heed the wisdom of the ancient classics: "Let us dedicate ourselves to what the Greeks wrote so many years ago: to tame the savageness of man and make gentle the life of this world." That the savageness could not be tamed was demonstrated, with a dreadful Greek irony, three months later, when Kennedy himself was murdered. The lines he cited on the night of King's death were used as the epitaph on his own tombstone.

RFK's allusion to the Greeks turned out to be prophetic. However Jacqueline Kennedy may have labored to make Camelot the official myth of the Kennedy administration, when we have tried to make sense of the Kennedys and their story—to try to find the larger, "mythic" structure beneath the details—we have turned to the Greeks; to Greek tragedy, in particular. It's not hard to see why. Athenian drama returns obsessively—as we do every November 22—to the shocking and yet seemingly inevitable spectacle of a fallen king: of power and beauty and privilege violently laid low. Many tragic plots, moreover, revolve around the ramifications of family curses, of "original sins" committed by a patriarch that come back to haunt later, innocent generations. Both of these narratives, in their different ways, haunt the story of the Kennedy family and of the assassination in particular; both, you suspect, have something to do with the curiously enduring grip exerted by the events that transpired in Dallas in 1963.

The family-curse theme, especially, is one we like to invoke in thinking about the Kennedys. The motif is nowhere stronger than in the *Oresteia* itself. When the Chorus speaks of suffering and pain, it looks as if they're referring to current events: the queen Clytemnestra's plot to murder her husband, Agamemnon, in revenge for his decision to sacrifice their virgin daughter Iphigenia—the sole means, according to a dire prophecy, for the Greek general to obtain favorable winds for his fleet to sail to Troy. But this act, it turns out, is merely a grim continuation of a cycle of carnage that goes back generations, as the Chorus knows only too well: to Agamemnon's father, Atreus, who murdered his brother's children; to Atreus's father, Pelops, who won his bride by violence and betrayal, and was cursed by the man he betrayed; to Pelops's father, Tantalus, a king so favored by the gods that he used to dine with them, until he murdered his own son and fed his flesh to his divine hosts to test whether they were, in fact, all-knowing.

As indeed they are. The point of many tragedies is that the gods deftly pull strings that are invisible to the mortals whose destinies they manipulate: in the space between the immortals' bird's-eye view of the cosmos and our only partial knowledge of things, we mortals stumble, and catastrophe blooms. Works like the *Oresteia*, with its cyclical patterns of violence and retribution, or Sophocles' *Oedipus*—whose hero learns, to his horror, that he cannot foil the "plot" the gods have written for him, as every escape only enmeshes him further in a destiny that was ordained at his birth—seem to confirm that there is an invisible but palpable order in things.

We, too, often seek to discern a kind of order—to find a plot—in the hodgepodge of events we call history. When people talk about the harrowing catalog of sorrow and violent death in the Kennedy family—not only the uncannily twinned assassinations but the wartime midair explosion that killed JFK's older brother, Joseph P. Kennedy Jr.; the two airplane crashes that killed his sister Kathleen and his son, JFK Jr.; the lobotomy and institutionalization of his sister Rosemary; Chappaquiddick; the murder scandal involving a

87

nephew of Ethel Kennedy; the drug addictions and early deaths of some of RFK's children—they often mention, in the same breath, the alleged crimes of the family patriarch, Joseph P. Kennedy. (The bootlegging, the election-fixing, the Mob connections, Gloria Swanson.) In referring to a "Kennedy Curse," they are, essentially, thinking "tragically": thinking the way Aeschylus thought, assuming that there is a dark pattern in the way things happen, a connection between the sins of the fathers and the sufferings of the children and their children afterward.

The tragic conviction that there are long-hidden reasons for the fall of kings finds its most extreme expression today in the obsessive desire to find "plots" of another kind in the Kennedy story: the conspiracy theories. With their Rube Goldbergesque ingenuity, with their elaborateness directly proportional to their preposterousness, these can end up looking suspiciously like madness. (That other favorite tragic subject.) But the impulse to expose, to bring secret crimes to light, to present evidence of deeds done in the past to an audience in the present, is one that itself lies at the heart of Greek drama. You could say that all Athenian tragedy is about the process of discovery, of learning that the present has a surprising and often devastating relationship to the past. Take Oedipus: faced with a plague on his city, he's informed by an oracle that he must find the killer of the previous king—only to learn, as the play unfolds, that the killer was he. Another way of saying this is that all tragedy is about the way that we live: slowly uncovering the deeper meanings of things, often long after we can do anything about them.

Hence, however extreme its manifestations over the years, the tragic yearning to go back, to get it right this time, to use our present knowledge to understand what we couldn't understand then is a vital part of our response to the Kennedy drama—another reason why it remains so insistently alive.

But if the Kennedy backstory reminds us irresistibly of tragedy and its gloomy theodicies, JFK himself powerfully recalls a key character from epic—from Homer's *Iliad*, the grandest of epics and the source for so many tragic plots. And yet the character he reincarnated isn't, in fact, the one so many people think of.

The linchpin of the poem is the wrath of the semidivine Achilles, the greatest of all the Greek warriors besieging Troy, and its dreadful and ultimately unexpected ramifications: an insult to this young warrior's honor in Book 1 sets in motion a train of events that, two-thirds of the way through, results in the death of his bosom friend, Patroclus, at the hands of the Trojan prince Hector. Achilles subsequently takes revenge, slaying Hector in combat and desecrating his unburied body: violence that is shadowed by Achilles' knowledge that his own death is fated to follow Hector's. Many readers are familiar with the poignant choice that Achilles has made in coming to fight at Troy—to die young and gloriously rather than live a long, uneventful life; to a large extent that choice has, since Homer, defined our understanding of what heroism is. As a result, the temptation to identify JFK as an Achilles figure has been powerful. One reason we return obsessively to his story is that it feels like a real-life affirmation of the primitive wisdom we recognize in Achilles' famous choice: that human life is a zero-sum equation, that everlasting renown comes at the price of a brief life.

And, yet, if JFK's story resonates strongly for us, it's because he reminds us of a slightly less glamorous—but equally powerful—character: Hector. Achilles is a free agent, a loner—an only child whose aged father is back home in Greece, far from the action, a warrior who thinks first and foremost of, about, and for himself. (Obsessed with his honor and reputation, he shows no great *esprit de corps*.) Hector, by contrast, is characterized from the start as bound up in a web of political, social, and family relationships: he is the prince of the city, on whose shoulders its defense depends ("Hector" means something like "the one who holds things together"), the dutiful son of the aged king and queen, Priam and Hecuba, the responsible older brother to numerous siblings whom he must often whip into shape (not least the playboy Paris, whose adultery with another man's wife set the war in motion), and, above all, the husband of a beautiful young wife, Andromache, and the father of an enchanting child, Astyanax.

So while Achilles has the glamour of extremity, it is Hector, more than any other character, who feels real to us: bound by competing obligations, anchored to his world and its claims. Homer poignantly dramatizes the conflict between the warrior's public and private selves in a famous scene in Book 6. Here Hector comes off the battlefield to seek out his wife and infant son, but the baby recoils in terror from his father, who, still in armor, is unrecognizable to him. It's only when Hector removes his helmet that the family unit can cohere once more.

For this reason, when Hector dies, he dies not only as a warrior and a prince but also as a husband and a father. Whatever we now know about his personal life (and however reckless his foreign policy may now seem), at the time of his death JFK was very much a Hector figure: the battle-tested hero of the PT-109 incident, the defender of his "city"—and also, as thousands of photographs and television clips seemed to demonstrate, the charming family man with the perfect wife and the enchanting children. The loss of such a person afflicts us both as citizens and as individuals: his death is a trauma both to the nation and to his family. Because it is a trauma, we constantly revisit it, as much to convince ourselves that such a thing could happen as to hope, each time we go back, that it might turn out differently.

There is another, larger and culturally more vital narrative that the events surrounding JFK's death share with the *Iliad*. When we talk about November 1963, we are referring not just to the assassination but to the entire weekend: the brutal murder, the roses lying abandoned and drenched in gore, the bloodstained stockings, the shocked absorption of the news, the grim business of handling the body, conveying it, and preparing it for burial. And then, gradually, amid the horror and confusion, the reassertion of order and ritual: the lying in state, the military guard, the procession of heads of state, the black-clad widow, the children in their Sunday best, the tiny salute, the religious ceremony, the cemetery, the bugle, the shots, the folded flag. The tension between the formal perfection of the public rites and the uncontrollable intensity of the private emotions generates a deep poignancy. John-John's iconic salute touches us for the same reasons that Astyanax's recoil from his helmeted father does: in both cases, the intrusion of the military and its symbols into what ought to be the cocooned realm of the domestic sphere— of childhood itself—strikes us as unbearable.

The arc from harrowing carnage to high ceremony structures the final third of the *Iliad*, too. After he slays Hector, who has killed Patroclus, Achilles, maddened by grief, drags his enemy's body back and forth before the walls of Troy—from which the dead man's family and countrymen watch in anguished horror, like the audience of a tragedy—and around Patroclus's tomb. The desecration of the dead body, the refusal to obey religious convention and give it back to the family for burial, is a mark of Achilles' inability to let go of—to "bury"—his own grief. In the end, the gods themselves insist on what we might call "closure," pointing out that even a man who loses a brother or a son "grieves, weeps, and then his tears are done." In the final book of the poem, the aged king of Troy, Priam, ransoms his dead son's body from Achilles, takes it home to the walled city, and there gives it a proper funeral.

After the trauma of Hector's death and the ongoing degradation of his body, there is an odd courtliness about the exchange between Priam and the man who killed his son: a sudden, wrenching flowering of civilized behavior. (A truce is called so that the Trojans can leave their walled city and go into the surrounding forests to cut wood for Hector's funeral pyre.) As if to remind us of that other world far from the mayhem of battle, the funeral is dominated by the women in Hector's life, who are the only eulogists. His mother speaks, his wife speaks, and even Helen, whose actions precipitated the war in which he died, speaks. Then the body is burned, the bones are gathered and buried. The last line of the entire epic—"This was the funeral of Hector, breaker of horses"—emphasizes the importance of the ritual closure: that simple verse quietly lays to rest not only the Trojan prince but the whole noisy epic, with its mad quarrels and awful carnage and odd moments of privacy and tenderness, its battles and sex and scheming.

The end of the *Iliad* is, in other words, a narrative about grief yielding to mourning, about the way in which civilization responds to violence and horror. This dark solace is one that only culture can provide. Our endless need to replay the events of November 1963— by which I mean all of the events, from Friday to Monday, from the murder to the funeral—is not only about a perverse, almost infantile need to revisit a scene of primal horror. (Although our own refusal to let go of Kennedy's body—expressed most strongly in our endless looping of the Zapruder film, which, like a tragedy, turns the death of the king into a kind of entertainment—certainly shows an Achilles-like unwillingness to bury the past.) It also bears witness to our desire to hear, once again, a very old tale that is not only the story of a fallen warrior and how he died but the story of what we did after he fell, of how the bloodied body was washed and anointed and clothed and grandly entombed and eulogized—all of these activities presided over, in 1963 as in antiquity, by the attentive widow, alert to the symbolic power of ritual details. It is a story, in the end, that only civilization can tell, one in which, however miraculously, calamity is alchemized into a kind of beauty.

Epic itself, a poem that we listen to (or, now, that we read), a beautiful work about often ugly things, war and madness and violence, is an example of that alchemy. So is tragedy, which often takes the stories we know from epic and turns them into something we watch—into spectacles of suffering and death that, through the mystery of art, become both ennobled and ennobling. Many commentators over the years have remarked on the special role that television played in our absorption of the news of that weekend, from the first blurry bulletins on Friday afternoon to the meticulously directed images of the funeral. But what's telling is that, fifty years later, we watch—with a fascination apparently undimmed by the passage of five decades—the same news bulletins, the same footage, the same "news," although, of course, it is no longer new.

This suggests that the conclusion to be drawn is not about "the role of the media"—about news and how we get it—but about *drama*: about our need, as ancient as the Greeks, to see certain elemental plots reenacted before our eyes, at once familiar but always fresh. As superficially shocking as their outcomes may be, these plots tell us things about the world that we know (or at least suspect) to be true: that nature can avenge herself brutally on culture (Euripides' *Bacchae*), that hidden sins of generations past visit suffering on the next generation (Aeschylus's *Oresteia*), that rulers and heroes who are remarkably brilliant and gifted are often crippled by secret flaws (Sophocles' *Oedipus*); that, like Iphigenia, a character who recurs so often in tragedy, innocent young girls will be sacrificed to the ambitions of greedy men.

And of course—the oldest tragic plot point of all, the plot that some believe to be at the root of tragedy as a genre, the reason why drama exists in the first place—that the king, the beautiful, powerful, elite, and talented figure on whose glittering figure all eyes are happy to rest, in whom we seek a model ruler, warrior, husband, and father, is, by virtue of those very excellences, conspicuous, marked out as a sacrificial victim. Hero and victim: our ambiguous relationship to the great—our need to idolize and idealize them, inextricable from our impulse to degrade and destroy them—is the motor of tragedy, which first elevates and then topples its heroes; not coincidentally, that strange relationship has characterized our half-century-long response to the Kennedy story, oscillating dizzyingly, as it has done almost from the start, between the impulse to idealize and urge to demystify.

And so the present keeps replaying the past, repeating those old stories, the narratives that lurk behind the plays and myths, tales and characters so hardwired into our cultural circuitry that we can forget why we knew them in the first place. But when they reappear, we recognize them. This is why, when certain real-life calamities do occur—the sinking of the *Titanic*; the death of Diana, Princess of Wales; the murder, in broad daylight, of John Fitzgerald Kennedy on this day half a century ago—they feel less like aberrations than like fulfillments. Millennia before they played out in real life, we were writing the scripts, waiting for them to come true. The question isn't why we keep going back, after so many years, but how we could do anything else.

—*The New Yorker*, Page-Turner, November 22, 2013

Epic Fail?

SINCE THE END of the first century AD, people have been playing a game with a certain book. In this game, you open the book to a random spot and place your finger on the text; the passage you select will, it is thought, predict your future. If this sounds silly, the results suggest otherwise. The first person known to have played the game was a highborn Roman who was fretting about whether he'd be chosen to follow his cousin, the emperor Trajan, on the throne; after opening the book to this passage—

> *I recognize that he is that king of Rome,*
> *Gray headed, gray bearded, who will formulate*
> *The laws for the early city . . .*

—he was confident that he'd succeed. His name was Hadrian.

Through the centuries, others sought to discover their fates in this book, from Rabelais in the early sixteenth century (some of whose characters play the game, too), to Charles I, who, during the English Civil War—which culminated in the loss of his kingdom and his head—visited an Oxford library and was alarmed to find that he'd placed his finger on a passage that concluded, "But let him die before his time, and lie / Somewhere unburied on a lonely beach." Two and a half centuries after Charles's execution, as the Germans marched toward Paris at the beginning of World War I, a classicist named David Ansell Slater, who had once viewed the very volume that Charles had consulted, found himself scouring the same text, hoping for a portent of good news.

What was the book, and why was it taken so seriously? The answer lies in the name of the game: *sortes vergilianae*. The Latin noun *sortes* means "lots"—as in "drawing lots," a reference to the game's element of chance. The adjective *vergilianae*, which means "having to do with Vergilius," identifies the book: the works of the Roman poet Publius Vergilius Maro, whom we know as Virgil.

For a long stretch of Western history, few people would have found it odd to ascribe prophetic power to this collection of Latin verse. Its author, after all, was the greatest and the most influential of all Roman poets. A friend and confidant of Augustus, Rome's first emperor, Virgil was already considered a classic in his own lifetime: revered, quoted, imitated, and occasionally parodied by other writers, taught in schools, and devoured by the general public. Later generations of Romans considered his works a font of human knowledge, on subjects from rhetoric to ethics to agriculture; by the Middle Ages, the poet had come to be regarded as a wizard whose powers included the ability to control Vesuvius's eruptions and to cure blindness in sheep. However fantastical the proportions to which this reverence grew, it was grounded in a very real achievement represented by one poem in particular: the *Aeneid*, a heroic epic in twelve chapters (or "books") about the mythic founding of Rome, which some ancient sources say Augustus commissioned and which was, arguably, the single most influential literary work of European civilization for the better part of two millennia.

Virgil had published other, shorter works before the *Aeneid*, but it's no accident that the epic was a magnet for the fingers of the great and powerful who played the *sortes vergilianae*. Its central themes are leadership, empire, history, and war. In it, an upstanding Trojan prince named Aeneas, son of Venus, the goddess of love, flees Troy after its destruction by the Greeks and, along with his father, his son, and a band of fellow survivors, sets out to establish a new realm across the sea, in Italy, the homeland that's been promised to him by divine prophecy. Into that traditional story Virgil cannily inserted a number of showstopping glimpses into Rome's future military and political triumphs, complete with cameo appearances by Augustus himself—the implication being that the real-life empire arose from a god-kissed mythic past. The emperor and his people alike were hooked: within a century of its author's death, in 19 BC, citizens of Pompeii were scrawling lines from the epic on the walls of shops and houses.

People haven't stopped quoting it since. From the moment it appeared, the *Aeneid* was the paradigmatic classic in Western art and education; as one scholar has put it, Virgil "occupied the central place in the literary canon for the whole of Europe for longer than any other writer." (After the Western Roman Empire fell, in the late fifth century AD, knowledge of Greek—and, hence, intimacy with Homer's epics—virtually disappeared from Western Europe for a thousand years.) Virgil's poetry has been indispensable to everyone from his irreverent younger contemporary Ovid, whose parodies of the older poet's gravitas can't disguise a genuine admiration, to Saint Augustine, who, in his *Confessions*, recalls weeping over the *Aeneid*, his favorite book before he discovered the Bible; from Dante, who chooses Virgil, *l'altissimo poeta*, "the highest poet," as his guide through Hell and Purgatory in *The Divine Comedy*, to T. S. Eliot,

99

who returned repeatedly to Virgil in his critical essays and pronounced the *Aeneid* "the classic of all Europe."

And not only Europe. Alexander Hamilton, Thomas Jefferson, and Benjamin Franklin liked to quote Virgil in their speeches and letters. The poet's idealized vision of honest farmers and shepherds working in rural simplicity was influential, some scholars believe, in shaping the Founders' vision of the new republic as one in which an agricultural majority should hold power. Throughout the nineteenth century, Virgil was a central fixture of American grammar school education; the ability to translate passages on sight was a standard entrance requirement at many colleges and universities. John Adams boasted that his son John Quincy had translated the entire *Aeneid*. Ellen Emerson wrote her father, Ralph Waldo, to say that she was covering 120 lines a day; Helen Keller read it in braille. Today, traces of the epic's cultural authority linger on: a quotation from it greets visitors to the Memorial Hall of the National September 11 Memorial & Museum in New York City. Since the turn of the current century, there have been at least five major translations into English alone, most recently by the American poet David Ferry, in the final installment of his translation of Virgil's complete works.

Still, the *Aeneid*—notoriously—can be hard to love. In part, this has to do with its aesthetics. In place of the raw archaic potency of Homer's epics, which seems to dissolve the millennia between his heroes and us, Virgil's densely allusive poem offers an elaborately self-conscious "literary" suavity. (The critic and Columbia professor Mark Van Doren remarked that "Homer is a world; Virgil, a style.") Then, there's Aeneas himself—"in some ways," as even the Great Courses website felt compelled to acknowledge, "the dullest character in epic literature." In the *Aeneid's* opening lines, Virgil announces that the hero is famed above all for his *pietas*, his "sense of duty": hardly the sexiest attribute for a protagonist. If Aeneas was meant to be a model proto-Roman, he has long struck many readers as a cold fish; he and his comrades, the philosopher György Lukács once observed, live "the cool and limited existence of shadows." Particularly in comparison with his Homeric predecessors, Aeneas comes up short, lacking the cruel glamour of Achilles or Odysseus's beguiling smarts.

But the biggest problem by far for modern audiences is the poem's subject matter. Today, the themes that made the epic required reading for generations of emperors and generals, and for the clerics and teachers who groomed them—the inevitability of imperial dominance, the responsibilities of authoritarian rule, the importance of duty and self-abnegation in the service of the state—are proving to be an embarrassment. If readers of an earlier era saw the *Aeneid* as an inspiring advertisement for the onward march of Rome's many descendants, from the Holy Roman Empire to the British one, scholars now see in it a tale of nationalistic arrogance whose plot is an all-too-familiar handbook for repressive violence: once Aeneas and his fellow Trojans arrive on the coast of Italy, they find that they must fight a series of wars with an indigenous population that, eventually, they brutally subjugate.

The result is that readers today can have a very strange relationship to this classic: it's a work we feel we should embrace but often keep at arm's length. Take that quote in the 9/11 Museum: "No day shall erase you from the memory of time." Whoever came up with the idea of using it was clearly ignorant of the context: these high-minded words are addressed to a pair of nighttime marauders whose bloody ambush of a group of unsuspecting targets suggests that they have far more in common with the September 11 terrorists than with their victims. A century ago, many a college undergrad could have caught the gaffe; today, it was enough to have an impressive-sounding quote from an acknowledged classic.

Another way of saying all this is that while our forebears looked confidently to the text of the *Aeneid* for answers, today it raises troubling questions. Who exactly is Aeneas, and why should we admire him? What is the epic's political stance? Can we ignore the parts we dislike and cherish the rest? Should great poetry serve an authoritarian regime—and just whose side was Virgil on? Two thousand years after its appearance, we still can't decide if his masterpiece is a regressive celebration of power as a means of political domination or a craftily coded critique of imperial ideology—a work that still has something useful to tell us.

Little in Virgil's background destined him to be the great poet of empire. He was born on October 15, 70 BC, in a village outside Mantua; his father, perhaps a well-off farmer, had the means to provide him with a good education, first in Cremona and Milan and then in Rome. The inhabitants of his native northern region had only recently been granted Roman citizenship through a decree by Julius Caesar, issued when the poet was a young man. Hence even after his first major work, a collection of pastoral poems called the *Eclogues*, gained him an entrée into Roman literary circles, Virgil must have seemed—and perhaps felt—something of an outsider: a reserved country fellow with (as his friend the poet Horace teased him) a hick's haircut, who spoke so haltingly that he could seem downright uneducated. His retiring nature, which earned him the nickname *parthenias* ("little virgin"), may have been the reason he decided not to remain in Rome to complete his education. Instead, he settled in Naples, a city with deep ties to the culture of the Greeks, which he and his literary contemporaries revered. In the final lines of the *Georgics*, a long didactic poem about farming that he finished when he was around forty, the poet looked back yearningly to the untroubled leisure he had enjoyed during that period:

> *And I, the poet Virgil, nurtured by sweet*
> *Parthénopé [Naples], was flourishing in the pleasures*
> *Of idle studies, I, who bold in youth*
> *Played games with shepherds' songs.*

I'm quoting David Ferry's translation of the poem. But the word that Ferry translates as "idle" is somewhat stronger in the original: Virgil says that his leisure time was *ignobilis*, "ignoble," a choice that suggests some guilt about that easygoing Neapolitan idyll. And with good reason: however "sweet" those times were for Virgil, for Rome they were anything but. The poet's lifetime spanned the harrowing disintegration of the Roman Republic and the fraught birth of the Empire—by any measure, one of the most traumatic centuries in European history. Virgil was a schoolchild when the orator and statesman Cicero foiled a plot by the corrupt aristocrat Catiline to overthrow the Republic; by the time the poet was twenty, Julius Caesar, defying the Senate's orders, had crossed the Rubicon with his army and set in motion yet another civil war. It was another two decades before Caesar's great-nephew and heir, Octavian, defeated the last of his rivals, the renegade general Antony and his Egyptian consort, Cleopatra, at the Battle of Actium, and established the so-called Principate—the rule of the *princeps* ("first citizen"), an emperor in everything but name. Soon afterward, he took the quasi-religious honorific "Augustus."

The new ruler was a man of refined literary tastes; Virgil and his patron, Maecenas, the regime's unofficial minister of culture, are said to have taken turns reading the *Georgics* aloud to him after his victory at Actium. Augustus no doubt liked what he heard. In one passage, the poet expresses a fervent hope that Rome's young new leader will be able to spare Italy the wars that have wreaked havoc on the lives of the farmers whose labor is the subject of the poem; in another, he envisages the erection of a grand temple honoring the ruler.

Because we like to imagine poets as being free in their political conscience, such fawning seems distasteful. (Robert Graves, the author of *I, Claudius*, complained that "few poets have brought such discredit as Virgil on their sacred calling.") But Virgil cannot have been alone among intelligent Romans in welcoming Augustus's regime as, at the very least, a stable alternative to the decades of internecine horrors that had preceded it. If Augustus did in fact suggest the idea for a national epic, it must have been while Virgil was still working on the *Georgics*, which includes a trailer for his next project: "And soon I'll gird myself to tell the tales / Of Caesar's brilliant battles, and carry his name / In story across . . . many future years." He began work on the *Aeneid* around 29 BC and was in the final stages of writing when, ten years later, he died suddenly while returning home from a trip to Greece. He was buried in his beloved Naples.

The epic's state of completion continues to be a subject of debate. There's little doubt that a number of lines are metrically incomplete, a fact that dovetails with what we know about the poet's working method: he liked to joke that, in order to preserve his momentum while writing, he'd put in temporary lines to serve as "struts" until the "finished columns" were ready. According to one anecdote, the dying Virgil begged his literary executors to burn the manuscript of the epic, but Augustus intervened, and, after some light editing, the finished work finally appeared. In the epitaph he composed for himself, Virgil refers with disarming modesty to his achievement: "Mantua gave me birth, Calabria took me, now Naples / holds me fast. I sang of pastures, farms, leaders."

Virgil was keenly aware that, in composing an epic that begins at Troy, describes the wanderings of a great hero, and features book after book of gory battles, he was working in the long shadow of Homer. But instead of being crushed by what Harold Bloom called "the anxiety of influence," he found a way to acknowledge his Greek models while adapting them to Roman themes. Excerpts of the work in progress were already impressing fellow writers by the mid-20s BC, when the love poet Propertius wrote that "something greater than the *Iliad* is being born."

The very structure of the *Aeneid* is a wink at Homer. The epic is split between an "Odyssean" first half (Books I through VI recount Aeneas's wanderings as he makes his way from Troy to Italy) and an "Iliadic" second half (Books VII through XII focus on the wars that the hero and his allies wage in order to take possession of their new homeland). Virgil signals this appropriation of the two Greek classics in his work's famous opening line, "Arms and a man I sing": the

Iliad is the great epic of war ("arms"), while the *Odyssey* begins by announcing that its subject is "a man"—Odysseus. Virtually every one of the *Aeneid*'s 9,896 lines is embedded, like that first one, in an intricate web of literary references, not only to earlier Greek and Roman literature but to a wide range of religious, historical, and mythological arcana. This allusive complexity would have flattered the sophistication of the original audience, but today it can leave everyone except specialists flipping to the endnotes. In this way, Virgil's Homeric riff prefigures James Joyce's twenty centuries later: whatever the great passages of intense humanity, there are parts that feel like a treasure hunt designed for graduate students of the future.

It is hardly surprising that readers through the centuries have found the *Aeneid*'s first half more engaging. As in the *Odyssey*, there are shipwrecks caused by angry deities (Juno, the queen of the gods, tries to foil Aeneas at every turn) and succor from helpful ones (Venus intervenes every now and then to help her son). There are councils of the gods at which the destinies of mortals are sorted out; at one point, Jupiter, the king of the pantheon, assures the anxious Venus (and, by implication, the Roman reader) that the nation her son is about to found will enjoy *imperium sine fine*, "rule without end." As for the mortals, there are melancholy reunions with old friends and family and hair-raising encounters with legendary monsters. Virgil has a lot of fun retooling episodes from the *Odyssey*: his hero has close calls with Scylla and Charybdis, lands on the Cyclops' island just after Odysseus has left, and—in an amusing moment that does an end run around Homer—decides to sail right past Circe's abode.

And like Odysseus, Aeneas is dangerously distracted from his mission by a beautiful woman: Dido, the queen of the North African city of Carthage, where the hero has been welcomed hospitably after he is shipwrecked. Venus, eager for her son to find a safe haven there, sends Cupid to make Dido fall in love with Aeneas in Book I, and throughout Books II and III the queen grows ever more besotted with her guest, who holds her court spellbound with tales of his sufferings and adventures. His eyewitness account of the sack of Troy, in Book II, remains one of the most powerful depictions of military violence in European literature, with a disorienting, almost cinematic oscillation between seething, smoke-filled crowd scenes and claustrophobic moments of individual panic. At one point, Aeneas, fleeing the smoldering ruins, somehow loses track of his wife, Creusa; in a chillingly realistic evocation of war's chaos, we never learn how she dies. As for Dido, her affair with the hero reaches a tragic climax in Book IV. Aeneas, reminded by the gods of his sacred duty, abandons her, and she commits suicide—the emotional high point of the epic's first half. (The curse she calls down on her former lover is the passage that King Charles selected when he played the *sortes vergilianae*.)

The *Aeneid*'s first part ends, as does the first half of the *Odyssey*, with an unsettling visit to the Underworld. Here there are confrontations with the dead and the past they represent—Dido's ghost doesn't deign to acknowledge the apologetic Aeneas's protestations—and encounters, too, with the glorious future. One of the spirits that Aeneas meets is his father, Anchises, whom he'd carried on his back as they fled Troy, and who has since died; as Anchises guides his son through the murky landscape, he draws his attention to a fabulous parade of monarchs, warriors, statesmen, and heroes who will distinguish the history of the future Roman state, from the mythic king Romulus to Augustus himself. As they witness this pageant, the old man imparts a crucial piece of advice. The Greeks, he observes, excelled at the arts—sculpture, rhetoric—but Rome has a far greater mission in world history:

> *Romans, never forget that this will be*
> *Your appointed task: to use your arts to be*
> *The governor of the world, to bring to it peace,*
> *Serenely maintained with order and with justice,*
> *To spare the defeated and to bring an end*
> *To war by vanquishing the proud.*

This conception of Rome's strengths—administration, governance, jurisprudence, war—in relation to Greece's will be familiar to anyone who's taken a World Civ course. What's so confounding is that, after receiving this eloquent advice on the correct uses of power, Aeneas—as the second half of the poem shockingly demonstrates—doesn't take it.

Books VII through XII, with their unrelenting account of the *bella horrida bella* ("wars, horrible wars") that Aeneas must wage to secure his new homeland, are clearly meant to recall the *Iliad*—not least, in the event that sets them in motion. After the hero arrives in Italy, he favorably impresses a local king named Latinus, who promises his daughter, Lavinia, as a wife for Aeneas. The problem is that the girl has already been chosen for a local chieftain named Turnus, who, smarting from the insult, goes on to command the forces trying to repel the Trojan invaders. And so, like the war recounted in the *Iliad*, this one is fought over a woman who has been stolen from her rightful mate—the difference being that this time it's the Trojans, not the Greeks, who invade a foreign country and ravage a kingdom in order to retrieve her. One challenge presented by the mythic Trojan origins of the Roman people was that the Trojans lost their great war; reshaping his source material, Virgil found a way to transform a story about losers into an epic about winners.

But what does it mean to be a winner? Anchises instructs his son that, to be a Roman, he must become (in Ferry's translation) "governor of the world." This rendering of Virgil's phrase *regere imperio populos* is rather mild. John Dryden's 1697 translation far better conveys the menace lurking in the word *imperium* ("the right to command"): "'tis thine alone, with awful sway, / To rule Mankind; and make the World obey."

Just what making the world obey looks like is vividly illustrated in another vision of the future that the *Aeneid* provides. In Book VIII, there is a lengthy description of the sumptuous shield that Vulcan, the blacksmith god, forges for Aeneas before he meets Turnus and the Italian hordes in battle. The decorations on the shield meld moments both mythic and historical, past and future, from Romulus and Remus being suckled by the she-wolf to a central panel depicting the Battle of Actium, with Augustus and his brilliant general Agripp on one side facing off against Antony and Cleopatra on the other. (She's backed by her foreign "monster gods": that "monster" is a telling bit of Roman jingoism that Ferry inexplicably omits.) The shield also includes an image of Augustus marching triumphantly through the capital as its temples resound with the joyful singing of mothers, while—that other product of *imperium*—a host of conquered peoples are marched through the streets: nomads, Africans, Germans, Scythians.

Yet one battle into which Aeneas carries his remarkable shield ends with the hero unaccountably failing to adhere to the second part of his father's exhortation: to "spare the defeated." As the poem nears its conclusion, the wars gradually narrow to a single combat between Aeneas and Turnus, who, by that point, has slain a beautiful youth called Pallas, Aeneas's ward and the son of his chief ally. In the closing lines of the poem, Aeneas fells Turnus with a crippling blow to the thigh. While his enemy lies prostrate before him, the hero hesitates, sword in hand; but, just as thoughts of leniency crowd his mind—he is, after all, famous for his sense of duty, for doing the right thing—he sees that Turnus is wearing a piece of armor torn from Pallas's body. Seized with rage and grief, Aeneas rips open Turnus's breast with one blow, and the dead man's soul "indignant fled away to the shades below."

That is the last line of the poem—an ending so disorientingly abrupt that it has been cited as evidence by those who believe that Virgil left his magnum opus incomplete when he died. One fifteenth-century Italian poet went so far as to add an extra book to the poem (in Latin verse) tying Virgil's loose ends into a neat bow: Aeneas marries Lavinia and is eventually deified. This ending was so popular that it was included in editions of the *Aeneid* for centuries afterward.

As recently as the early twentieth century, the *Aeneid* was embraced as a justification of the Roman—and, by extension, any—empire: "a classic vindication of the European world-order," as one scholar put it. (This position is known among classicists as the "optimistic" interpretation.) The marmoreal perfections of its verse seemed to reflect the grand façades of the Roman state itself: Augustus boasted that he found Rome a city of brick and left it a city of marble.

But in the second half of the last century more and more scholars came to see some of the epic's most wrenching episodes as attempts to draw attention to the toll that the exercise of *imperium* inevitably takes. This "pessimistic" approach to the text and its relation to imperial ideology has found its greatest support in the account of Aeneas's treatment of Dido. That passionate, tender, and grandly tragic woman is by far the epic's greatest character—and indeed the only one to have had a lasting impact on Western culture past the Middle Ages, memorably appearing in works by artists ranging from Purcell to Berlioz to Mark Morris.

After the gods order Aeneas to abandon Dido and leave Carthage—he mustn't, after all, end up like Antony, the love slave of an African queen—he prepares to sneak away. But Dido finds him out and, in a furious tirade, lambastes the man she considers to be her husband for his craven evasion of a kind of responsibility—emotional, ethical—quite unlike the political dutifulness that has driven him from the start:

> *What shall I say? What is there for me to say? . . .*
> *There is nowhere where faith is kept; not anywhere.*
> *He was stranded on the beach, a castaway,*
> *With nothing. I made him welcome.*

In uttering these words, Dido becomes the *Aeneid*'s most eloquent voice of moral outrage at the promises that always get broken by men with a mission; in killing herself, she becomes a heartbreaking symbol of the collateral damage that "empire" leaves in its wake.

Aeneas's reaction to her tirade is telling. Unable to bring himself to look her in the eye, he looks instead "at the future / He was required to look at":

Pious Aeneas, groaning and sighing, and shaken
In his very self in his great love for her,
And longing to find the words that might assuage
Her grief over what is being done to her,
Nevertheless obeyed the divine command
And went back to his fleet.

You wish that Ferry hadn't translated the Latin word *pius* in the first line of this passage as the English word it so closely resembles, "pious"; here more than anywhere else, *pius* means "dutiful," embodying a steadfast obedience to the gods' plan that overrides every other consideration. Much of the *Aeneid* is fueled by this torturous conflict between private fulfillment and public responsibility, which was to become a staple of European literature and drama, showing up in everything from Corneille to *The Crown*. (You sometimes get the impression that Virgil himself would like to be free of his poetic duty to celebrate the empire. In Book V, a long set piece about a sailing competition that Aeneas holds for his men, filled with verve and humor, feels like a vacation for the poet, too.)

When Aeneas does reply to Dido, he's as cool as a corporate lawyer, rattling off one talking point after another. (Dido has a kingdom of her own, so why shouldn't he?) But how are we to reconcile this Aeneas with the distraught figure we're left with at the end of the poem, a man who goes berserk when he's reminded of the loss of his

young ward and who brutally slays a captive supplicant? The contra-
diction has led to persistent questions about the coherence of Virgil's
depiction of his hero. When critics aren't denouncing Aeneas's lack
of personality ("a stick who would have contributed to *The New
Statesman*," Ezra Pound sniffed), they're fulminating against his lack
of character. "A cad to the last" was Robert Graves's summation.

And as with the hero so, too, with the epic itself: for many readers,
something doesn't add up. If the *Aeneid* is an admiring piece of
propaganda for empire triumphant, whose hero emblematizes the
necessity of suppressing individuality in the interest of the state,
what do you do with Dido—or, for that matter, with Turnus, who
could well strike readers today as a heroic native resisting colonial
incursion, an admirable prototype of Sitting Bull? And if it's a veiled
critique of empire that movingly catalogues the horrible costs of
imperium, what do you do with all the imperial dazzle—the shield,
the parade of future Romans, the apparent endorsement of the hero's
dogged allegiance to duty?

Latin is a rather chunky language. Unlike Greek, which is far more
supple, it has no definite or indefinite articles; a page of Latin can
look like a wall of bricks. As such, it's particularly difficult to adapt
to dactylic hexameter, the waltzlike, oom-pah-pah meter of epic
poetry, which the Romans inherited from the Greeks. One of Virgil's

achievements was to bring Latin hexameter verse to an unusually high level of flexibility and polish, stretching long thoughts and sentences over several lines, gracefully balancing pairs of nouns and adjectives, and finding ways to temper the natural heaviness of his native tongue. Alfred, Lord Tennyson, called the result "the stateliest measure ever moulded by the lips of man."

David Ferry more than succeeds in capturing the stateliness, as his translation of the Proem, the epic's introductory lines, into English blank verse shows:

> *I sing of arms and the man whom fate had sent*
> *To exile from the shores of Troy to be*
> *The first to come to Lavinium and the coasts*
> *Of Italy, and who, because of Juno's*
> *Savage implacable rage, was battered by storms*
> *At sea, and from the heavens above, and also*
> *By tempests of war, until at last he might*
> *Bring his household gods to Latium, and build his town,*
> *From which would come the Alban Fathers and*
> *The lofty walls of Rome.*

Alone among recent translators, as far as I am aware, Ferry has honored the crucial fact that, in the original, this is all one long flowing sentence and one thought: from Troy to Rome, from past to present, from defeat to victory.

But there's more to Virgil than high polish. You might compare Ferry's rendering to that of the 2007 Oxford World Classics translation by Frederick Ahl, which is far more attentive to some crucial vocabulary:

Arms and the man I sing of Troy, who first from its seashores,
Italy-bound, fate's refugee, arrived at Lavinia's
Coastlands, how he was battered about over land, over high deep
Seas by the power above! Savage Juno's anger remembered
Him, and he suffered profoundly in war to establish a city,
Settle his gods into Latium, making this land of the Latins
Future home to the Elders of Alba and Rome's mighty ramparts.

Ahl here preserves some crucial diction that disappears in Ferry's translation. "Juno's anger remembered," for instance, is a smart solution for the poet's pointed description of the goddess's rage as *memorem*, "remembering": the motif of savage wrath growing out of a compulsive remembering, a pathological inability to forget past hurts, is vital to the epic from these first lines to its final moments. Ferry's bland "implacable" does nothing to convey this all-important motif.

Ahl's translation also preserves a certain oddness in Virgil's verse that Ferry's elegance smooths away. Because the *Aeneid's* instantaneous status as a classic made its style a standard, it's difficult to appreciate how innovative and idiosyncratic Virgil's poetry once felt. One favorite device, for instance, is called "hypallage," in which an adjective is pointedly displaced from the noun it should, logically, modify. Take the last line of the Proem, with its climactic vision of what Ferry renders as "the lofty walls of Rome." What Virgil actually wrote was stranger: "the walls of lofty Rome." The poet knew what he was doing—"lofty walls" is about architecture, but "lofty Rome" is about empire. Here and elsewhere, Ferry's stately rendering has the effect of "correcting" the original's strangeness. As such, it is likely to leave you wondering why critics both ancient and modern have scratched their heads over Virgil's poetics—his occasionally jarring or archaic diction, his "tasteless striving for effect" (as Augustus's friend and general Agrippa complained), his "use of words too forcible for his thoughts," as A. E. Housman put it two millennia later. It's these arresting qualities that made Virgil feel modern to his contemporaries—something it's almost impossible to feel about him in this translation and so many others.

In a way, Virgil may be the victim of his own literary sophistication. The archaic force of Homer's epics makes itself felt despite the moral and cultural distance that separates them from us; the elemental qualities of their protagonists impress themselves on us, however strange their mores. This is why even adaptations that take great liberties—Alice Oswald's *Memorial* or Christopher Logue's *All Day Permanent Red*, both searing riffs on the *Iliad*—manage to feel true to the originals while completely reworking them. But for all that it's the product of a civilization much closer to our own than the Greeks', Virgil's poetry has proved curiously difficult to pin down, to make feel modern. In an essay on Virgil in English translation, the Oxford scholar Colin Burrow summed up the problem: "Virgil has not found an Ezra Pound ... or a Christopher Logue to wrench him into modernity."

It may be that we don't need to rely on a translation to drag the *Aeneid* into the modern era. Maybe it's always been here, and we're just looking at it from the wrong angle—or looking for the wrong things. Maybe the inconsistencies in the hero and his poem that have distressed readers and critics—the certainties alternating with doubt, the sudden careening from coolness to high emotion, the poet's admiring embrace of an empire whose moral offenses he can't help cataloguing, the optimistic portrait of a great nation rising haunted by a cynical appraisal of realpolitik at work—aren't problems of interpretation that we have to solve but, rather, the qualities in which this work's modernity resides.

This, at any rate, is what was going through my mind one day fifteen years ago, when, I like to think, I finally began to understand the *Aeneid*. At the time, I was working on a book about the Holocaust, and had spent several years interviewing the few remaining survivors from a small Polish town whose Jewish population had been obliterated by what you could legitimately call an exercise of *imperium*. As I pressed these elderly people for their memories, I was struck by the similarities in the way they talked: a kind of resigned fatalism, a forlorn acknowledgment that the world they were trying to describe was, in the end, impossible to evoke; strange swings between an almost abnormal detachment when describing unspeakable atrocities and sudden eruptions of ungovernable rage and grief triggered by the most trivial memory.

Months later, when I was back home teaching Greek and Roman classics again, it occurred to me that the difficulties we have with Aeneas and his epic cease to be difficulties once you think of him not as a hero but as a type we're all too familiar with: a survivor, a person so fractured by the horrors of the past that he can hold himself together only by an unnatural effort of will, someone who has so little of his history left that the only thing that gets him through the present is a numbed sense of duty to a barely discernible future that can justify every kind of deprivation. It would be hard to think of a more modern figure.

Or, indeed, a more modern story. What is the *Aeneid* about? It is about a tiny band of outcasts, the survivors of a terrible persecution. It is about how these survivors—clinging to a divine assurance that an unknown and faraway land will become their new home—arduously cross the seas, determined to refashion themselves as a new people, a nation of victors rather than victims. It is about how, when they finally get there, they find their new homeland inhabited by locals who have no intention of making way for them. It is about how this geopolitical tragedy generates new wars, wars that will, in turn, trigger further conflicts: *bella horrida bella*. It is about how such conflicts leave those involved in them morally unrecognizable, even to themselves. This is a story that both the Old and the New Worlds know too well; and Virgil was the first to tell it. Whatever it meant in the past, and however it discomfits the present, the *Aeneid* has, alas, always anticipated the future.

—*The New Yorker*, October 15, 2018

As Good as Great Poetry Gets

"OUTSIDE HIS POEMS Cavafy does not exist." Seventy-five years after the death of "the Alexandrian" (as he is known in Greece), the early verdict of his fellow poet George Seferis—which must have seemed rather harsh in 1946, when the Constantine Cavafy who had existed in flesh and blood was still a living memory for many people—seems only to gain in validity. That flesh-and-blood existence was, after all, fairly unremarkable: a middling job as a government bureaucrat, a modest, even parsimonious routine, no great fame or recognition until relatively late (and even then hardly great), a private life of homosexual encounters kept so discreet that even today its content, as much as there was content, remains largely unknown to us.

All this—the mediocrity, the obscurity (whether intentional or not)—stands in such marked contrast to the poetry, with its haunted memories of seethingly passionate encounters in the present and its astoundingly rich imagination of the remote Greek past, from Homer to Byzantium, from Alexandria and Rome to barely hellenized provincial cities in the Punjab, that it has been hard not to agree with Seferis that the "real" life of the poet was, in fact, almost completely interior; and that outside that imagination and those memories, there was little of lasting interest.

As the man and everyone who knew him have passed into history, the contrast between the life and the art has made it easy to think of Cavafy in the abstract, as an artist whose work exists untethered to a specific moment in time. This trend has been given impetus by the two elements of his poetry for which he is most famous: his startlingly contemporary subject (one of his subjects, at any rate) and his appealingly straightforward style. Certainly there have always been many readers who appreciate the so-called historical poems, set in marginal Mediterranean locales and long-dead eras and tart with *mondain* irony and a certain weary stoicism. ("Ithaca gave you the beautiful journey; / without her you wouldn't have set upon the road. / But now she has nothing left to give you," he writes in what is perhaps his most famous evocation of ancient Greek culture, which tells us that the journey is always more important than the inevitably disappointing destination.)

But it is probably fair to say that Cavafy's popular reputation currently rests almost entirely on the remarkably prescient way in which those other, "sensual" poems, as often as not set in the poet's present, treat the ever-fascinating and pertinent themes of erotic longing, fulfillment, and loss; the way, too, in which memory preserves what desire so often cannot sustain. That the desire and longing were for other men only makes him seem more contemporary, more at home in our own times.

As for the style, it is by now a commonplace that Cavafy's language, because it was so bare of common poetic devices—image, simile, metaphor, specialized diction—is tantamount to prose. One of the first to make this observation was Seferis himself, during the same 1946 lecture at Athens in which he passed judgment on Cavafy's life: "Cavafy stands at the boundary where poetry strips herself in order to become prose," he remarked, although not without admiration. "He is the most anti-poetic (or a-poetic) poet I know." Bare of its own nuances, that appraisal, and others like it, have inevitably filtered into the popular consciousness and been widely disseminated—not least because the idea of a plainspoken, wholly modern Cavafy, impatient with the frills and fripperies characteristic of his Belle Epoque youth, dovetails nicely with what so many see as his principal subject, one that seems to be wholly contemporary, too.

No one more than Cavafy, who studied history not only avidly but with a scholar's respect for detail and meticulous attention to nuance, would have recognized the dangers of abstracting people from their historical surroundings; and nowhere is this more true than in the case of Cavafy himself. To be sure, his work—the best of it, at any rate, which is as good as great poetry gets—is indeed timeless in the way we like to think that great literature can be, alchemizing the particulars of the poet's life, times, and obsessions into something relevant to a wide public over years and even centuries. But the tendency to see him as one of us, as someone of our own moment, speaking to us in a voice that is transparently, recognizably our own about things whose meaning is self-evident, threatens to take a crucial specificity away from him—one that, if we restore it to him, makes him seem only greater, more a poet of the future (as he once described himself).

I am referring here, of course, to the particulars of the "life" that Seferis denied him, which is to say to his place and time. By "place" I mean the fervid if declining peripheries of the cosmopolitan Greek diaspora (Alexandria always; never Athens); by "time" I mean the nineteenth century, which—astoundingly, it sometimes seems— Cavafy inhabited for more than half his life. That time deeply colored the poet's early style (many readers will be surprised to learn that much of his output, until he was nearly forty, was in sonnet form), while the place had a lasting influence on his themes, particularly his lifelong penchant for exploring the margins, the obscurer realms of Greek history and geography—Seleucia and Antioch and Cyrene, the second century BC and the fifth and seventh and fourteenth AD—and, of course, the obscurer realms of erotic experience as well. Being on the margins is, in fact, the key to this poet's work, both "historical" and "sensual." To fail to appreciate Cavafy's unique perspective, one that (as it were) allowed him to see history with a lover's eye and love with a historian's eye, is to be deprived of a chance to see the great and moving unity of the poet's project.

In one sense, it was indeed an unexceptional life—or at least, no more exceptional or distinguished than the lives of certain other great poets, in whom the richness of the work stands in striking contrast to the relative uneventfulness of the life (Emily Dickinson, say). Constantine Petrou Cavafy—the Anglicized spelling of the Greek Kavafis was one that Cavafy and his family invariably used— was born in Alexandria in 1863, the youngest of seven surviving sons of parents whose families were not at all untypical of the far-flung Greek diaspora, with its hints of vanished empire. Their roots could be traced not only to the Phanar, the Greek community clustered around the Patriarchate in Constantinople, and to Nichori (Turkish

Yeniköi) in the Upper Bosporus, but also to Caesarea, to Antioch, and to Jassy, in present-day Moldavia.

His father, Peter John Cavafy, was a partner in a flourishing family business devoted to corn and cotton export that eventually had offices in London and Liverpool as well as in several cities in Egypt; after moving from Constantinople to London, he finally settled in Alexandria, where he would be considered one of the most important merchants in the mid-1850s (not coincidentally, a time when the Crimean War resulted in a steep rise in the price of grain). The poet's mother, Haricleia Photiades, the daughter of a diamond merchant from Constantinople, counted an archbishop of Caesarea and a prince of Samos among her relations.

What effect the memory of such glory and prestige—carefully tended and endlessly polished by his mother long after she'd become a widow living in not very genteel poverty—might have had on her impressionable and imaginative youngest son, we can only guess at; but it is surely no accident that so much of Cavafy's poetry is torn between deep sentiment about the lost riches of the past and the intelligent child's rueful, sharp-eyed appreciation of the dangers of glib nostalgia. For his father's premature death, when Constantine was only seven, would bring hard times to Haricleia and her sons, from which the family fortunes would never really recover. Peter John had lived well but not wisely.

For several years the widow Cavafy and her three younger sons ambled back and forth between Paris and London and Liverpool, relying on the generosity of her husband's brothers. They stayed in England for five years, where Cavafy acquired the slight British inflection that, we are told, accented his Greek. When it became clear that the surviving brothers had hopelessly bungled their own affairs, Haricleia returned to Alexandria in 1877, when Cavafy was fourteen. With the exception of a three-year sojourn in Constantinople, from 1882 to 1885, following the British bombardment of Alexandria (a response to Egyptian nationalist violence against some of the city's European inhabitants; the bombardment largely destroyed the family home), Cavafy would never live anywhere else again.

For some time, the life he lived there was, as he later described it to his friend Timos Malanos, a "double life." The poet had probably had his first homosexual affair around the age of twenty, with a cousin, during his family's stay in Constantinople; there is no question that he continued to act on the desires that were awakened at that time once he returned to Alexandria. By day, when he was in his middle and late twenties, he was his corpulent mother's dutiful son (he called her, in English, "the Fat One"), working gratis as a clerk at the Irrigation Office of the Ministry of Public Works in the hopes of obtaining a salaried position there. (This he eventually did, in 1892, remaining at the office with the famously Dantesque name—the Third Circle of Irrigation—until his retirement thirty years later.) From seven-thirty to ten in the evening he was expected to dine with the exigent and neurotic Haricleia. Afterward, he would escape to the city's louche quarters.

One friend recalled that he kept a room in a brothel on the Rue Mosquée Attarine; another that he would return from his exploits and write, in large letters on a piece of paper, "I swear I won't do it again." Like many bourgeois homosexual men of his era and culture (and indeed later ones), he seems to have enjoyed the favors, and company, of lower-class youths: another acquaintance would recall Cavafy telling him that he'd once worked briefly as a dishwasher in a restaurant in order to save the job of one such friend, who'd been taken ill. About the youths and men he slept with we know little. We do know, from an extraordinary series of secret notes that he kept about his habitual masturbation, that the amusing Alexandrian nickname for that activity—"39," because it was thought to be that many times more exhausting than any other sexual activity—was not entirely unjustified:

> And yet I see clearly the harm and confusion that my actions produce upon my organism. I must, inflexibly, impose a limit on myself till 1 April, otherwise I shan't be able to travel. I shall fall ill and how am I to cross the sea, and if I'm ill, how am I to enjoy my journey? Last January I managed to control myself. My health got right at once, I had no more throbbing. 6 March 1897.

At about the same time he'd settled in his rather dreary job, he began to write and publish seriously. Apart from that, the life he led, as he got older, wasn't noticeably different from that of many a mid-level provincial functionary. He enjoyed gambling, in moderation; he played the stock market, not without success. Apart from his constant and extensive reading of ancient and modern historians in a variety of languages, his tastes in literature were hardly remarkable. His library of about three hundred volumes contained a quantity of what his younger Alexandrian friend the botanist J. A. Sareyannis later recalled, with a palpable shudder, as "unmentionable novels by unknown and forgotten writers." An exception was Marcel Proust, the second volume of whose *In Search of Lost Time* he borrowed from a friend not long after its publication. "The grandmother's death!" he enthused to Sareyannis. "What a masterpiece!

Proust is a great writer! A very great writer!" (Interestingly, he was less enthusiastic about the opening of *Sodom and Gomorrah*, which he dismissed as "pre-war.") He particularly enjoyed detective novels. Simenon was a favorite in his last years.

Almost a decade after his mother died, he came to live at the overstuffed apartment on Rue Lepsius (today the Cavafy Museum), where he would spend the rest of his life. For Sareyannis, it is only too clear, the poet's taste in décor was clearly no better than his taste in fiction:

> Cavafy's flat was on an upper floor of a rather lower-class, unkempt apartment house. Upon entering, one saw a wide hall laden with furniture. No walls were to be seen anywhere, as they were covered with paintings and, most of all, with shelves or Arabian *étagères* holding countless vases—small ones, large ones, even enormous ones. Various doors were strung along that hall; the last one opened onto the salon where the poet received his visitors.... It was crowded with the most incongruous things: faded velvet armchairs, old Bokhara and Indian stuffs at the windows and on the sofa, a black desk with gilt ornament, folding chairs like those found in colonial bungalows, shelves on the walls and tables with countless little columns and mother-of-pearl, a *koré* from Tanagra, tasteless turn-of-the-century vases, every kind of Oriental rug, Chinese vases, paintings, and so on and so on. I could single out nothing as exceptional and really beautiful; the way everything was amassed reminded me of a secondhand furniture store....Whether Cavafy himself chose and collected those assorted objects or whether he inherited them, I do not know; what is certain is that Cavafy's hand, his design,

could not be felt in any of that. I imagine that he just came slowly to love them, with time, as they were gradually covered with dust and memories, as they became no longer just objects, but ambiance.

The cluttered, déclassé surroundings, the absence of aesthetic distinction, the startlingly conventional, to say nothing of middlebrow, taste: Cavafy's apartment, like his job, gave little outward sign of the presence of a great artistic mind—the place from which the poetry really came. The more you know about the life, the more Seferis's pronouncement that Cavafy existed only in his poetry seems just.

Most evenings, as he grew older, found him at home, either alone with a book or surrounded by a crowd of people that was, in every way, Alexandrian: a mixture of Greeks, Jews, Syrians, visiting Belgians, established literary figures such as Nikos Kazantzakis, a critic or two, younger friends, and aspiring writers. (Among the latter, eventually, was Alexander Sengopoulos, known as Aleko, who was very possibly the illegitimate son of one of Cavafy's brothers— acquaintances remarked on a striking family resemblance—and would eventually be his heir.)

To these friends and admirers the poet liked to hold forth in a voice of unusual charm and authority and in the mesmerizing if idiosyncratic manner memorably described by E. M. Forster, who met Cavafy during World War I, when Forster was working for the Red Cross in Alexandria. It was Forster who would do more than anyone to bring Cavafy to the attention of the English-speaking world, and it is to him that we owe the by now canonical description of the poet as "a Greek gentleman in a straw hat, standing absolutely motionless at a slight angle to the universe." Cavafy, the novelist recalled,

may be prevailed upon to begin a sentence—an immense complicated yet shapely sentence, full of parentheses that never get mixed
and of reservations that really do reserve; a sentence that moves with
logic to its foreseen end, yet to an end that is always more vivid and
thrilling than one foresaw. . . . It deals with the tricky behaviour of
the Emperor Alexius Comnenus in 1096, or with olives, their possibilities and price, or with the fortunes of friends, or George Eliot,
or the dialects of the interior of Asia Minor. It is delivered with equal
ease in Greek, English, or French. And despite its intellectual richness and human outlook, despite the matured charity of its judgments, one feels that it too stands at a slight angle to the universe:
it is the sentence of a poet.

The life, in other words, was idiosyncratically hybrid: the fervent,
unseen artistic activity on the one hand, the increasingly tame pleasures of a middling bourgeois existence on the other; the fusty apartment in the tawdry *quartier* echoing with the abstruse, rather
baroque conversation. Not coincidentally, "abstruse" and "baroque"
describes a particular literary manner—characteristic of the Hellenistic authors who had flocked to the era's cultural capital two millennia earlier, and who were so beloved of Cavafy—known as
"Alexandrian."

In 1932, Cavafy, a lifelong smoker, was diagnosed with cancer of
the larynx. That summer he traveled to Athens for the tracheotomy
that would deprive him forever of the famous voice; from that point
on, he was forced to communicate in a distorted whisper and, later
on, by means of penciled notes. He returned home in the autumn,
after declining an invitation from his wealthy friend Antony Benakis,
a collector and the brother of Penelope Delta, to stay with him in

Athens. ("Mohammed Aly Square is my aunt. Rue Cherif Pasha is my first cousin, and the Rue de Ramleh my second. How can I leave them?") After first refusing and then allowing himself to be visited by the Patriarch of Alexandria, he died in the Greek Hospital in Alexandria on April 29, 1933, his seventieth birthday: an elegant closure that is nicely suggested by what is said to have been his last act. For we are told that on one of the pieces of paper that had become his sole mode of communication, he drew a circle; and then placed a small dot in the middle of that circle. Whatever he may have meant by that glyph, certain people will recognize in it an apt symbol. It is the conventional notation, used by writers when correcting printer's proofs, for the insertion of a period, a full stop.

"In the poems of his youth and even certain poems of his middle age he quite often appears ordinary and lacking in any great distinction," Seferis remarked during his 1946 lecture—another rather severe judgment whose underlying shrewdness cannot be denied, when we go back to so many of the poems Cavafy wrote in his thirties and even early forties, with their obvious debts to other writers and thinkers, their evasions and obfuscations. And then, as Seferis went on to say, "something very extraordinary happens." As will be evident by now, little about the external events of Cavafy's life helps to account for that remarkable evolutionary leap. Only by tracing the course of his interior life, his intellectual development, from the 1890s to the 1910s is it possible to discern the path by which (to paraphrase that other great Greek poet again) Cavafy went from being a mediocre writer to a great one.

As a young littérateur in the 1880s and 1890s, when he was in his twenties and thirties, he was steadily writing quantities of verse as well as contributing articles, reviews, and essays, most in Greek but some in English (a language in which he was perfectly at home as the result of those adolescent years spent in England), on a broad range of idiosyncratic subjects to Alexandrian and Athenian journals ("Coral from a Mythological Viewpoint," "Give Back the Elgin Marbles," Keats's *Lamia*). Such writings, as well as the historical poems that belong to this early period, already betray not only a deep familiarity with a broad range of modern historians, which he read in Greek, English, and French, but also the meticulous attentiveness to primary sources in the original languages—classical and later Greek and Roman historians, the early Church Fathers, Byzantine chroniclers—that we tend to associate with scholars rather than poets.

The writings of those early years indicate that Cavafy was struggling to find an artistically satisfying way in which to unite the thematic strands that would come to characterize his work, of which the consuming interest in Hellenic history was merely one. (That interest, it is crucial to emphasize, rather strikingly disdained the conventional view of what constituted "the glory that was Greece"— which is to say, the Archaic and Classical eras—in favor of the long post-classical phase, from the Hellenistic monarchies through late antiquity to the fall of Byzantium.) There was, too, the poet's very strong identity as a product of the Greek diaspora, an Orthodox Christian, and the scion of that once-distinguished Phanariot family who saw, in the thousand-year arc of Byzantine history, not a decadent fall from idealized classical heights—the standard Western European attitude, crystallized by Gibbon—but a continuous and coherent thread of Greek identity that seamlessly bound the antique past to the present.

And finally, there was homosexual sensuality. However tormented and secretive he may have been about his desire for other men, Cavafy came, after a certain point in his career, to write about that desire with an unapologetic directness so unsensational, so matter-of-fact, that we can forget that barely ten years had passed since Oscar Wilde's death when the first of these openly homoerotic poems was published. As the poet himself later acknowledged, he had to reach his late forties before he found a way to unify his passion for the past, his passion for "Hellenic" civilization, and his passion for other men in poems that met his rigorous standards for publication.

The earliest poems we have date to the poet's late teens, when he was sojourning with his mother's family in and around Constantinople. These include dutiful if unpersuasive exercises on Romantic themes (ecstatic encomia to the lovely eyes of fetching lasses; a Grecified adaptation of Lady Anne Barnard's ballad on love and loss in the Highlands); some flights of Turkish Orientalism, complete with smoldering beauties locked up in harems.

As time passed, he was drawn more and more to recent and contemporary currents in Continental literature. The Parnassian movement of the 1860s and 1870s, in particular, with its eager response to Théophile Gautier's call for an "Art for Art's sake," its insistence on elevating polished form over earnest subjective, social, and political content, and particularly its invitation to a return to the milieus and models of the antique Mediterranean past, had special appeal. That so many of Cavafy's poems from this period are sonnets or variations on the sonnet form is a testament to the influence of the Parnassians, who prized the form for its rigorous technical requirements.

From the Parnassians it was but a short step to Baudelaire, a Greek translation of whose *Correspondences* constitutes part of one 1892 poem; and, ultimately, to Symbolism. It is not hard to see the allure that Baudelaire's elevation of the poet as a member of an elite—a gifted seer whose special perceptions were denied to the common mass—had for the young poet, in whom a rarefied taste for the past, as well as a necessarily secret taste for specialized erotic pleasures, coexisted. Lines from the second half of "Correspondences According to Baudelaire" suggest how thoroughly the young Alexandrian had absorbed the lessons of the pioneering French modernist:

> *Do not believe only what you see.*
> *The vision of poets is sharper still.*
> *To them, Nature is a familiar garden.*
> *In a shadowed paradise, those other*
> *people grope along the cruel road.* ...

With Cavafy, the inevitably self-justifying preoccupation with the notion of an artistic elite ("Cavafy's attitude toward the poetic vocation is an aristocratic one," wrote Auden, a trifle indulgently)— an attitude irresistible, as we might imagine, to a tormented closeted gay man—was paralleled by a lifelong fascination with figures gifted with second sight, extrasensory perception, and telepathic knowledge. It found its ideal historical correlative in the first century AD magus and sage Apollonius of Tyana, about whom Cavafy published three poems; as the corpus of poems left unfinished at the time of the poet's death makes clear, he was working on the draft of another toward the end of his life.

By the end of the 1890s he was experiencing a profound intellectual and artistic crisis precipitated by his engagement not with other poets but with two historians. A series of reading notes on Gibbon's *Decline and Fall of the Roman Empire*, made between 1893 and 1899, indicates a serious ongoing engagement with the great Enlightenment historian. The exasperated rejection of Gibbon's disdainful view of Byzantium and Christianity that we find in those notes betrays the strong influence exerted by the contemporary Greek historian Konstantinos Paparrigopoulos, whose *History of the Greek Nation* expounded a Romantic nationalist vision of a coherent Greek identity continuing unbroken from ancient to Byzantine to modern times. It was Cavafy's reading in these two historians that led him to reject his earlier, rather facile use of history as merely the vehicle for bejeweled verses in the Parnassian mode on "Ancient Days" (one of the thematic headings into which he'd group his poems: others were "The Beginnings of Christianity," "Passions," and "Prisons"), and inspired him to try to combine history and poetry in a more intellectually and aesthetically serious way.

This intellectual crisis coincided with a devastating series of deaths of friends and family members throughout the same decade (his two closest friends, three of his six brothers, an uncle, his mother, and his maternal grandfather would all die between 1886 and 1902) and with what he obscurely referred to as a "crisis of lasciviousness," which may or may not have had something to do with his intense attraction to a young playwright whom he met during a trip to Athens at the turn of the century.

Together, these cerebral, emotional, and erotic upheavals

culminated in a dramatic reappraisal of his life's work thus far: the "Philosophical Scrutiny" of 1902–1903, to which the poet, as he turned forty, ruthlessly subjected all of his poems written up to that point, both unpublished and published. (Hence the later appellation "Repudiated" for a group of poems he'd already published by that time and subsequently rejected.)

Cavafy himself dated his mature period to the year 1911—not coincidentally the year in which he published "Dangerous," the first of his poems that situated homoerotic content in an ancient setting. Nor is it a coincidence that the subject of this poem is a Syrian student living in Alexandria during the uneasy double reign of the sons of Constantine the Great, Constans and Constantius, in the fourth century AD, at the very moment when the Roman Empire was shifting from paganism to Christianity. As if profiting from that uncertain moment, and reflecting it as well, the young man feels emboldened to give voice to illicit urges:

> *Strengthened by contemplation and study,*
> *I will not fear my passions like a coward.*
> *My body I will give to pleasures,*
> *to diversions that I've dreamed of,*
> *to the most daring erotic desires,*
> *to the lustful impulses of my blood, without*
> *any fear at all....*

Both the "shady" character and the confusing fourth-century setting (to which he would return in his late masterwork "Myres: Alexandria in 340 AD"—the longest poem he ever published) are typical of what Seferis described as the characteristic Cavafian milieu: "the margins of places, men, epochs . . . where there are many amalgams, fluctuations, transformations, transgressions." As he neared the age of fifty, Cavafy had found, at last, a way to write without shame about his desire—a way that suggestively conflated the various "margins" to which he had always been drawn: erotic, geographical, temporal.

The painfully achieved reconciliation of Gibbon's eighteenth-century Enlightenment view of history and Paparrigopoulos's nineteenth-century Romantic national feeling, coupled with a startlingly prescient twentieth-century willingness to write frankly about homosexual experience, made possible the "unique tone of voice," as the admiring Auden described it, that is the unmistakable and inimitable hallmark of Cavafy's work. Ironic yet never cruel, unsurprised by human frailty, including his own ("Cavafy appreciates cowardice also," Forster wrote, "and likes the little men who can't be consistent or maintain their ideals"), yet infinitely forgiving of it, that tone takes its darker notes from the historian's shrewd appreciation for the ironies of human action (which inevitably result, as did the life-altering business misfortunes of his father and uncles, from imperfect knowledge, bad timing, missed opportunities, or simply bad luck); yet at the same time is richly colored by a profound sympathy for human striving in the face of impossible obstacles. (Which could be the armies of Octavian or taboos against forbidden desires.) And it is inflected, too, by the connoisseur's unsparing and unsentimental grasp of both the pleasures and the pain to which desire makes us vulnerable.

Such appreciation, such sympathy, such understanding are made possible only by time—the medium that makes history possible, too. For many readers, even sophisticated ones, Cavafy is a poet who wrote essentially two kinds of poems: daringly exposed verses about desire whose frank treatment of homoerotic themes put them decades ahead of their time, and makes them gratifyingly accessible; and rather abstruse historical poems, filled with obscure references to little-known and confusingly homonymous Hellenistic or Byzantine monarchs, and set in epochs one was never held responsible for learning about and places that fringed the more shadowy margins of the Mediterranean map.

But to divide the poet's work in this way is to make a very serious mistake. Cavafy's one great subject, the element that unites virtually all of his work, is time. His poetry returns obsessively to a question that is, essentially, a historian's question: how the passage of time affects our understanding of events. The expanse of time in question could be the millennia that have elapsed since 31 BC, when the Hellenophile Marc Antony's dreams of an Eastern Empire were pulverized by Rome (the subject of seven poems) or the mere years that, in the poem "Since Nine—," have passed since those long-ago nights that the narrator spent in bustling cafés and on crowded city streets. That short space of time has since been filled with the deaths of loved ones whose value he only now appreciates, sitting alone in a room without bothering to light the lamp. What matters to Cavafy, and what so often gives his work both its profound sympathy and its rich irony, is the understanding, which as he knew so well comes too late to too many, that however fervently we may act in the dramas of our lives—emperors, lovers, magicians, scholars, Christians, catamites, stylites, pagans, artists, saints, poets—only time reveals whether the play is a tragedy or a comedy.

The references to long-vanished eras, places, and figures that we so often find in Cavafy's poetry, and which indeed are unfamiliar even to most scholars of classical antiquity, are, for this reason, never to be mistaken for mere exercises in abstruse pedantry. Or, indeed, for abstruseness at all. A poem that casually invokes, say, the autumnal thoughts of the Byzantine emperor Manuel Comnenus in the year 1180 functions quite differently from the way in which invocations of arcane material can function in (to take the well-known example of a contemporary) *The Waste Land* of T. S. Eliot—where the self-consciously rarefied quality of the numerous allusions is part of the texture of the poem, part of its Modernist project.

Cavafy, by contrast, may be said simply to have inhabited his various pasts so fully that they are all equally present to him. Not for nothing are a striking number of his poems about nocturnal apparitions of those who have vanished into history. In "Caesarion," for instance, a poem written in 1914 and published in 1918—the intervening years, the years of the Great War, saw the publication of a number of poems on alluring dead youths—the beautiful (as he imagines) teenage son of Caesar and Cleopatra materializes one night in the poet's apartment:

> *Ah, there: you came with your indefinite*
> *charm...*
>
> *...*
>
> *And I imagined you so fully*
> *that yesterday, late at night, when the lamp*
> *went out—I deliberately let it go out—*
> *I dared to think you came into my room,*
> *it seemed to me you stood before me...*

Such apparitions do not always belong to the distant past. In "Since Nine—," published in 1918 and written the year before, an "apparition" of the poet's own "youthful body" suddenly materializes in front of him one evening as he sits alone in a darkened room; in an unfinished poem of the same period, "It Must Have Been the Spirits," the poet's own soul, together with the image of a louche youth he'd encountered years ago in Marseille, takes form before his eyes, replacing a décor that is itself a suggestive mélange of past and present (a commonplace settee, a piece of archaic Greek statuary). Although in the latter poem the narrator attributes his supernatural vision to the excess of wine he'd drunk the previous night—hence the title—such apparitions are, therefore, hardly anomalous in his creative life, and symbolize a crucial theme of the entire body of work: the presence of the past in our own present.

To Cavafy, figures such as that of the dead princeling and the long-forgotten French boy all inhabit the same era—the vastly arcing past that his own imagination inhabited so fully—and were therefore as alive and present to him as the whores who lived in the brothel below his apartment on the Rue Lepsius. ("Where could I better live?" he once remarked, in the *mondain* tone we recognize from his verse. "Under me is a house of ill repute, which caters to the needs of the flesh. Over there is the church, where sins are forgiven. And beyond is the hospital, where we die.") It is the responsibility of the reader to inhabit that past as fully as possible, too, if only during the brief space during which he or she explores these poems. Otherwise, the meaning of many of these poems will be obscure, if not opaque. The reader who, put off by that opacity, seeks out the contemporary poems while skipping over the historical poems is missing the point of Cavafy's work—is, like so many of his characters, tragically mistaking the clouded part for the clear and brilliant whole.

—From the Introduction to *C. P. Cavafy: The Complete Poems*
(Knopf, 2009)

II. Moderns

The Last Minstrel

HALFWAY THROUGH the first installment of the four-volume autobiographical novel *Mercy of a Rude Stream*, which the late Henry Roth wrote in the ninth decade of his long and tormented life, an immigrant Jewish schoolboy named Ira Stigman, the author's fictional stand-in, is called on by his grade school teacher to recite from Sir Walter Scott's 1805 poem *The Lay of the Last Minstrel* at a school assembly. "Breathes there the man, with soul so dead," the poem goes, "who never to himself hath said, / this is mine own, my native land!" Ira is so honored because he'd previously recited the poem in the classroom with great fluency; but at the large public assembly he falters, and the words come out "stiff and mechanical." Humiliated, Ira chides himself afterward for having disappointed his teacher:

> Why couldn't he do the same thing well a second time, or time after time, regularly, uniformly, the way some people could? The way an actor did, the way that a certain soldier did who went to every school and gave enthralling imitations of the noises made by different pieces of ordnance....

The juxtaposition of the tongue-tied Jewish immigrant pupil and the swashbuckling Scottish text may seem, at first, comical—an amusing set piece about immigrant aspiration. But Roth's choice of poem was a pointed one. Scott's convoluted tale of a sixteenth-century Border feud, complete with nobles, tombs, goblins, kidnapped bairns, duels, and ghosts, is steeped in rich local color; and the poem is preoccupied not only (as the lines Ira recites suggest) with sentimental allegiance to one's homeland but, more subtly, with the way in which the poet in particular derives his art from his connection to his country and traditions. The conceit of Scott's poem, after all, is that the sixteenth-century tale is being recited by a seventeenth-century minstrel who has barely survived Cromwell's anti-Stuart purges: the minstrel is "the last of all the bards," now cut off from a once-rich tradition. The stanza that Ira Stigman recites ends with a vehement curse on anyone who is so "concentred all in self" as to feel no connection to his native land.

A deep connection to native traditions—and the trauma of being separated from them—can be seen as the dominating theme of Henry Roth's work and of his strange life. In 1934, at the age of twenty-eight, he published what would be his only published work for six decades, until the bizarre reflorescence represented by *Mercy of a Rude Stream*. That early novel, *Call It Sleep*, is now considered a classic of modern American fiction: according to some, it is the greatest novel of the early-twentieth-century immigrant experience. As befitting a novel that owes so much to (and sometimes borrows so much from) Joyce, the book is an artist's bildungsroman: the story of how an imaginative immigrant child's aesthetic consciousness emerges from the conflict between the Old World and the New.

The subjects of immigrant assimilation, cultural adaptation, and artistic identity had, by the time of the publication of *Call It Sleep*, already been treated in novels by Jewish writers, the best known of which was Abraham Cahan's *The Rise of David Levinsky* (1917). What gave Roth's novel its particular urgency was the way in which the author conflated his young protagonist's crisis of confused cultural allegiances with a psychologically prior and more devastating drama of divided loyalties, one transcending the particularities of Jewish-American experience. The child David Schearl, Roth's earliest fictional doppelgänger, is caught in the ongoing and vitriolic conflict between his adoring, saintly mother, Genya, a woman who is trapped in romantic memories of the old country—we know that she never learns English—and his emotionally and physically abusive father, Albert. A tormented, pathetically striving, would-be entrepreneur, Albert in nearly every scene threatens his small child with blows or with words of a near-biblical portentousness. ("Shudder when I speak to you.") The Oedipal triangle at the heart of Roth's first novel was, as we would eventually learn, an all-too-faithful replica of the author's tortured early years.

Famously, *Call It Sleep* disappeared soon after its publication: the reviews were warm, but the public was cool. It wasn't until it was revived thirty years later as an Avon paperback—and highly praised on the front page of *The New York Times Book Review* by Irving Howe, the first step in its elevation to the status of a classic—that the book caught the imagination of the reading public and became, quite unexpectedly, a best seller. (One possible explanation for the delayed popularity of the book is nostalgia: by the time it became a success, the children of the Great Immigration were in their mid-sixties, too.) But by that time, Roth had disappeared as completely as his book. Although he'd published his novel while hobnobbing with a bohemian Greenwich Village crowd in the 1930s, reporters and fans who wanted to track him down when fame finally came for him were directed to a bleak little house in rural Maine, devoid not only of a television but also of books, in which Roth lived in austere circumstances with his wife and two sons, eking out an improbable living as, of all things, a waterfowl farmer.

The materially and, apparently, intellectually impoverished life that Roth had ended up living, when contrasted to the rich promise evident in his only novel, raised a question that seized the imagination of his newfound audience and would be asked for decades to come, one that was pungently put by his sister, Rose (who had typed the manuscript of *Call It Sleep*): "How could he give up a God-given talent and fool around with chickens and ducks?" Roth himself often gave two reasons for his long silence, both of which have to do with the trauma that can result when an artist is separated from his cultural roots. The first was that the author, a committed Communist at the time his book was published, was deeply wounded by party-line criticisms that his book was overly aesthetic and "bourgeois"; he felt himself to be incapable of producing the grand, proletarian, socialist-realist work that was expected of him. (Maxwell Perkins, nonetheless, is said to have seen promise in the hundred or so pages that Roth later produced but eventually burned.) The second was that his alienation specifically from his Jewish origins, from the roiling immigrant culture of his childhood, had cut him off from the material that was most fertile for his artistic purposes.

It was for these reasons, Roth would say after *Call It Sleep* was republished, that he had come to suffer what would be known as one of the most famous cases of writer's block in American publishing history. (He did publish a few short stories in *The New Yorker*, but the world was waiting for another novel.) Only in the 1990s, when nearly another generation had passed and Roth was at the end of his life, did a different, more sensational reason for the author's long silence come to light. In the second volume of *Mercy of a Rude Stream* (or MORS—the Latin word for "death"—as the sour-humored author liked to call the series), Ira Stigman—who in the first volume is, to all appearances, an only child, as *Call It Sleep*'s David Schearl had been—is suddenly given a sister, Minnie, with whom by the novel's end he is carrying on a perfervid incestuous relationship. Minnie was clearly as much a surprise to *Mercy*'s publisher as she was to readers: she doesn't appear in the family trees printed at the front of the novels until volume 3. Far more disturbing was the implication that, like virtually every other aspect of the novel, the incestuous relationship between brother and sister was a direct reflection of the facts of the author's life.

Immediately before this controversial volume was published, Roth's editor persuaded him to inform his sister about its depiction of incest; in response, a distraught Rose begged Henry to eliminate the references to incest and threatened him with legal action in the event that he kept the manuscript intact. In part to protect his publisher from the threat of libel, Roth made a video in which he confirmed that he had begun to experiment sexually with his sister when he was twelve and she ten, and that by the time they were sixteen and fourteen, respectively, they were engaging in sexual intercourse. "A sneaky mini-family" was how Roth referred to this relationship in volume 2 of MORS, entitled *A Diving Rock on the Hudson*, "a tabooed one." (Ira also begins a relationship with his first cousin, Stella, and this too mirrored a real-life sexual relationship between Roth and his cousin Sylvia.) Eventually, the incest story found its way into *The New York Times* and *The New York Observer*.

The secret history of paralyzing sexual shame provided what

Roth's biographer, Steven G. Kellman, calls "another, more compelling reason for his legendary writer's block." This theory inevitably puts you in mind of another blockage—the one suffered by MORS's unfortunate Ira Stigman when he tries and fails to recite Walter Scott's poem, that celebration of artistic rootedness. Suddenly, the abject, immobilized inability of the elderly Roth's fictional doppelgänger to "do the same thing well a second time, or time after time, regularly, uniformly, the way some people could" seems like a symbol for his creator's blockage, the dire consequences of his awful secret.

Whatever the reasons for his long silence, the eleventh-hour burst of productivity that so improbably followed Roth's prolonged dry spell has been seen as rescuing him from the tragic (if intriguing) narrative of crippling childhood trauma, placing him instead at the heroic center of another, equally intriguing narrative: the tale of shame that, by means of a public confession, is transformed into a healing "closure," which allows life to go on at last. In Roth's case, closure helped produce a final epic that he completed immediately before his death.

This, as its title suggests, is the tale that gets told in Kellman's strangely flat biography, *Redemption: The Life of Henry Roth*. You don't envy Kellman his task. As is often the case with bitter, chronically depressed, self-destructive people (artists and others), Roth's life was essentially a monotonous one: the story of childhood miseries that are fated to be internalized and reenacted again and again in an adult life that, because of that perpetual replaying, is itself "blocked." We learn that Roth the smothered mama's boy sought out maternal women as partners in passionate but ultimately unsuccessful relationships. (His feelings for his wife, Muriel, a musician who was his own age, were, apparently, not so much passionate as deeply affectionate.) Roth the abused child beat his own sons. Roth the victim of withering paternal disapproval thought he was worthless, and made his willfully self-punishing life choices accordingly, from his career to the Spartan décor of his house to his adult choice of reading material. (The editor responsible for reviving *Call It Sleep* in 1964 was shocked to find that the onetime aficionado of Dante and Joyce now limited himself to *The Saturday Review of Literature* and the *Bulletin of the Atomic Scientists*.) Roth denounced his father as a "miserably, moody, infantile tightwad," but that's precisely how he himself ended up.

The great problem with the story that Kellman wants to tell is that his tale of redemption only makes sense—is only a "redemption," is only a tale worth telling—if you see Roth's final work as a success, as a culminating achievement of a long-repressed talent. If it isn't, then Roth's story becomes less dramatic, a story not about tortured geniuses but about the fact that there are always people who need to believe in them.

Reading Kellman's biography is an unsatisfying experience for a number of reasons. His writing is dreary and pedantic. A comparative literature professor at the University of Texas, he pursues pointless tangents whenever they will display his copious research: when Henry goes off to Peter Stuyvesant High School in the autumn of 1920, we get an excursus about the career of the eponymous seventeenth-century Dutchman; when Henry befriends an Irish boy, a disquisition about the Great Famine is not far behind. The tone falters frequently. There are unlovely solecisms ("drowses off"), feeble attempts at—you must suppose—jokes ("At fifteen, Henry Roth was still a defective dictionary; he lacked definition"), and, sometimes, an irritating parochialism. (He notes at one point that Stuyvesant High School produced three Nobel laureates—"all of them Jews." Nu?) There are, too, careless errors throughout: Albert Camus died in 1960, not 1980.

More seriously for a book that is, like this one, necessarily preoccupied with details of early-twentieth-century immigrant Jewish life and culture, the author's acquaintance with this material can seem casual. For small-town Galician Jews like Roth's parents, to be married in a religious rather than a civil wedding (and, hence, for their offspring to be considered "bastards" by the state) was not at all, as Kellman implies, a dramatic anomaly; to characterize relations between cousins as "incestuous" has a sensational allure but is inaccurate. (First-cousin marriages were hardly uncommon among the Jews of Eastern Europe.) And to suggest that the Molotov–Ribbentrop pact of 1939 was "a Faustian agreement that extinguished the hopes of any Jew living on the European continent" suggests an imperfect familiarity with twentieth-century European history—or, perhaps, geography. The pact enabled Hitler to invade western Poland and turn his attention to Western Europe; but for Jews like Roth's relatives who lived in eastern Poland, which came under Soviet control, the pact bought two more years of safety from Nazi terror.

For all the excessive detail and the sometimes silly theorizing about his psychology ("Roth's attraction to mathematics . . . reflected the meticulous prose of *Call It Sleep*"), Kellman's life of Roth feels redundant: anyone who cares enough about Henry Roth to read a biography of him has already read about his life. This is certainly so in the case of those who have read *Call It Sleep*, which as we now know faithfully reproduces not only the bitter psychological dynamics of the young Roth's childhood but also many of its key events and characters: the arrival of mother and child in the "Golden Land" whose promise is so swiftly to prove false for the elder Schearls; tense relationships with tenement neighbors, early sexual experimentation, a particularly gruesome beating by his father, quasi-comical power struggles with the rabbi who runs his religious school, eager attempts at friendships with non-Jewish boys, and so on.

What makes *Call It Sleep* superior to the many first novels that consist of little more than recast autobiography is a remarkable and precocious artistry that even today seems strikingly original. It's true that the stark Oedipal triangle of Roth's novel is decked out with a Freudian symbolism that strikes us today as heavy-handed. At the nadir in his relationship with his wife, Albert Schearl hangs a pair of bull's horns in their tenement flat; David's symbolic death and resurrection at the climax of the book—he has run away from home after Albert discovers him playing with a rosary—take place after he accidentally electrocutes himself, a mishap that results from a highly symbolic sexual initiation: he thrusts the handle of a zinc milk-can ladle into the narrow groove between the electrified rails of a streetcar track.

But a genuine and still-arresting achievement of *Call It Sleep* is the way the author manipulates languages to represent his characters' dilemmas of emotional and cultural identity—the tension between "concentred selves" and their surrounding culture. David Schearl's move from the shtetl (and later the ghetto) into the American mainstream, from Austrian Galicia to New York City, is presented as an abandonment of the emotionally narrow yet reassuringly homogeneous Yiddish-speaking world of his unhappy mother for the vivifying but often frightening multilingual milieu of the streets, where Irish, Italian, and Yiddish voices melt together in a confusing, exultant cacophony. Roth is particularly interested in the sounds of immigrant culture, and for that reason exactingly represents the awkward English of the new immigrants—phonetically. ("Between de legs," a neighbor girl instructs the terrified David, "Who puts id in is de poppa.") The narrative climax of the book is also the climax of its ongoing preoccupation with language and speech: as a crowd of horrified onlookers surrounds the unconscious David after his electrocution, Roth lets us hear their voices all at once in a twenty-two-page tour de force that owes an obvious debt to Joyce:

> "Lectric shot; Doc!"
> "De hospital!"
> "Knocked him cold!"
> "Shock?"
> "'Zee dead?"
> "Yea, foolin' aroun' wid de—"
> "Shawt soicited it, Doc!"
> "Yea, boined!"
> "Vee sin id Docteh!"
> "Git back, youz!...I'll spit right in yer puss!"

With even bolder ingenuity, in order to confound further any facile assumptions about which culture is the "mainstream" for the novel's troubled people, the young Roth had the original idea of representing the Schearls' Yiddish speech not as it sounds to the

American reader (awkward, halting, foreign) but as it sounds to the speaker: natural, even idealized—a pure English that is often poetic ("The sweet chill has dulled," the mother tells her son. "Lips for me...must always be cool as the water that wet them"), and never less than beautifully proper ("Love, marriage, whatever one calls it, does that to one, makes one uncertain, wary. One wants to appear better than one is"). Even the awful father speaks in the cadences of one of the Prophets: "She's jesting with the angel of death!" he snarls at one point, threatening his wife's rebellious sister. As for David himself, his interior voice is always represented, intriguingly and with great effectiveness, as a fragmented stream of consciousness in which the debt to Joyce is again clear:

—Dark yet up. Dark...First, second, third is light. Mine Dark. Dark mine only. Papa stop. Stop! Stop, papa. Light it now. Ain't mad no more. Light it, mama. Now! One, two, three, now! One, two, three, now! Now! Aaa! Ain't! Ain't! Ow! Run away, mama! Don't let him! Run away! Here! Here I am! Run! Mama! Mama! Mama!

It is only when Roth's characters speak English that we're made brutally aware of how awkwardly "foreign" they still in fact are, how helpless they are in this new world. Confronted with an Irish policeman after her son has gotten lost, this same eloquent mother is reduced to a stiff, mechanical stutter: "Herr—Mister. Ve—er—ve go?"

As you listen to these rich and varied registers of speech, you can't help feeling that Roth's Yiddish-speakers are also the "last minstrels" of their particular linguistic music, and it is only too clear that a profound emotion moved Roth as a young writer to commemorate them. Indeed, as if unable to bring himself to contemplate the implication of assimilation, the author pulls away at the end of his book; the struggle between cultures ends in an ambiguous and cozy truce when, after his miraculous recovery from near electrocution, David falls into the deep slumber to which the title refers.

Such artistry is, it must be said, almost entirely absent from the four dense volumes that make up Roth's late-life revisitation of his early years, *Mercy of a Rude Stream*. (The title, from *Henry VIII*, cites Cardinal Wolsey's complaint that he has been left "Weary and old with service, to the mercy / Of a rude stream that must for ever hide me.") In cramped, exhaustive, and exhausting detail, these novels recreate Roth's life on a minute, almost day-by-day basis. (Kellman often cites them as sources for his claims about events in Roth's life, a methodology that is problematic at best.) Everything, once again, is here: Ira's early childhood seems identical to Roth's, starting in the family's first apartment in Brownsville, moving eventually to the homogeneous Yiddish world of East Ninth Street, and ending with the traumatic relocation to multicultural Harlem when Roth/Ira is nine years old—a displacement, Roth later claimed, that he never got over. Down to the appearances, personalities, and professions of various relatives, Ira's large and noisy extended family exactly duplicates that of the author, including the patriarch, a maternal grandfather who never reconciles himself to the multicultural hubbub of Harlem and cries out that he is "besieged by the barbarians, the Goths, the Vandals, the Teutonim." In *Mercy*, this grandfather becomes the voice of traditional values, a fact that makes the series' most arresting scene—in which Ira and his first cousin have a sexual encounter within a few feet of their sleeping grandparent—the more shocking. One way to try to make sense of the sprawling novel is to see it as an allegory about the depravity that results from the abandonment of tradition.

There are, too, the by-now familiar parents, dutifully transcribed from the author's childhood; the description of Ira's father, Chaim Stigman, as "a mean, stingy, screwy little louse" in volume 4 pointedly reminds us of Roth's father. There is the beginning of the sexual relationship with the sister, and later on the commencement of the other "incestuous" relationship with the first cousin; then the tortured adolescence, the stirrings of a literary impulse, the abortive friendships with track-star friends, with handsome non-Jewish boys; an episode of neurotic kleptomania that gets Ira (and got Roth) kicked out of one junior high school; the time he won a writing contest with a story called "Impressions of a Plumber," which was published in the City College magazine *Lavender* when the young author was nineteen. The name of the story and the name of the publication are both real.

All this takes up four volumes, at the conclusion of which Ira, now a young man, finds the strength to tear himself away from his family and move in with his older lover, Edith Welles. As if to acknowledge how barely fictionalized this epic "novel" is, the fictional characters bear, in almost every case, the initials of their real-life counterparts: Edith Welles, for instance, is closely modeled on Roth's lover Eda Lou Walton, a poet and professor who took him in and who supported him through the writing of *Call It Sleep*.

There is, to be sure, something oddly impressive about the sheer scale of Roth's *Mercy* books; it's as if, in their minute, exacting, unsentimental recreation of the smallest details of his existence, the shame-filled author were consciously, bitterly creating an anti–*Call*

It Sleep, an autobiographical novel stripped of artistry—as if literary style, as if beauty itself, were falsifications that the now-elderly author, perhaps vindictively, wanted to eradicate. He traces detailed genealogies and trudges through dreary cityscapes out of little more than an obligation to documentary completeness:

> Their apartment, a large one with six rooms, only two flights up, and supplied with steam heat, electricity and hot running water—and even striped awnings above the two front-room windows—was located in the middle of the block—in the middle of 115th Street, between Park and Madison Avenues. It was called in Yinglish a *shaineh b'tveen*, meaning—literally—a lovely between.

More than anything else in that pedestrian passage, the explication of *shaineh b'tveen* indicates strongly that we are no longer in the poetic world of *Call It Sleep*. In *Mercy*, the world is being observed from the outside—a shift in perspective that of necessity eliminates the thrilling play with points of view that gave the first novel its great distinction. The inclusion of a Yiddish glossary at the back of each of the four novels feels like an admission of defeat, and lends the whole enterprise the slightly dejected aura of an academic anthropology treatise.

The one attempt at artistic innovation takes the form of an ongoing dialogue, threaded through the narrative, between the elderly author of this extended reminiscence and his word processor, which he portentously dubs "Ecclesias." But this device is striking only for the obviousness of its attempts to create some sense of narrative momentum. (There are heavy-handed hints about future developments, not least the incest in the second volume: "When will you redress the omission, introduce the crucial factor?" "In good time, Ecclesias, in good time....") At one point, Ecclesias comments, ominously, "Well, salvage whatever you can, threadbare mementos glimmering in recollection." Much of MORS, come to think of it, feels like a grim salvage operation.

As such, as a dogged transcription of a life, *Mercy of a Rude Stream* will be of interest mainly to those who are fascinated by the writer himself. Such people, in fact, may be said to have been responsible for the entire project—foremost among them the young men ("sons of Henry," as they were called) who, fervent with belief in a great American Jewish genius, kept in touch with Roth, read his drafts, and served as midwives over a number of years to the work that eventually became *Mercy of a Rude Stream*. Already in September 1968 Roth was confiding about the existence of an autobiographical work in progress to a young Italian admirer, describing it, with typical self-deprecation, as a "landscape of the self; to epitomize its meaning for myself and others, I offer you the title, *Portrait of the Artist as an Old Fiasco*." Not quite a year later Roth described his project to an editor—all too accurately, as it turned out—as "a rambling interminable multivolume opus." Work began in earnest in 1979, and by the early 1990s the four hundred or so pages that Roth, nearly crippled by rheumatoid arthritis, had managed to produce persuaded Robert Weil, a young editor at St. Martin's Press, to purchase the long-awaited second novel of Henry Roth for publication. After heroic amounts of editing, painstakingly detailed by Kellman (his biography was also published by Weil), the first volume, *A Star Shines Over Mt. Morris Park*, was published in 1994 to polite reviews that, whenever possible, focused on the improbable "miracle" represented by the writing of the book rather than on its qualities.

To my mind, the final verdict must remain that of a *New Yorker* editor who, faced with a manuscript about life in Maine that Roth submitted in 1967—an early trickle of the torrent that was to follow—rejected it, saying, "It struck us as a lifeless piece of work.... The feeling here is that a writer's problems are only likely to be interesting to other writers."

The critical attention given to Kellman's biography, which was widely covered in the press and was the subject of substantial essays in *The New Yorker* and *The New York Times Book Review*, suggests that Roth's problems, perhaps more than the work itself, are what is interesting about him—if not to many readers, then certainly to other writers, for whom the subject of writer's block is, naturally, a fraught one. As, of course, is the subject of other writers' sex lives. Together, the two neuroses that twist themselves through Roth's life like strands of psychological DNA—the sexual and the creative, the incest and the writer's block—make for an irresistible subject.

And yet the facts of Roth's life—all of the facts, soberly considered—suggest that the incest has, from the start of this controversy, been a red herring: a flashy, attention-getting, ultimately misleading distraction, just as the drama of his final work's appearance was attention-getting but ultimately empty. If you want to know why Roth stopped writing, you must look at the work, and at the whole life. *Call It Sleep* ends when its hero is eight; *Mercy of a Rude Stream*, when its hero, at nineteen, falls into the arms of an older woman. After the late-hour success of *Call It Sleep*, when Roth was in his mid-sixties, he told an interviewer, "I just failed at maturity, at adulthood." The real cause of Roth's inability to write persuasively after *Call It Sleep*, with its masterly rendering of a child's worldview, was an old, undramatic one: once he'd exhausted the subject of child-hood, the only one that was, to him, psychologically as well as artistically urgent, Roth had nothing to write about. If we must seek psychological explanations for his strange creative tragedy, it's to the parents, I suspect, rather than the sister that we should look. The only period of his life in which Roth seems to have been able to write authentically was during his relationship with the maternal Eda Lou Walton, who like his own mother had created a safe and nurturing environment for the much younger Roth. (Walton liked to call him "child.") As for the other parent, it seems clear that from the start Roth had internalized the voice of the punishing, brutal father: by middle age, he'd convinced himself that he was, in the end, nothing more than "a schmo who had married a shiksa"—his father's characterization of him even after the late-season success of *Call It Sleep*.

Whatever else *Mercy of a Rude Stream* may be, it is, indeed, powerful testimony to an immense self-loathing. One of the reasons that those four volumes are so hard to get through is that Ira Stigman is intentionally made to be a repulsive character—David Schearl stripped of any appealing traits whatsoever. If Roth's purpose in *Mercy* was a self-conscious rejection of the poetry, the romance of artistic creation, that infuses every page of *Call It Sleep*, then we may say that, like so many abused children, Roth in later life was enacting the parts of both victim and oppressor. His mean-spirited and unpersuasive public rejection of James Joyce (at a 1981 Bloomsday conference at the University of New Mexico he offended the organizers with his anti-Joyce ramblings) was an all-too-obvious attempt to kill off a father figure; but the last creative act of his life was to kill off David Schearl, his best-beloved child.

Kellman writes that he approached Roth "as a mystery to be pondered." But what if the mystery is no mystery? The unhappy evidence of *Mercy of a Rude Stream* suggests that Henry Roth, like so many other impassioned writers—Ralph Ellison, Harper Lee, Margaret Mitchell, a list that Roth kept in his Maine cabin—wrote the only novel he had in him. The desire to see him as a tormented "genius," the obsession with his writer's block, his sex life, with his final, "redemptive" resurrection, reflects more about the commentators than it does about their subject. In our garrulous age, "concentred all in self," the traumatized artist who has lost the ability to speak is a far less unnerving figure than the one who has simply run out of things to say.

—*The New York Review of Books*, December 15, 2005

Brideshead, Revisited

HOLY WEEK OF 1937 found Evelyn Waugh—thirty-three years old, solidly established in his literary career, and on the verge of a second marriage—at a Benedictine monastery in Ampleforth, in Yorkshire, where, as he noted in his diary, he whiled away the time "entertaining dumb little boys and monks." It was not his first sojourn with these particular monks. He had come to Ampleforth before, and would come again, with his old friend Alfred Duggan, a stepson of Lord Curzon, whom Waugh had first befriended at Oxford, and whose alcoholism the novelist was, with a touching doggedness, trying to cure—not least in the hopes of returning Duggan to the Catholic faith he had abandoned. (Some of these retreats were more successful than others; on one of them, Duggan appeared to be behaving until he suddenly disappeared, only to be discovered later, in the midst of a major binge, in Scarborough.) During his prenuptial visit of March 1937, however, Waugh was alone, apart from the dumb boys and monks, and his diary records nothing more dramatic than a visit to Castle Howard, the fabulous country seat that Vanbrugh had designed for the Earls of Carlisle, members of the recusant Howard family, who eventually left it to a cadet branch.

Great country houses forsaken by their loftily titled owners were likely to have been much on Waugh's mind just then. The preceding summer had seen a wrenching social drama played out, following the premature death of another of his Oxford friends, Hugh Lygon. Along with his older brother, Lord Elmley, "Hughie" had been a glamorous figure at the center of the Hypocrites, the outré "aesthetic" set with whom Waugh fell in not long after he went up at the beginning of 1922. Outrageousness ran in the family: Hughie's father was the disgraced Earl Beauchamp, who several years earlier had been forced to resign most of his titles and leave the country when it was revealed—by his vindictive brother-in-law, the Duke of Westminster—that he was homosexual. In August 1936 Hughie, whose life after Oxford had failed to gel, died while traveling in Germany, precipitating an anguishing crisis for his father, who was by now living in Venice.

Only months before, when the earl's estranged wife had also died suddenly, he was intimidated into staying away from the funeral by the threat of arrest on morals charges, a warrant for which had been issued by the Home Office at Westminster's insistence. Now, devastated by the death of his son, the earl insisted on returning to Madresfield, the great house in Worcestershire he had not seen in six years, in order to attend Hughie's funeral—at whatever the cost. As it turned out, the Home Office was moved to suspend the warrant, and Beauchamp was allowed to return. He was left in peace during the few extended visits to his ancestral home that he was able to make in the two remaining years of his life.

The better part of a decade would pass before the filaments of associations triggered by Waugh's visit to Yorkshire in the spring of 1937—threads that connected Castle Howard, with its great lantern and magnificent fountain, to Madresfield, with its tragically abandoned chatelaine and its disgraced patriarch exiled to Venice; that linked Alfred Duggan and his desperate struggles with alcoholism, the monastic retreats at Ampleforth followed by binges at country inns, to poor Hughie Lygon, whose enchantingly debauched undergraduate days gave no sign of the rather failed adulthood to come—would weave themselves into the fabric of a novel. At least in certain ways, it was a book unlike anything he had written before.

By this time England had been at war for five years, as had Waugh: he'd enlisted as a marine in 1939 and had seen service in various theaters in Europe and North Africa. When, in January 1944, the novelist asked for a leave to work on a new book, he and his country had entered a drab period that his friend Christopher Sykes, in his biography of the writer, recalled as one of "shortening rations, increasing discomfort and more and more an all-pervading shabbiness." The description was meant, as was a similar one by Waugh himself, to account for the peculiar characteristics of the novel he began working on that winter, which, in its feeling depiction of spiritual anguish and erotic torment in a great aristocratic family between the wars, seemed to abandon the blithely acerbic social and political satire of the breezy novels of the 1930s that had made him famous—*Vile Bodies* (1930), *Black Mischief* (1932), *A Handful of Dust* (1934), *Scoop* (1938)—for something lushly nostalgic, even sentimental:

> It was a bleak period of present privation and threatening disaster—the period of soya beans and Basic English—and in consequence the book is infused with a kind of gluttony, for food and wine, for the splendours of the recent past, and for rhetorical and ornamental language...

In the same text—a preface to a later edition of the book—Waugh went on to say that he had written it "with a zest that was quite strange to me and also with impatience to get back to the war," which no doubt accounts for its remarkably speedy composition.

Yet despite the fervor of his inspiration and the smoothness of the writing—and his belief, expressed in a letter he sent to a friend soon after finishing, that the novel he had produced, his largest to date, was "a masterpiece"—he was pessimistic about the new book's prospects. Its subject, after all, was the unpopular one of religion: the Roman Catholic Church generally and, more specifically, what he called "the operation of divine grace on a group of diverse but closely connected characters." "The general criticism," he wrote to his mother, Catherine,

> is that it is religious propaganda. That shows how opinion has changed in 80 years. No one now thinks a book which totally excludes religion is atheist propaganda. 80 years ago every novel included religion as part of the normal life of the people.

"It would have a small public at any time," he wrote to his agent and friend A. D. Peters. "I should not think six Americans will understand it."

Waugh hated being wrong in general and, you suspect, particularly with regard to Americans, for whom he had the same reflexively snobbish disdain that he had for so many; yet he cannot fail to have been gratified by how mistaken he was in this case. For *Brideshead Revisited* ended up having a very big public indeed: since its publication, a few months before the war ended, it has been enthusiastically received by readers, American as well as British, and is now generally considered to be his most popular novel.

And yet the book's popularity tends to bemuse connoisseurs of

Waugh's writing, who, entirely apart from considerations of *Brides-head*'s internal flaws—not least, the fatal unpersuasiveness of a crucial female character—find distasteful the novel's excesses of nostalgic sentimentality and its rather purple rhetoric, which seem to stray disastrously from the amusing tartness and impressive economy that characterize his earlier, satiric works. To them, it is an irritating irony that the most popular of Waugh's novels is, in fact, the least Wauvian.

Brideshead Revisited may nonetheless be seen as a work that, rather than breaking with its predecessors, merely shifts emphasis, amplifying certain qualities that had always been present in the author's work while eschewing others. After dabbling in art, carpentry, and illuminated manuscripts, and after a none too spectacular stint as a teacher at a boys' school, Waugh made his name as a writer at the age of twenty-five, in 1928, with the publication of *Decline and Fall*, which traces the increasingly farcical adventures of a hapless Oxbridge undergraduate who becomes a teacher at a boys' school after he's unjustly sent down as a result of a run-in with an upper-class boor. Like much of Waugh's fiction, this one borrowed heavily from his own life—which, however, did not include an unwitting participation in a prostitution ring run by an elegant socialite.

The figure of the well-intentioned, well-educated young man who becomes the perplexed victim of circumstances beyond his control, one whose haplessness and passivity deflects attention onto the sinister and manipulative world around him—a highly useful kind of character if you happen to be writing social satire—would recur fruitfully in Waugh's work. He appears in *Vile Bodies*, a caustic satire of the vacuity of the lives led by the Bright Young Things in the 1920s ("when it comes to the point there doesn't seem to be anything I much want to do"), as well as *Scoop*, Waugh's satire of modern journalism, in which, as a result of a confusion about names, a young country squire who's mistaken for a famous young writer gets sent to Africa to cover a civil war and ends up being successful, mostly by dint of his utter cluelessness.

The structure of these novels—the hero, after all, always manages to be saved and restored to the class to which he belongs—allowed Waugh to poke sometimes rather strained fun at the high and mighty: there are upper-class characters with names like Lady Circumference and Lord Zinc, and a prime minister called Mr. Outrage. But for all the fun the author had at its expense, he never quite rejected that world entirely, either. While a good deal of Waugh's impish satire is more or less what you'd expect of a clever and ambitious twenty-something with enough contact with the great world to know what its foibles were, what's intriguing is that, from the start of his career, the deep and reflexive conservatism that would later inspire dismay in even his closest friends ("his political opinions were utterly ridiculous," Sykes, his biographer, would write) was in fact always present. In a famous passage that gives *Vile Bodies* its title, the narrator provides a long list of the various kinds of parties at which the frivolous young of the age exhausted themselves: "Masked parties, Savage parties, Victorian parties, Greek parties, Wild West parties, Russian parties, Circus parties . . . all that succession and repetition of massed humanity. . . . Those vile bodies. . . ." This is deliberately contrasted with a wholly different kind of party being given at the "last survivor of the noble town houses of London," at which the guests are the parents of those other party-goers. These dignified older folk constitute, in the narrator's eyes,

> a great concourse of pious and honourable people . . . their women-folk well-gowned in rich and durable stuffs, their men-folk ablaze with orders . . . unaffected, unembarrassed, unassuming, unambitious people, of independent judgment and marked eccentricities, kind people who cared for animals and the deserving poor, brave and rather unreasonable people, that fine phalanx of the passing order. . . .

The assumptions that underlay the blithe collocation of "animals and the deserving poor" are ones that Waugh himself wasn't interested in investigating. At twenty-seven he was already mired in nostalgia for a more authentic British past and nettled by impatient disdain for the modern era. (The glamorous and vacuous socialite with whom the hero of *Decline and Fall* falls in love decides to raze her country house, a perfectly preserved masterpiece of Tudor architecture called King's Thursday, in favor of an angular modernistic structure designed by an architect called Dr. Silenus.) Small wonder that *Vile Bodies* closes with an apocalyptic coda set in "the biggest battlefield in the history of the world": like all great satirists, Waugh was a moralist, and it's clear that for him, the sinning world must be purged by blood. You can't help wishing he'd taken on the biography of Swift that he once considered writing.

This is why the finest of his early novels, *A Handful of Dust*, is also the grimmest. The tale of a country aristocrat whose wife capriciously leaves him for another man (as Waugh's first wife left him), whose enchanting young son and heir subsequently dies pointlessly, and who ends up lost and given up for dead in the Amazon jungle, forced by a wily but illiterate native to read Dickens aloud every day—all this, while his beloved country seat is being taken over by poor relatives—the book attains a forceful purity, a quality of longtime concerns now distilled to an essence, not shared by the breezy novels that came before. Waugh's later description of *A Handful of Dust* as the tale of a "civilized man's helpless plight" among "savages at home" could be said to summarize the plots of all the early work; but only this one achieves a dark economy that gives the satire of contemporary society and its morally vacant denizens emotional as well as comic impact.

A Handful of Dust was the penultimate novel that Waugh completed before the war started. Its classically tragic action—the progressive stripping away of worldly comforts that leaves the characters to confront higher if often cruel truths—clearly worked on his mind in the terrible intervening years, as he cast about for a new subject. He would later describe *Brideshead Revisited* as the story of a family whose "physical dissolution . . . has in fact been a spiritual regeneration."

Brideshead's plot (which became familiar to many who viewed the popular 1981 Granada TV miniseries adaptation) suggests the seriousness of Waugh's intentions in creating his parable about sin, grace, and redemption—a story that had more than casual significance for its author. Born into an upper-middle-class Anglican family, to a publisher father, Waugh was received into the Catholic Church in

1930, after the first flush of his literary fame and not long after his first wife, also called Evelyn, left him. Like the characters in *Vile Bodies*, he had lived fast, crashed hard, and seemed to be looking for meaning.

In the novel, the family to be redeemed is a vastly wealthy and highly aristocratic one, the Flytes, whose head bears the title Marquis of Marchmain. They are Catholic—not, in fact, one of the great recusant families like the Howards, but an old Anglican family whose head, Lord Marchmain, converted in order to win his Catholic bride, with whom he had four children and from whom he has, for reasons unspecified, since been estranged. He has long been living in Venice with his Italian mistress while his wife, Lady Marchmain, attempts to exert control over her four often wayward children. Here you can see the way in which the Madresfield saga made itself felt in Waugh's creative imagination.

All these characters are seen through the eyes of an outsider, Charles Ryder. A Waugh-like figure, Charles ogles the great world to which he cannot quite belong; he's a moneyed upper-middle-class youth with artistic interests who's drawn into the rarefied and troubled world of the charming but unhappy Flytes when he is befriended by, and soon becomes the lover of, the second son, Sebastian, at Oxford. More an observer than an actor, Charles is a subtler variation on the passive heroes of Waugh's earlier, patently comic novels. Here, however, the inertia suggests a spiritual vacancy, an inchoate yearning to attach himself to something significant. (It is no accident that when Charles becomes a successful painter, his subject is great houses about to be demolished—inert objects with a past but no future.)

That significance is provided, in the end, by the Flytes themselves. Charles's infatuation with the family inevitably brings him into contact, and conflict, with the strong Catholic faith from which even the most wayward members of the family cannot ultimately extricate themselves. As Sebastian careers from one alcoholic crisis to another (an element of the text clearly inspired by Waugh's experience with Alfred Duggan), unable and unwilling to be saved, Charles switches his affections to his lover's capricious sister, Julia, who by now is mired in an unhappy, childless marriage: yet another of the book's many dead ends. By the end of the novel, not only does the lapsed Lord Marchmain return home to England and, after much agonizing on the part of his family, consent to take Extreme Unction (a scene closely modeled on the death of Waugh's friend Hubert Duggan, Alfred's brother), but Charles himself has a conversion experience.

Waugh wrote that the novel was about "the unmerited and unilateral act of love by which God continually calls souls to Himself." The undeserving souls in question are, for the most part, masterfully etched in all their rather pointed unworthiness: Bridey, the older brother, who has a deep but wholly unexamined piety, his intellectual and spiritual conventionality pointedly reflected (with an implicit snobbishness typical of Waugh) in his choice of a middle-class widow—her name is Beryl—as his wife; Julia, who is punished with childlessness for her youthful frivolousness and barren adulteries; the enchanting Cordelia, the youngest daughter, deeply religious (but not to the point of having a "calling") and the happiest of all the children, who turns out "plain."

None, however, is as affecting as the "magically beautiful" Sebastian ("with that epicene quality which in extreme youth sings aloud for love and withers at the first cold wind"), whose tragic inability to make a life for himself, tormented as he is by the conflict between his desire and his faith—the latter represented by the person of his mother, the quietly imperious Lady Marchmain, a woman who cannot see that her desire to control her family's happiness competes with God's own plan for them—is the heart of the book. He is its most persuasive and touching character, at once all too recognizably human and yet an effective symbol in the novel's parable. Sebastian, who *pace* Matthew Arnold thinks a butterfly as beautiful as a cathedral, has a pure if childish appreciation for the beauty of Creation. A kind of holy fool, he ends up a wrecked drunk who works as a porter in a monastery in Morocco—a desert saint.

By the end of the story, the great family has been dispersed. The parents are dead, the great palace of Brideshead (modeled, as we know, on Castle Howard) bequeathed away from the childless Bridey, the chapel closed, the children absent. But this dissolution has led to spiritual regeneration. Julia and Cordelia have gone off to the Middle East to perform good works during the war, Lord Marchmain has been shriven, Charles converts. For Waugh, all this represented a happy ending. There's a crucial scene about halfway through *Brideshead Revisited* that finds Lady Marchmain reading to her children during a particularly difficult night for the family (Sebastian has been bingeing in secret); what she reads is one of G. K. Chesterton's *Father Brown* stories, a passage in which, as Cordelia later reminds Charles, God's mysterious way of calling souls to himself is suggested by means of a homely metaphor:

I've caught him with an unseen hook and an invisible line, which is long enough to let him wander to the ends of the world, and still to bring him back with a twitch upon the thread.

Brideshead, whose second half is called "A Twitch Upon the Thread," is meant to illustrate that process.

At the time this surprisingly earnest book was published, not everyone was convinced, despite its critical and commercial success. Edmund Wilson, among others, lambasted the awkward juxtaposition of the moral parable with the patent classism, deplored the rank sentimentality, and disdained the self-indulgent excesses of a rather overcooked style. This last is a particularly shocking sin in a writer who had distinguished himself by the high lapidary polish of his witty prose. You would not find, in the earlier work, sentences like, "My theme is memory, that winged host that soared about me one grey morning of war-time." (The author, too, came to find *Brideshead*'s style mortifying: "rhetorical and ornamental language, which now with a full stomach I find distasteful.")

Pretty much everyone, too, agreed that the character of Julia was particularly thin and unconvincing—a serious flaw in a narrative intended to build up to the emotionally fulfilling but spiritually fruitless affair between her and Charles, the failure of which ultimately sets him in the direction of God. Julia is all too clearly there to represent the next rung on the erotic and spiritual ladder that Charles must ascend as he progresses to heterosexual maturity from the homosexual phase of his youth. (A phase that Waugh himself had passed through, with considerable relish, at Oxford: his friend Harold Acton—one model for the novel's flamboyantly homosexual Anthony Blanche—later, and with what you can't help thinking was a wink, described him in those days as "a prancing faun.") Waugh himself seems to have suspected that this was a flaw. To his friend Nancy Mitford he wrote that if the love affair "falls flat . . . the book fails plainly."

Your sense that Julia is simply a mechanism to chart the main character's progress en route to a foreordained destination brings you to the heart of the problem with *Brideshead Revisited*. All of the criticisms made at the time the novel was published are valid but not necessarily fatal. You suspect that a large part of what gives the book its perennial allure is, if anything, its lush evocations of how the titled rich once lived; the novel turns us into stand-ins for Charles Ryder, pressing our noses against the mullioned windows of great houses as we crane our necks for a glimpse of what happens within. (A taste for such glimpses has been indulged regularly on television over the past four decades, from *Upstairs, Downstairs* in the 1970s to *Downton Abbey* and *The Crown* today.) Charles himself never forgets that he is merely well-to-do but not upper-class. And thank God he is: the conversational sparring matches between him and his eccentric father, brilliantly enacted in the 1981 series by a touchingly young Jeremy Irons and a gleefully mischievous John Gielgud, provide some welcome comic relief to the humorless Flytes. But such flashes of the old Wauvian humor are rare here. What has exerted a powerful spell in this novel is its sentimentality—particularly those honeyed evocations of undergraduate romance, of Oxford and its "soft air of a thousand years of learning"—however artistically questionable it, too, may be.

The fatal problem with this religious book is the problem with so many religious texts, which is one of question-begging: they don't add up in the end unless you already believe in the operating premise. Long before Christopher Sykes, himself a Catholic, ever thought of writing Waugh's biography, he had complained about this, remarking when the novel was first published that it was "solely addressed to believing Catholics and admirers of the Catholic Church. The general reader is rather left in the cold." Which is to say that there's nothing in the novel itself that persuades you that the sudden death-bed gesture of faith made by Lord Marchmain, let alone Charles's subsequent conversion, was the result of coherent psychological processes, working themselves out organically; you just have to take it on—well, faith. The family's dissolution is beautifully evoked, but the spiritual regeneration remains a mystery. It happens because the author wills it to happen.

This reminds you that there's another way to interpret the passage from *Father Brown* that Lady Marchmain so eagerly reads, and this alternate reading of the parable of the fish twitching on the line helps you, finally, to understand just why it is that *Brideshead* is preaching only to the converted. An invisible figure whose creations have the appearance of free will and yet are always controlled by the unseen master who's busily manipulating invisible strings: this could be God, but it could also be a novelist. In religion, you yearn to feel the strings, because they reassure you that the creator is at the other end. In the traditional realistic novel, by contrast, you're not supposed to notice them. In *Brideshead*, you do.

I suspect that some people will, like me, be inspired by the recent British film adaptation of *Brideshead* to revisit the novel and, perhaps, to struggle to make sense of this grand and often grandiose, affecting yet somehow unpersuasive work, whose failures more than its successes tell us a good deal about Waugh. If so, the inspiration to return to the original text may be counted among the very few merits that the movie possesses. Undoubtedly anticipating resistance to their film by the millions who embraced the meticulously written and beautifully acted miniseries, the British makers of the new film have asserted that theirs is a bold "new interpretation" that will simultaneously "engage with" and "remake" Waugh's novel. But the remaking involved in this adaptation—designed, as they put it, "for our own time"—amounts to a rewriting, one that grossly distorts not just the lineaments of Waugh's novel but the deep moral meaning it sought, however imperfectly, to achieve.

Now as when Waugh first complained about the phenomenon, serious considerations of religion and religious belief make for uncomfortable subjects in mass entertainment. In consequence, those responsible for the new version clearly decided to frame Charles's fascination with the Flytes as one based almost exclusively on money and position. Gone are the novel's thoughtful disquisitions about grace and redemption, which the 1981 miniseries scrupulously reproduced, and which in fact saved it from accusations of mere class voyeurism—what the American author Tom Wolfe referred to "plutography." In this *Brideshead*, Charles is just another middle-class wannabe ogling his rich friends' nice houses and clothes, like someone leafing through the latest issue of *Town & Country* in a dentist's office.

But while the makers of this film profess an interest in "caste" (a "very contemporary and fresh" subject, one of the screenwriters has said), they don't seem to have spent much time studying the caste they're representing—a particularly damaging lapse, given the crucial importance for Waugh's theological theme of the disparity between the Flytes' material wealth and its appurtenances—that is, their class—and their spiritual poverty. In the novel, Sebastian's upper-class Oxford friends are represented as displaying to their aristocratic friend's new middle-class lover a "polite lack of curiosity which seemed to say: 'We should not dream of being so offensive as to suggest that you never met us before'": a significant representation of a *noblesse oblige* so inbred that it makes itself felt as politeness. These youths, with their rarefied politesse, are transformed in the new movie into guffawing hooligans who grill poor, drab Charles about his social credentials. "I don't remember *you* at Eton," one of them sneers.

Another way in which the movie compensates for its lack of serious interest in matters religious is to ratchet up the romance: this *Brideshead* is less a dramatization than what you might call a melodramatization. In Waugh's novel, Sebastian takes Charles to Venice during the summer after their first meeting, an idyll that turns out to be a last fleeting moment of happiness for Sebastian before his alcoholic disintegration (which poor Charles, shut out from his friend's spiritual anguish, cannot yet comprehend). Since the movie gives no serious consideration to the subject of spiritual anguish—which is merely flashily alluded to in a lugubrious voice-over at the beginning: "one emotion remains my own, as pure as that faith from which I am still in flight: guilt!"—it must produce another, more obvious motivation for Sebastian's decline. This motivation turns out to be a seething love triangle involving Charles, Sebastian, and Julia.

The screenwriters have thus retooled Waugh's carefully built plot. In the novel, Charles pointedly refers to Sebastian as "the forerunner" of Julia, a kind of *figura* for his more mature love, but in the new movie Charles schleps poor Julia along to Venice, where an overwrought—and, it must be said, very swishy—Sebastian catches sight of her and Charles smooching during Carnival. This and other hectic reconfigurations of the action, squeezed into a couple of hours, gives the film a jumbled, incoherent feel. The miniseries, by contrast, which stretched Waugh's tale over eleven episodes, made *Brideshead Revisited* seem tauter than it actually is.

The excision, to all intents and purposes, of the religious preoccupation of the novel wreaks particular havoc with a crucial, subtle character: Lady Marchmain. If you don't take her faith seriously, she becomes a predictable type: the castrating Catholic matriarch whose steely, unlovable nature is visually reflected in the rigid curls of her armor-stiff coif—a recusant Margaret Thatcher, a Phyllis Schlafly *avant la lettre*. One of the achievements of Claire Bloom's portrayal of this strange figure in the miniseries was that it evoked the delicate complexities of a character whose only sin—a great one, to be sure—was to compete with God.

Every nuance of Bloom's performance—the arresting quiet of her speech, with its assumption of inevitable obedience; the neurotic, almost controlling crispness in the way she articulated the often unvoiced *ti* in "Sebastian," or her fussily perfect pronunciation of "Zürich"—suggested a desperate desire to control in a character whom Waugh, for one, saw not as cruel but as "tragic." (This description is taken from a document available to anyone with a Web browser: the remarkable set of notes that Waugh composed for the benefit of a Hollywood producer who in 1947 was contemplating a film version.) Emma Thompson's Lady Marchmain, in the new film, is, by contrast, a cliché—a tight-lipped harridan who drives her children to drink. There is no sign here of the marchioness

Marchmain's fatal "charm," about which Charles, at Oxford, is warned by one of Sebastian's friends—and which is the thing about the Flytes that lures Charles to Brideshead in the first place, the honey in which he gets fatefully stuck.

These are but a few of the new adaptation's many failures to make sense of the material on which it is supposedly based. The most serious, of course, is that the shift in emphasis from God to Mammon makes utter nonsense of the end, the twin climaxes, of the story: if Waugh's novel, with its serious intentions and anguished spiritual questioning, couldn't bring off a convincing ending ("extravagantly absurd," Edmund Wilson concluded), then how could this film, with its soap opera antics and coarse clichés, possibly lead anyone to believe in the tale's twofold spiritual culmination—the deathbed repentance, the triumphant conversion? The makers of this movie neither know nor care. All of them, by the way, are British. You can only imagine what Evelyn Waugh would make of a world so topsy-turvy that it's not the savage Americans but the civilized English who, faced with his vexed but still somehow impressive work, "do not understand."

—*The New York Review of Books*, October 9, 2008

Hail, Augustus!

COMPARED TO JOHN WILLIAMS'S earlier novels, *Augustus*—the last work to be published by the author, poet, and professor whose once-neglected *Stoner* has become an international literary sensation in recent years—can seem like an oddity. For one thing, it was the only one of his four novels to win significant acclaim during his lifetime: published in 1972, *Augustus* won the National Book Award for fiction. (Williams was born in Texas in 1922 and died in Arkansas in 1994, after a thirty-year career teaching English and creative writing at the University of Denver.) More important, the novel's subject—the life and history-changing career of the first emperor of Rome—seems impossibly remote from the distinctly American preoccupations of Williams's other mature works, with their modest protagonists and pared-down narratives.

Butcher's Crossing (1960) is the story of a young Bostonian who, besotted with Emersonian Transcendentalism, goes west in 1876 to explore the "wilderness." There, he believes, lies "the central meaning he could find in all his life"; there, too, he ends up participating in a savage buffalo hunt that suggests the costs of the American dream. *Stoner* (1965) traces the obscure and, to all appearances, unsuccessful life of an assistant professor of English at the University of Missouri in the early and middle years of the last century—a man of desperately humble origins who sees the Academy as an "asylum," a place where he finds at last "the kind of security and warmth that he should have been able to feel as a child in his home." (The author repudiated his first novel, *Nothing But the Night*, published in 1948, about a dandy with psychological problems.)

It would be difficult to find a figure ostensibly less like these idealistic and, ultimately, disillusioned minor figures than the real-life world leader known to history as Augustus, whose many and elaborate names, given and taken, augmented and elaborated, acquired and discarded over the eight decades of his tumultuous and grandiose life, stand in almost comic contrast to the simple disyllables Williams gave those two other protagonists. Both characters, as readers will notice, share their creator's name—William Andrews, William Stoner—a choice that inevitably hints at an element of autobiography.

No such temptation exists in the case of *Augustus*. The emperor who gave his lofty name to a political and literary era was born Gaius Octavius Thurinus in 63 BC, the year in which the statesman Cicero foiled an aristocrat's attempted coup d'état against the Republic. The offspring of Gaius Octavius, a well-to-do knight of plebeian family origins, he was raised in the provinces about twenty-five miles from Rome. While still a teenager, the sickly but clever and ambitious youth sufficiently impressed his maternal great-uncle, Julius Caesar, to be adopted by him; he was thereafter known as Gaius Julius Caesar Octavianus ("Octavian").

In 44 BC, following Caesar's assassination and his subsequent deification by decree of the Senate, the canny nineteen-year-old, eager to capitalize on his dead relative's prestige and thereby enhance his standing with Caesar's veterans, referred to himself as Gaius

Julius Caesar Divi Filius ("Son of the Divine"). By the time he was twenty-five, having avenged Caesar's murder by vanquishing Brutus and Cassius at Philippi, the new Gaius Julius Caesar had shrewdly maneuvered himself to the center of power in the Roman world as one of three military dictators or "triumvirs." (Another was Marc Antony, with whom he would eventually quarrel and go to war.) At this point the "Gaius" and "Julius" disappeared, to be replaced by "Imperator": a military title used by troops to acclaim successful leaders, and the root of the English word "emperor."

Within another decade this "Imperator Caesar Divi Filius" had successfully wrested absolute control of the vast Roman dominions from his one remaining rival, Antony, whom he defeated at Actium in 31 BC and who committed suicide a year later, along with his paramour Cleopatra. (As the imperator gave the order to murder Cleopatra's teenaged son Caesarion—a potential rival, since the youth's father had been Julius Caesar—he remarked that "too many Caesars is no good thing.") Master of the world at thirty-three, he then set about consolidating his power, craftily legitimating his autocratic rule under the forms of traditional republican law, and establishing the legal, political, and cultural foundations for an empire that would persist, in one form or another, for the next fifteen centuries.

One title that this astonishingly adept figure never used was *rex*, "king"—a word much loathed by the Romans, some of whom killed his great-uncle partly out of fear that he wanted to be one. The master of the world referred to himself as *princeps*, "first citizen." In 27 BC, ostensibly in gratitude to the new Caesar for ending a century of civil bloodshed and establishing political stability at home and abroad, the Roman Senate voted him an additional honorific name that had suggestive religious associations: *augustus*, "the one to be revered." The name by which he has come to be known, then, bears no resemblance whatsoever to the one he was born with.

No resemblance to his former self: it is here that the hidden kinship between *Augustus* and its two predecessors lies. A strong theme in Williams's work is the way that our sense of who we are can be irrevocably altered by circumstance and accident. In his Augustus novel, Williams took great pains to see past the glittering historical pageant and focus on the elusive man himself—one who, more than most, had to evolve new selves in order to prevail. The surprise of his final novel is that its famous protagonist turns out to be no different in the end from this author's other disappointed heroes; which is to say, neither better nor worse than most of us. The concerns of this spectacular historical saga are intimate and deeply humane.

The life of the first emperor is in one distinctive way an ideal vehicle for a historical novel: Augustus is a figure about whom we know at once a great deal and very little, and hence invites both description and invention.

The biographies and the gossip, the recording and conjecturing began in the emperor's own lifetime. One *Life* was written by a friend and contemporary of Augustus's who appears as a character in Williams's novel: the philosopher and historian Nicolaus of Damascus, erstwhile tutor to the children of Antony and Cleopatra. The emperor himself composed an official autobiography, the *Res Gestae Divi Augusti* ("Deeds Accomplished by the Divine Augustus"), which was clearly intended as a form of political propaganda. Inscribed on bronze tablets that were affixed to the portals of his mausoleum, it was reproduced in inscriptions throughout the Empire.

If we are to believe Tacitus, writing a century after Augustus's reign, the obscurity of the emperor's nature and aims was already a subject of discussion among his contemporaries. In his *Annals*, that historian paraphrases a debate that took place at the time of the emperor's death, at the age of seventy-seven, in 14 AD:

Some said "that he was forced into civil war by the duty owed to a father [Julius Caesar], and by the necessities imposed by the state, in which at the time the rule of law had no place...and that there was no other remedy for a country at war with itself than to be ruled by one man."

And yet:

It was said, on the other hand, "that duty toward a father and the exigencies of state were merely put on as a mask: it was in fact from a lust for domination that he had stirred up the veterans by bribery... he wrested the consulate from a reluctant Senate and turned the arms that had been entrusted to him for a war with Antony against the republic itself. Citizens were proscribed and lands divided... Undoubtedly there was peace after all this, but it was a peace that dripped blood."

The emperor may well have cultivated a certain opacity as a means of maintaining control: if his motives were hard to guess, so too would his actions be. Small wonder that his official seal was the enigmatic, riddling Sphinx.

How to write about such a figure? In *Augustus*, the question is slyly put in the mouth of the emperor's real-life biographer, Nicolaus. "Do you see what I mean," the confounded scholar writes after a meeting with Augustus, whose notorious prudence he cannot reconcile with an equally notorious penchant for gambling. "There is so much that is not said. I almost believe that the form has not been devised that will let me say what I need to say." This is an in-joke on Williams's part: the form Nicolaus dreams of—which is of course the one Williams ended up using—is the epistolary novel, a genre that wasn't invented until fifteen centuries after Augustus. And yet its roots go right back to his reign. The Roman poet Ovid—also a character in *Augustus*, providing gossipy updates on the doings of the imperial court—composed a work called *Heroides* ("Heroines"), a sequence of verse epistles by mythical women to their lovers.

The epistolary form, so long associated with romantic subjects, is in fact ideally suited to Williams's quasi-biographical project. (And, as he must have known, to this particular historical period: it had been used with great success in *The Ides of March*, Thornton Wilder's 1948 novel about Caesar's assassination.) The portrait that *Augustus* creates, refracted through not only (invented) letters but also journal entries, senatorial decrees, military orders, private notes, and unfinished histories, is at once satisfyingly complex and appropriately impressionistic, subjective. The authors of the invented epistles and documents are, with very few exceptions, real-life characters, and Williams, who expressed impatience with historical fiction that crudely "updated" the past, clearly relished the opportunity to impersonate some well-known figures.

184

Here, then, is the wit and also the preening of Cicero, the orator who, despite his opposition to Julius Caesar, was allied at one point with the young Octavian, whom at first he dangerously underestimates. ("The boy is nothing, and we need have no fear...I have been kind to him in the past, and I believe that he admires me...I am too much the idealist, I know—even my dearest friends do not deny that.") Here too is the worldly Ovid, his report to his friend and fellow love-poet Propertius about a day at the races in the emperor's box nicely filigreed with self-conscious poeticisms: "The sun was beginning to struggle up from the east through the forest of buildings that is Rome...."

Even those historical figures who left few traces of their writing style appear in the novel fully fleshed and, as far as the historical record permits us to know, true to life. Maecenas, the well-born patron of the arts who served as the new emperor's unofficial cultural czar, and who was a friend of Horace and Virgil as well as of Augustus (the emperor ridiculed his friend's effete style), is presented as a prickly aesthete ("much has been said about those eyes, more often than not in bad meter and worse prose") with a hint of steel. Augustus's ambitious third wife, Livia, the mother of his eventual successor, Tiberius, comes across as coolly pragmatic and no more excessively conniving than most of the people around her: a far more persuasive character than the Grand Guignol poisoner of Robert Graves's *I, Claudius*. "Our futures are more important than our selves," Williams's Livia matter-of-factly writes to her son, demanding that he divorce his beloved wife in order to enter into a dynastic match with Augustus's daughter, Julia, whom he loathes.

Williams has the excellent idea of using invented excerpts from a now-lost memoir by Marcus Agrippa—Augustus's great friend from youth, the leader of his military victories, his eventual son-in-law, and the father to his heirs—to give the tersely prosaic, "official" version of events:

> And after the triumvirate was formed and the Roman enemies of Julius Caesar and Caesar Augustus were put down, there yet remained in the West the forces of the pirate Sextus Pompeius, and in the East the exiled murderers of the divine Julius....

To Agrippa, Williams gives the habit of beginning his sentences with "and," a tic that makes the prose feel idiosyncratic, persuasive. Indeed, a possible criticism of the earlier novels is that the author occasionally works so hard to make the writing "beautiful" that it sometimes works against believability; Will Andrews in *Butcher's Crossing* often expresses himself in a high style at odds with his extreme youth. The ventriloquism imposed by *Augustus*'s epistolary form saves Williams from this vice: he works to sound like his characters, not like himself. It is his most rigorous work.

One shrewd choice that he made in writing *Augustus* was the decision to withhold the emperor's own voice until the end, where we get to hear it at last in a long (again fictional) letter to Nicolaus of Damascus, the real-life biographer. This coda constitutes the novel's climax; not surprisingly, the emperor's account of his past doesn't square with many of the suppositions and speculations that have preceded it. For instance, it now emerges that what a friend had understood at the time to be the young Octavian's cry of grief and confusion on hearing the news of Caesar's assassination was—at least as the aged emperor would now have his friend believe—merely an expression of "nothing ... coldness," followed by a feeling of triumph: "I was suddenly elated. . . . I knew my destiny." And indeed, as if to underscore the unbridgeable distance between what is perceived and what is true, between the official and unofficial, public and private narratives of our own lives, Williams intersperses this climactic fictional mini-autobiography with italicized excerpts from the *Res Gestae Divi Augusti*. Where does the truth of a life lie? After reading Nicolaus's authorized biography (and reflecting on his own official autobiography), Williams's Augustus wryly comments that "when I read those books and wrote my words, I read and wrote of a man who bore my name but a man whom I hardly know." Anyway, as we know, "who bore my name" is itself problematic, given how many names—and, by implication, identities—the emperor had.

To the historical novelist, if not to the historian, that unknowability can be an advantage. Like the best works of historical fiction about the classical world—Marguerite Yourcenar's *Memoirs of Hadrian*, Wilder's *The Ides of March*, Graves's Claudius novels, Mary Renault's evocation of fifth-century Athens in *The Last of the Wine* —*Augustus* suggests the past without presuming to recreate it.

To have attempted simply to paint a picture of the past would, in any event, have left no room for the serious literary concern at the heart of *Augustus* and Williams's other works. In a 1985 interview, he described what he saw as the common theme of *Stoner* and *Augustus*:

I was dealing with governance in both instances, and individual responsibilities, and enmities and friendship. . . . Except in scale, the machinations for power are about the same in a university as in the Roman Empire....

The effect of power (and of struggles for power) on individuals is, in fact, a theme of the episode in Augustus's reign that first captured Williams's imagination and would set the novel in motion. In the early 1960s, not long after the publication of *Butcher's Crossing*, he first learned about the devastating scandal that had rocked both the empire and the imperial family: in 2 BC, Augustus was forced to exile his beloved daughter and only child, Julia, to a tiny island called Pandateria. One of the charges was adultery—a violation of the strict morality laws her father had instituted as part of his campaign to renew old-fashioned Roman virtues in his new state. (By that point, Julia, trapped in her marriage to Tiberius, whom she loathed, was notorious for her flagrant affairs.) Another charge was treason: there is a strong suggestion that some of the men whom she took as lovers were part of a faction opposed to Tiberius's succession.

In this tale of a spirited woman whose passions brought her into disastrous conflict with her obligations, Williams perceived a compelling theme: what he called "the ambivalence between the public necessity and the private want or need." This tension is one that his Julia, among the novel's subtlest and most arresting characters—intelligent, ironic, rebellious, worldly, philosophical—tartly comments upon in the Pandateria journal Williams invents for her:

It is odd to wait in a powerless world, where nothing matters. In the world from which I came, all was power; and everything mattered. One even loved for power; and the end of love became not its own joy, but the myriad joys of power.

It is no accident that *Augustus* falls into two main sections: the first recounts the emperor's unlikely, triumphant rise to power, whereas the second, anchored by Julia's journal entries, maps the disintegration of his family and personal happiness—largely as the result of his machinations to perpetuate his power through ill-conceived dynastic marriages. Which is to say, Part I is about success in the public, political sphere, and Part II about failure in the private, emotional sphere—the latter being a potential cost, Williams suggests, of the former.

The conflict between individuals and institutions is also at work in *Stoner*—the book that Williams wrote immediately after learning of the Julia story: to some extent, the contours of Julia's story are inverted by *Stoner*'s narrative, which presents a hero who repeatedly submerges his private wants to his larger obligations. There is an unhappy marriage alleviated too briefly by an affair with a sympathetic graduate student. (The novel's great failure is the portrait of Stoner's harridan of a wife: engineered to make Stoner miserable, she is far nastier than she needs to be.) There is fatherhood. Williams is particularly good on the tenderness of father–daughter relationships, both here and in *Augustus*.

And there is the dogged devotion to a middling career, which is delicately supported by a few cautious allies and dangerously open to threats from one or two academic enemies Stoner has inevitably made in the course of things. One of these, embittered by Stoner's (justified) criticism of a dishonest protégé, successfully thwarts his academic progress and personal happiness over the course of many years—a disaster that Stoner could have avoided had he not stuck so ferociously to his principles in exposing the protégé's phoniness, a victory over phoniness that turned out to by pyrrhic. In *Augustus*, a character called Salvidienus, a bosom friend of the emperor's youth who ultimately betrays him, observes in his "Notes for a Journal" that "every success uncovers difficulties that we have not foreseen, and every victory enlarges the magnitude of our possible defeat." This is another of Williams's major themes.

Yet Williams's work cannot be reduced to a series of parables about individuals struggling with, and within, institutions. Among other things, such an approach can't account for *Butcher's Crossing*, a work in which the strictures of society and its institutions are almost wholly absent; their absence is what creates some of the dreadful outcomes in that novel, which charts the characters' descent, during and after the buffalo hunt, into a precivilized, asocial stupor. ("Their food and their sleep came to be the only things that had much meaning for them.") The main theme at play in all three of Williams's mature novels is larger—the discovery that, as Stoner puts it to the mistress he must abandon for the sake of his family and his job, "we are of the world, after all." All of Williams's work is preoccupied by the way in which, whatever our characters or desires may be, the lives we end up with are the often unexpected products of the friction between us and the world itself—whether that world is nature or culture, the deceptively Edenic expanses of the Colorado Territory or the narrow halls of a state university, the carnage of a buffalo hunt or the proscriptions of the Roman Senate. At one point in *Augustus*, a visitor to Rome asks Octavian's boyhood tutor what the young leader is like, and the elderly Greek sage replies, "He will become what he will become, out of the force of his person and the accident of his fate."

An inescapable and sober conclusion of all three novels is that the friction between "force of person" and "accident of fate" becomes, more often than not, erosion: a process that can blur the image we had of who we are, revealing in its place a stranger. Just before *Butcher's Crossing*'s Will Andrews leaves for the buffalo hunt, a kindly whore whom he yearns for but can't bring himself to sleep with—his loss of innocence will take another form, during and after the hunt—warns the soft-skinned and handsome young man that he'll change and harden. This prophecy comes quite literally true at the height of the slaughter of the buffalo: "In the darkness Andrews ran his hand over his face; it was rough and strange to his touch; ... he wondered if Francine would recognize him if she could see him now."

Similarly, Stoner understands at the end of his life that whatever his ideals may have been, they have yielded to chance and necessity, which have made him other than what he had hoped to be:

> He had dreamed of a kind of integrity, of a kind of purity that was entire; he had found compromise and the assaulting diversion of triviality. He had conceived wisdom, and at the end of the long years he had found ignorance. And what else? he thought. What else?

So, too, Williams's *Augustus*, whose many names reflect with particular vividness the processes of unexpected evolution and irreversible erosion so fascinating to this author. In the last of the letters that Augustus addresses to Nicolaus, Stoner's word "triviality" tellingly reappears, as the dying emperor ruefully acknowledges "the triviality into which our lives have finally descended." What occasions this thought is Augustus's weary realization that the peace and stability for which he has struggled for so long, sacrificed so much, and staked his career and reputation on may not, after all, be what the Roman, or indeed any people, want. "The possibility has occurred to me that the proper condition of man, which is to say that condition in which he is most admirable, may not be that prosperity, peace, and harmony which I labored to give to Rome." He has founded his empire, in other words, on a misconception.

This painful concluding irony is typical of Williams. It bears a strong resemblance, for instance, to the awful end of *Butcher's Crossing*, when the buffalo hunters return at last to civilization after the slaughter only to find that, during the months of their absence, the bottom has dropped out of the market for buffalo hides—which means that all their labor, all the slaughter, the deprivations and sacrifices, have been in vain. In *Augustus*, the irony is painfully underscored in a brief coda that takes the form of the last of the many documents the author so imaginatively invents: a letter written forty years after the emperor's death by the now elderly Greek physician who had attended him on his deathbed. In it the writer, having weathered the reigns of the cruel Tiberius and the mad Caligula, celebrates the advent of a new emperor who "will at last fulfill the dream of Octavius Caesar." That emperor is Nero.

And yet Williams didn't see his heroes as failures. Nor should we. In the long interview he gave a few years before his death, the author remarked that he thought Stoner was "a *real* hero":

A lot of people who have read the novel think that Stoner had such a sad and bad life. I think he had a very good life.... He was doing what he wanted to do, he had some feeling for what he was doing, he had some sense of the importance of the job he was doing. He was a witness to values that are important...You've got to keep the faith.

"Keep the faith." These characters may have grown away from the selves they thought they would be, but what they come to understand is that the life that they have made is equal to "themselves"—the dwellings they must inhabit, and which, in the end, they must find the courage to inhabit alone.

This knowledge is tragic, but not necessarily sad. At the end of the affair that threatens the modest life he has painstakingly, confusedly created, Stoner gently tells his lover, Katherine, that at least they haven't compromised themselves: "We have come out of this, at least, with ourselves. We know that we are—what we are." Similarly, William Andrews returns from the buffalo hunt dimly aware that his dream of oneness with Nature was a glib fantasy, and that the lessons he took away from his encounter with the wild were different from the ones he imagined he'd be learning, the "fancy lies" a bitter, older partner contemptuously dismisses: he sees at last that "there's nothing, nothing but yourself and what you could have done." As with Greek tragedies, Williams's novels expose the process by which "what you could have done" is gradually stripped away from a character, leaving only what he did do—which is to say, the residue that is "yourself."

So too with the Imperator Caesar Divi Filius Augustus, who in the last pages of Williams's final novel stoically embraces the truth that, in *Butcher's Crossing*, the hero's partner sourly complained about. To confront one's self, stripped of pretense and illusion, is the climax to which every life inevitably leads, however great or humble:

I have come to believe that in the life of every man, late or soon, there is a moment when he knows beyond whatever else he might understand, and whether he can articulate the knowledge or not, the terrifying fact that he is alone, and separate, and that he can be no other than the poor thing that is himself.

This is the conclusion to which many good biographies, to say nothing of some very good novels, also lead. "The poor thing that is himself" is hardly the way that most of us would think about the first Roman emperor. It is the achievement of Williams's novel that, by its end, we are able to do so, and to think of that end as a satisfying one.

—Introduction to John Williams, *Augustus*
(New York Review Books, 2014)

Weaving New Patterns

Toward the beginning of Ingmar Bergman's *Fanny and Alexander*, a film at once deeply autobiographical and infused with improbable enchantments both bright and dark, a beautiful young boy wanders into a beautiful room. The room is located in a rambling Uppsala apartment belonging to the boy's widowed grandmother, Helena Ekdahl, once a famous actress and now the matriarch of a spirited and noisy theater family. As the camera follows the boy, Alexander, we note the elaborate fin-de-siècle décor, the draperies with their elaborate swags, the rich upholstery and carpets, the pictures crowding the walls, all imbued with the warm colors that, throughout the first part of the film, symbolize the Ekdahls' warm (when not overheated) emotional lives. Later, after the death of Alexander's kindhearted father, Oscar, who is the lead actor of the family troupe, his widow rather inexplicably marries a stern bishop into whose bleak residence she and her children must move. (It's no coincidence that the play Oscar was producing at the time of his death was *Hamlet*.) At this point, the film's visual palette will be leached of color and life; everything will be gray, black, coldly white.

But for now, vivacity and sensuality and even fantasy reign. On a mantelpiece, an elaborate gilt clock ticks, its golden cherubs preparing their mechanized dance. Nearby, a life-size white marble statue of a nude woman catches the boy's eye. When he blinks, she seems,

Galatea-like, to come to life, one arm moving as if to beckon him to pleasures he has not yet even imagined; he blinks again, and the statue is just a statue once more. At that moment a violent rattling wakes him from his reverie: the maid is pouring coal into a stove.

The tension between the fantastical and the mundane, imagination and reality—symbolized above all by the difference between the aesthetically and emotionally extravagant Ekdahls and the tight-lipped bishop and his dour household—is one with which Bergman's film is deeply preoccupied, from its opening shot of Alexander staring into a toy theater, to the scene a few moments later with the magically animated statue, to its final seconds, during which the grandmother recites the first lines of Strindberg's *A Dream Play*: "On a flimsy framework of reality, imagination spins, weaving new patterns."

To those familiar with Bergman's life as well as his work, the opening of *Fanny and Alexander* is likely to provoke musings on the patterns that the imagination weaves on the framework of reality. For the room we see in the film is a version of a room that Bergman knew as a boy, which he describes in his 1987 autobiography, *The Magic Lantern*:

> I can see the shimmering green of the drawing room, green walls, rugs, furniture, curtains, ferns in green pots. I can see the naked white lady with her arms chopped off. She is leaning slightly forward, looking at me with a small smile. A gilt clock under a glass dome stands on the bulging bureau with its gold fittings and feet...

This room—so clearly the model for the one in *Fanny and Alexander*—was part of the luxurious Uppsala apartment of the director's widowed maternal grandmother, Anna Åkerblom, the matriarch of a noisy, comfortably well-off, emotionally colorful clan that, just as clearly, was the model for the fictional Ekdahls. The apartment, along with Anna's summer house in Dalarna, would become places of refuge for the young Bergman as the marriage between his parents—Anna's high-spirited and willful daughter Karin and Erik Bergman, the impoverished, "nervous, irritable, and depressive" Lutheran pastor whom she married against her family's wishes—disintegrated.

Bergman would recreate both the setting and the family in film after film, from early masterpieces such as *Smiles of a Summer Night* and *Wild Strawberries* (in both of which we find avatars of the refreshingly unsentimental grandmother; the beautiful, headstrong, confused mother; the severe, humorless father; the rambunctious families) to *Fanny and Alexander* a quarter-century later. But as he entered old age and grew increasingly exasperated with filmmaking (in *The Magic Lantern* he writes dismissively of the "perfectionist restriction" he felt characterized his later work), the director turned to another medium, one that would allow him to revisit one particular "framework of reality"—his parents' lives and doomed marriage—and weave an entirely new kind of pattern from it. That medium was fiction.

Confronted with works like Bergman's novels—excursions by a famous creative artist into a genre other than the one that made him famous; works, moreover, that are explicitly autobiographical—the reader is tempted to waver between curiosity ("What light can these works shed on his films?") or disdain, dismissing them as vanity projects.

Bergman himself—who, it is worth reminding American readers, wrote essays, articles, plays, and an opera as well as the screenplays for his films—could be a harsh critic of his prose. In the autobiography he reminisces about the criticism he received early on when he was praised as a producer but condemned for his writing, and he goes on to agree with their verdict: "I wrote badly, affectedly." Later in life, when his sister, Margareta, asked him to look over some writing of her own, he reflected on the "strained, labored style" that he found in both their work. (Ingmar didn't refrain from telling Margareta exactly what he thought of her work, a reaction that "murdered," as he later put it, her literary ambitions: an instance of cruelty that was hardly atypical of this family, as his autobiographical writings make clear.)

Yet there are few signs of strain—stylistic, artistic, or otherwise—in the three works of fiction Bergman produced in a remarkable creative rush between the ages of seventy-three and seventy-eight. *The Magic Lantern* oscillates, sometimes uncomfortably, between family memoir and career retrospective. With its summoning of old ghosts, it seems to have freed up some new creative energies in Bergman; the swiftness with which the three novels followed the autobiography is striking. *The Best Intentions*, a dramatization of his parents' improbable courtship and troubled marriage that's punctuated by conversations (real or imagined) with Erik and Karin (referred to in the novel by the pseudonyms "Anna" and "Henrik") in their old age, came out in 1991; *Sunday's Children*, which focuses on a precarious moment in the young Ingmar's relationship with his forbidding father, in 1993; and *Private Confessions*, a series of six dialogues, each featuring his mother at a crucial moment in her emotional and spiritual life, in 1996.

The Best Intentions, the longest of the three, is the most theatrical. A good deal of the novel consists of stacked chunks of dialogue, presented as if in a script, and embedded in passages that feel more like stage directions than expository prose. Here, for example, is a moment from the first few pages of the book, when the young divinity student Henrik Bergman—already set in his self-righteous ways—confronts his elderly grandfather, who has sought the youth out on behalf of his dying wife, who wants to make amends for the way she and her husband have treated the boy and his widowed mother. (We learn that, upon the premature death of Henrik's father, the Bergmans abandoned his widow, Alma, and young son to poverty: a circumstance that warps his character, as he himself later acknowledges, leaving him able to function only when he is in a state of "privation.") This crucial early moment tells us much about Henrik and indeed all the Bergmans—and much about the author's stylistic and thematic ambitions:

FREDRIK BERGMAN: Your grandmother and I have been talking about you over the past few days.

Someone out in the corridor laughs then walks quickly away. A clock strikes three quarters past the hour.

FREDRIK BERGMAN: Your grandmother says, and has said for a great many years, that we wronged you and your mother. However, I maintain that each and every man is responsible for his own life and his own actions. Your father broke away from us and moved elsewhere with his family. That was his decision and his responsibility…

HENRIK (*suddenly*): Grandfather, if you have summoned me here
to clarify your attitude towards my mother and myself; that I have
known for as long as I can remember. Everyone is responsible for
himself. *And* for his deeds. In that we are agreed. Please, may I go
now? I'm actually studying for my exams. I'm sorry that Grandmother is ill. Perhaps you would be so kind as to give her my regards?

Imprisoned as they are by their high sense of their own rectitude,
neither of these men, we know, will end well.

In *The Magic Lantern*, Bergman describes his parents as people
whose "beliefs, values, and traditions [were] of no use to them." In
The Best Intentions, he dramatizes that failure—the way in which
we are often confined as well as defined by of our understanding of
who we are; the tragic grip that history and character exert on our
ambitions and desires—in every branch of his family, as Åkerbloms
and Bergmans of various generations, not only Anna and Henrik
but their various relatives, repeatedly come together and make each
other miserable. The novel's slightly distancing, "dramatic" style,
which allows us to witness these interesting, intelligent, and often
wrongheaded characters as they go about their lives, letting us hear
what they say and see what they do without (as is possible in a novel)
making us privy to thoughts or motivations that aren't revealed in
dialogue or action, accentuates our sense of the "tragedy of character," of a dark fate moving inexorably to its conclusion.

This hybrid style, deployed across the novel's nearly four hundred
pages, allows Bergman to track his doomed protagonists' fates in
great detail and with considerable sweep. Take Henrik, whom the
narrative tracks from youth to old age, and who is revealed as someone who, over the course of that eight-decade-long arc, could never

break out of the straitjacketed assumptions of his paltry background —assumptions already firmly in place during that rigid exchange with his equally rigid grandfather. Fearful, awkward, smothered by his needy mother, Alma ("You're all I have, I live for you alone")—in a word, "eclipsed" by life, as his more self-aware wife will one day sum it up—he is all too clearly a man who uses the rigor and strictures of organized religion to prop up a hopelessly crippled inner self.

As such, he's the worst possible match for the vivacious, spoiled Anna Åkerblom, a young woman who is shown over the course of her life to be driven by confident ideas about how things ought to be, by preconceived notions about, rather than by the realities of, life. "Do you know what an *unbeatable combination* we will be," she excitedly tells young Henrik soon after her brother introduces him at one of the Åkerbloms' rambunctious dinners. "You a priest and me a nurse . . . You bandage the soul, and I the body." Anna blithely sees life as a grand play in which everyone has "roles"; on the day of her wedding she's "rather like an actress just about to go onstage in an incomparable, brand-new part." When her headstrong fantasies encounter reality, only disaster can result. Bergman's novel is the record of that disaster—of the "life catastrophe" (a recurring phrase in all three novels) that results when imagination weaves its webs in life rather than in art.

The only character who successfully distinguishes between imagination and reality, who has a clear vision of the disaster in the making after Anna and Henrik meet, is the girl's mother, Karin Åkerblom. Practical, strong-minded, competent at managing her two children and three stepsons, deliciously lacking in sentiment or romanticism, coolly sensible when everyone else is befuddled by self-interest or self-delusion, she is clearly an avatar of Bergman's maternal grandmother. As are her cinematic sisters: the colorful but practical-minded mother of Desirée Armfeldt in *Smiles of a Summer Night* ("I was given this estate in return for not writing my memoirs"), the frostily matter-of-fact mother of Isak Borg in *Wild Strawberries* ("Ten children and all dead except Isak," she crisply reminds him when he visits), and Helena Ekdahl in *Fanny and Alexander*, accepting of and yet bemused by her daughter-in-law's inexplicable second marriage.

It is hard not to think that Ingmar Bergman was channeling this impressive figure when he wrote, in *The Magic Lantern*, of his loathing of "tumult, outbursts, or emotional reactions," of his conviction that "self-discipline, cleanliness, light, and quiet ... calm, order, and cleanliness" were necessary to "approach the limitless world." Bergman was all too aware that within himself he was replicating the struggle between his parents and their families: the tormented, guilt-ridden, self-destructive Bergmans, the blithe, crisply competent Åkerbloms. (However coolly in control he may have been on a film set or backstage at the theater, in his life—certainly in his early married life—it was as if he were irresistibly drawn to recreating his parents' ménage, with its havoc and unhappiness, rather than the Åkerblom household. By the time he was thirty, when he'd already left one wife and child for a new wife and child, "home seethed with crying children and weeping women ... all escape routes were closed and betrayal was obligatory." *Plus ça change*.)

So Karin stands as a figure of reality, of the world as it is, while, in their different ways, both Anna and Henrik are figures of a twisted "art"—of the attempt to impose imagination or fantasy on an unresponsive world. This familiar Strindbergian theme is underscored in *The Best Intentions* by an ingenious device to which the author turns more than once: the juxtaposition of some documentary evidence from the "real life" that he's fictionalizing—a photograph he has found of this or that relative or an entry in someone's diary—with his novelistic reconstruction of the person or incident in question. This technique can shed ironic light on the characters—for instance, when Bergman quotes a (presumably real) diary entry by Henrik's mother, Alma, after she meets her future daughter-in-law the first time: "Henrik came with his fiancée. She is extremely beautiful and he seems happy. Fredrik Paulin called in the evening. He talked about tedious things in the past. That was inappropriate and made Henrik sad."

This text is cited, pointedly, at the end of a long passage that has dramatized precisely the moment that Alma so tersely summarizes: the visit by Anna, the interruption of the family friend, Fredrik. But what Alma neglects to mention—or rather, what Bergman the novelist has her neglect to mention—is that the "tedious thing" that Fredrik talked on and on about was the conflict between Henrik Bergman and his guilty grandparents. Fredrik reveals that the grandmother has, in fact, died, an event about which young Henrik, all too characteristically, shows no emotion. The extended passage that Bergman has created out of his grandmother's terse diary entry inevitably brings us back to his novel's opening scene, the dialogue between the unyielding young man and his unyielding grandfather—and thereby serves to remind us, at the very moment Henrik is to be married, of his crippling flaws—just as the citation of the diary entry sheds light on the self-involved silliness of the smothering mother, who fusses over the beauty of her future daughter-in-law while remaining blind to the flaws in her son that will, in the end, bring down their marriage.

Karin Åkerblom, needless to say, has no illusions about her daughter's intended. Quite early in *The Best Intentions*, she tries to talk sense to Henrik, who persists in his courtship of Anna out of a helpless conviction that he can somehow transform himself into someone who fits into her and her family's life. Karin dismisses Henrik and his delusions like someone swatting a fly away:

> I believe that the liaison with you, Mr. Bergman, would lead to catastrophe. That is a strong word and I know it may seem exaggerated, but nonetheless, I must use the word. *A life catastrophe.* I cannot think of a more impossible and fateful combination than between our Anna and Henrik Bergman. Anna is a spoiled girl, willful, strong-willed, emotional, tenderhearted, extremely intelligent, impatient, melancholy and cheerful at the same time. What she needs is a *mature* man who can nurture her with love, firmness and unselfish patience. You are a very young man, Mr. Bergman, with little insight into life, and with, I fear, early and deep wounds beyond remedy or consolation. Anna will despair in her helpless attempts to heal and cure. . . .

Which is, of course, precisely what happens, from the courtship itself through a near breakup to the early years of the marriage—a wretched arc that *The Best Intention* relentlessly evokes, leaving us, at the end, with the picture of an uneasy truce, of a husband and wife who are horribly aware of the colossal mistake they have made and yet have been, again and again, seemingly powerless to change course. (A quarrel in a church over whether to have a tiny or grandiose wedding, which almost shipwrecks the engagement, makes it clear—at least to the reader—what the problems in their relationship will be; but by this point the couple are too attached to their illusions about each other, and about what their life together will be, to change course.) Against the delusion stands the lone figure of Karin, a marvelous fictional creation—one of those appealing realists you encounter from time to time in European fiction, from Count Mosca in *The Charterhouse of Parma* to Aunt Sarah in Sybille Bedford's *A Legacy*, memorable secondary characters who perceive the emotional folly of the protagonists but can do nothing to stop them. As indeed they mustn't, since without the folly we wouldn't have the novel—or the novelist.

Without the folly so meticulously autopsied in *The Best Intentions* we wouldn't have *Sunday's Children* or *Private Confessions*, either. Each of these extremely short books can be read as a freestanding work. And yet like moons drawn into the gravitational field of a large planet, they are irresistibly attached to their more ample predecessor, shedding light on its characters and themes even as they slowly illuminate fascinating landscapes of their own.

In contrast to the fervent and verbose drama of *The Best Intentions*, *Sunday's Children* evokes with an almost Jamesian subtlety— you think of *What Maisie Knew*—a young child's growing consciousness of his parents' marital distress. (The title refers to the fact that, in fairy tales, a "Sunday's child" is thought to have clairvoyant powers.) It is the summer of 1926, and Bergman's fictional alter ego, Pu, and his older brother are beginning to sense that something is wrong between their parents (who, rather confusingly, are here given the real-life names of Bergman's parents, Karin and Erik).

The eight-year-old Pu is alert to a strangeness in the atmosphere. "He doesn't like listening when Mother and Father use that particularly friendly tone of voice."

The plot, such as it is, is gossamer. Early on, we learn that Erik has been invited to preach in Grånäs, a town some distance away, and has asked Pu to accompany him, which throws the troubled young boy's conflicted feelings into high relief. On the one hand, Pu, who along with his brother has suffered from Erik's physically violent outbursts, dreams of killing his father, of making him "pray and weep and scream with fear"; on the other, he craves Erik's attention. The tentative interaction between the father, who is all too aware of his son's ill-concealed reluctance to be with him—a reluctance justified by a moment of violence aboard the ferry taking them to the town where he will preach—and the son, who can barely account for his incoherent feelings, is the achievement of this slender work, at once delicately rendered and deeply moving.

Delicately rendered, because Bergman has the good sense not to press his themes and characters too far. Much of the novel is given to the ephemera of that long-ago summer, the meals and the outings, the confused encounters with adult sexuality (at one point Pu hears his older brother masturbating in the next bed but isn't quite sure what's going on), the elderly relatives with their endless talk of bodily functions gone awry. All this, as well as the crises and the real dramas, the fear of catastrophe and death, is the stuff of life, too: another recurrent Bergmanian theme. ("While we talk, life passes," a character muses, quoting Chekhov.) At one point in *The Seventh Seal*, the wandering Knight takes a moment from his grim, ongoing struggle with Death to enjoy a sunny afternoon picnic with the actor Jof and his family, announcing afterward that "I'll hold this memory between my hands as carefully as a bowl brimming with fresh milk. And it will be a sign for me and a source of great content." *Sunday's Children* holds such memories, too.

But the novel derives additional force from our reading of *The Best Intentions*. Among other things, it vividly depicts the side effects—"collateral damage" may be a better phrase—of the doomed union whose origins are laid bare in the earlier work: the damaged children reenacting on one another the parents' cruelties; the fearful atmosphere, the tensions always simmering just below the surface so agonizingly that some kind of explosion would, like a storm on a muggy summer day, come as a relief. There is in fact a storm in *Sunday's Children*, and it does come as a climax, but whether it provides any relief is open to question.

When the confrontation does come, it is fifty years too late, and one of the aggrieved parties isn't even there to fight. In a flash-forward to the 1960s, the fifty-year-old Bergman visits his now-widowed father, who has recently discovered and read his late wife's diaries, in which she refers to her marriage as a "life catastrophe." (That fateful phrase again.) Reading them, the narrator's elderly father declares, is a "living hell." These are strong words from a Lutheran pastor; but who is the punisher, and does his suffering have meaning? Or do we create our own hells? These are old questions for Bergman the filmmaker; but in his novel he refuses to show his hand. The past is the past, its pleasures and pains all dust: *Sunday's Children* holds that past, with the pleasure and the pain, gratefully in its hands. The embrace of an exquisite ambivalence gives to this work a persuasive reality far more effective than melodramatics could do—nowhere more so than at the very end, when an accident resulting from that summer storm appears to give young Pu what he has dreamed of. Whether he really wants it is, of course, another question entirely.

What we want and what we sacrifice to get it is the theme of *Private Confessions*. The title of the novel is an allusion to Martin Luther: as one of the characters reminds us early on, Luther didn't abolish confession, he recommended replacing it with "private conversations." The novel proceeds as a series of six such conversations, each one focusing on a pivotal moment in Anna's spiritual life as she navigates the disintegration in her marriage to Henrik.

Four of the six conversations take place in the 1920s, when Anna is in her late thirties and carrying on an adulterous affair with a young musician, Tomas. In the first, she seeks out Uncle Jacob for spiritual advice about her crisis, which she describes in terms that will, by now, be familiar to the reader of these novels. ("We are moving toward a catastrophe," Anna desperately says of her life with Henrik. "A life catastrophe.") In the second conversation, we see that she has heeded Jacob's advice to tell her husband the truth about her affair: a scene that, like similar moments in the previous novels, only confirms Henrik's inability to be other than he has always been—terrifying in his self-righteousness, incapable of yielding on even the smallest points. An argument that the two have over some spots he's noticed on a tablecloth, which escalates and ends up serving as a metaphor for the entire marriage, is one of the most unsettling scenes of marital discord I can recall reading.

The next two conversations provocatively disturb the chronology. The third, a charged encounter between Anna and her indomitable but ineffective mother, is set a few months before the one in which she approaches Jacob for his advice—suggesting that she has turned to the old pastor as a last resort, hoping to get from him support that she can't get from anyone else. The fourth, set two years before that, relates a botched assignation between Anna and Tomas, in which that young man's limitations, and the improbability of their affair, are made uncomfortably plain. Once again, we understand, Anna has set her sights on an inappropriate man. What the warped chronology reveals is that Anna, being Anna—she is, after all, the same headstrong woman we first met in *Best Intentions*—proceeds anyway.

Anna's ambiguities have already been evoked in an early passage that shows Bergman skillfully wielding a traditional technique he's avoided in the other novels—free indirect discourse. Here she tries to decide whether to reach out to Jacob or to her callow young lover:

> What if she tried to get hold of Tomas instead? Just to find out what mood he is in, not to tell him about confessions or press him to say anything consoling, or meaningful . . . She stands with her head lowered, her finger to her lips as if requesting silence. No, not Tomas, not at the moment. Not later, either; perhaps never. Confession presumably entails something shattering and final. Anyhow, something mysterious, which she does not dare include in her vision. There are short moments that muscle into life when she grasps the content, the exact content, of her situation. Then she reaches out and grasps the back of a chair and for a moment is utterly aware of the chill emanating from the sculptured white wood.

Once again, knowledge of the earlier novels fills out the picture: in the woman who, quite literally, grasps at concrete realities in a moment of emotional crisis, Anna reveals herself to be very much her mother's child. And yet, unlike her mother, she has never been able to tame her fantasies of what life ought to be like, to tailor the role she yearns to enact to the play she finds herself in.

The conflict evoked in this passage—between the abstract, spiritual world represented by the word "confession," on the one hand, and the concrete realities of life, on the other hand, here symbolized by the hard, carved wood of the chair back—haunts all of the conversations in this work, the most overtly religious of the three novels, but nowhere more strikingly than in the fifth part. We're now in the mid-1930s, and the middle-aged Anna has a final conversation with the dying Jacob, who's curious to know how her life turned out. But even this deathbed scene offers no pat resolutions, gives no obvious answers. In a scene that is wholly consistent with the Bergman aesthetic, both cinematic and literary, juxtaposing as it does the mysterious and sacred with the deeply mundane crudities of physicality, a solemn moment—Jacob and his wife take Communion together and ask the doubtful Anna to join them—is suddenly shattered when the elderly pastor vomits out the wafer and the wine.

Bergman is right to refer to the last of these "confessions" as both an epilogue and a prologue. For even though it is set decades before those earlier conversations, and the events that trigger them, take place, it brings us full circle to the beginning, not only of this novel but of the whole cycle, of the tragedy of character, self-delusion, and belated self-awareness, that lurks behind all three novels. Once again, Anna is talking to Jacob, but this time we get to overhear the conversation that set all the others in motion, providing crucial insight into why those others had to take place. It is 1907 and Anna is seventeen and about to be confirmed, but on the eve of the ceremony she seeks out "Uncle" Jacob, an old family friend, to express her reservations. The two have a long conversation about religion, during which Jacob reveals the "factual basis" for his belief in the miracle of Christianity. (He sees the remarkably swift growth of the early church as a miraculous historical proof of the validity of the church's message.) Anna, who, Jacob can't help noticing, is wearing a hat far too grown-up and sophisticated for her, appears to be unmoved, and the two leave the church and stroll in the strong wind along the water for a while. Suddenly the girl lets the wind whip the hat into the water, and in a moment of "astonished appreciation" Jacob realizes that she's done it to please him. In that moment, the whole of her future life seems to be laid bare. If she does decide to be confirmed, we understand, it will be for a trifle—because she doesn't want to disappoint Mamma and her guests, or have her "lovely confirmation dress" go to waste. Or perhaps because she wants to please this pastor whom she has decided she likes.

In the tormented young mother who appears in this and the other novels, Bergman has created one of his most memorable characters—one not quite like any of the women familiar from his cinematic work. In *Fanny and Alexander*, we know strikingly little about Alexander's mother: why a woman who's been married to the sensitive and charming actor-manager could choose the dour and cruel bishop, why she so readily accedes to his bizarre demand that she strip herself of her family, her friends, her clothes and jewels—and that her children do the same—before entering his household. ("Naked," she jokes when he asks her; but he's not laughing.) You could argue that we don't know because the film unfolds from the child's point of view, and that to Alexander, as to all small children, his parents, their motivations and actions, are opaque.

But once you've read Bergman's autobiographical novels—works dominated by his mother's "life catastrophe," to which he so obsessively returns, a mystery whose decipherment requires him to imagine, among other things, his mother losing her virginity, his mother making love to her lover—it's hard not to think that it was only in fiction that he could allow himself to fully reanimate the real-life Anna Åkerblom Bergman, to weave a bold new portrait of her. "The theater is my wife," he is said to have declared, "and the cinema is my mistress." In order to go back to the beginning, to return to and explore with such startling intimacy the archetype of all those other women, this great artist has to find a new mode of expression—one that was, so to speak, neither wife nor mistress. A virgin medium.

If this is so, then it is fitting that the final scene in *Private Confessions*, a novel whose closing lines conjure the image of a girl in her white confirmation dress, brings not only the book but the entire trilogy to its close. At the end of his life, it was perhaps inevitable that Bergman should return to its beginning—the primal moment from which everything would evolve. Earlier in the novel—this is during the second conversation, in which Anna confesses her adultery to Henrik—the author once again self-consciously intervenes in his narrative to opine (tongue in cheek, you have to think) that the concept of a "decisive moment" in a fictional narrative is just a figment of dramatists' imagination, something that rarely happens in real life:

> The truth is probably that such moments hardly exist but it just looks as if they do ... if looked at carefully, the moment is not at all decisive: for a long time, emotions and thoughts have consciously or unconsciously been flowing in the same direction. The actual breakthrough is a fact far back in the past, far back in obscurity.

Anna's decisive moment, at the end of the novel that her son devoted to reanimating her, seems to be a whim, but it says everything about her that we need to know. Whatever our intentions, however clever or clairvoyant we feel ourselves to be, however great our yearning to confess and start afresh, character, for all of us, is destiny. The unfolding of that destiny, the delving into the obscurity whence it proceeds, is the work of artists—filmmakers, playwrights, novelists. But the hidden logic that connects our end to our beginning is also the province of priests. Who better than the son of a pastor to know that the alpha and the omega are one and the same?

—*The New York Review of Books*, April 18, 2019

The End of the Road

"WE SHALL NEVER GET to Constantinople like this." This rueful aside, which comes toward the end of the first of the three books that the late Patrick Leigh Fermor devoted to his youthful travels on foot across Europe in the early 1930s, was to prove prophetic. "Like this" ostensibly refers to the author's weakness for detours. By this point in *A Time of Gifts*—written some four decades after that remarkable journey and first published in 1977—it is late in 1933, and the high-spirited, precocious, poetry-spouting eighteen-year-old, long since expelled from school ("a dangerous mixture of sophistication and recklessness," a housemaster clucked), weary of England, and hungry for adventure, finds himself in Czechoslovakia, having walked from the Hook of Holland through the Low Countries, southern Germany, and Austria, his battered copies of *The Oxford Book of English Verse* and Horace's *Odes* firmly, famously in hand.

His plan at this point was to follow the Danube all the way to the Black Sea, whence he would head south to Constantinople—the name by which the romantic-minded youth, his head brimming with memorized verse, insisted on calling Istanbul. But in Bratislava, with Hungary and the continuation of his southeasterly route shimmering just across the great river, he finds himself unable to resist a Czech friend's invitation to go north to see Prague, that "bewildering and captivating town."

Here, as often with this erudite and garrulous author—the dashing autodidact and World War II hero, considered by some to be the greatest travel writer of the twentieth century—the geographical digression becomes a narrative one. As the impecunious Leigh Fermor zigzags around the city, the guest of his better-heeled and well-connected friend (the blithe sponging off obliging students, postmistresses, madams, diplomats, and aristocrats is an amusing leitmotif of his travels), goggling at the castles and the bridges, the relics and the nightclubs, the text goggles and zigzags, too. And so we carom from the murder of the tenth-century Bohemian leader we know as "Good King Wenceslas" (actually, a duke; later a saint) to the brief *Mitteleuropäisch* reign of James I's daughter, the so-called Winter Queen; from swoony evocations of medieval architectural details ("in King Vladislav's vast Hall of Homage the ribs of the vaulting had further to travel, higher to soar") to the tale of the Defenestration of Prague in 1618; from Kabala, Rosicrucians, the "sad charm" of the Habsburgs, and the tomb of the creator of the Golem to a triumphant conclusion (via an offhand rumination about the identity of Shakespeare's Mr. W. H.) in which the teenaged narrator believes he has solved the mystery of where the mysterious "coast of Bohemia" in *The Winter's Tale* could possibly have been. It is only after all this that the Leigh Fermor of 1933 heads south once again, to the Danube and his planned itinerary.

So it is possible to take "we shall never get to Constantinople like this" as a humorous acknowledgment by the author of a helpless penchant for digressions literal and figurative, one that will be familiar to anyone who has read even a few pages of Leigh Fermor's books: the early one about the Caribbean, *The Traveller's Tree* (1950); a slender volume called *A Time to Keep Silence* (1957), about his visits to three monastic communities; *Mani* (1958) and *Roumeli* (1966), his two lively and impassioned books about Greece, the country he loved best and where he ended up living part-time; and of course the trilogy of his walk across Europe—*A Time of Gifts* and its sequel, *Between the Woods and the Water* (1986), the first two installments, now completed by the posthumous publication last year of an unfinished final volume, *The Broken Road*.

The author's chattiness, his inexhaustible willingness to be distracted, his susceptibility to geographical, intellectual, aesthetic, and occasionally amorous detours, constitute an essential and self-conscious component of the style that has won him such an avid following. It has more than a little in common with the "centrifugal lambency and recoil" he found in Central European design, the "swashbuckling, exuberant and preposterous" aesthetic that he so extravagantly admired in a picture of Maximilian I's knights, which he came across one night while leafing through a book on German history in the luxurious apartment of a charming girl he met and ended up staying with in Stuttgart. (The strange new city, the chance meeting, the aesthetic reverie, the hints of money and eros: this would prove to be the pattern of the young man's progress across the continent.) It is indeed odd that, among the many classical authors to whom Leigh Fermor refers in his writing (none more famously than Horace, verses of whose Soracte Ode the author found himself swapping, in Latin, with a German general he had kidnapped on Crete during World War II, an incident that was later turned into a film starring Dirk Bogarde), Herodotus doesn't figure more prominently. There is no ancient writer whose technique Leigh Fermor's more closely resembles. Expansive, meandering, circular, it allows him to weave what is, after all, a relatively

217

straightforward tale of a youthful backpacking hike into a vast and highly colored tapestry, embroidered with observations, insights, and lessons about the whole panorama of European history, society, architecture, religion, and art.

And yet the author's charming and useful tendency to lose track of his destination became a serious real-life problem in the case of the books about the walk across Europe—the most beloved of his works, which have achieved the status of cult classics particularly among adventure-bent youth. ("Those bibles of backpacking seekers everywhere": so Joshua Jelly-Schapiro, a young California-based writer and geographer who wrote the preface to a recent reissue of *The Traveller's Tree* by New York Review Books, which has now republished nearly all of the author's work.) However many the detours, Leigh Fermor's youthful journey did have a destination, which the author finally reached: he got to "Constantinople" on New Year's Eve, 1935, a little shy of his twenty-first birthday.

The two installments that he eventually published committed him inexorably to writing about that climactic arrival. *A Time of Gifts*, which ends with Leigh Fermor arriving at last in Hungary—he crosses the Danube from Slovakia in the spring, just in time to witness a magnificent Easter service at the Basilica of Estergom—closes with the legend "TO BE CONTINUED." *Between the Woods and the Water* concludes in much the same way. Having followed its young hero through many a Hungarian and Yugoslavian castle's "antlered corridor," the narrative of this second volume brings him at last to the Iron Gates, the gorge on the Danube that forms the boundary between Serbia and Romania. It is the Feast of the Dormition of the Virgin, Leigh Fermor is in his nineteenth summer, and the book bids him with an all-caps promise: "TO BE CON-

CLUDED." (That the climaxes of both works are marked by great religious events is not accidental: the *mondain* and sensual Leigh Fermor, who always knew how to find his way into a count's castle or a duchess's good graces—Somerset Maugham once dismissed him as a "middle-class gigolo for upper-class women"—was beguiled by religious ceremonials; and, perhaps not so paradoxically, by intense religious feeling.)

But the conclusion never came. When Leigh Fermor died in 2011, at ninety-six, he had been afflicted by a writer's block that had lasted a quarter of a century. Soon after the publication of *Between the Woods and the Water* in the 1980s, he was already worried that the subject was, in the words of his friend and biographer Artemis Cooper, "stale" and "written out." In the early 1990s, his wife, Joan, wrote to a friend that he was "sadly stuck"; not long after, Charlotte Mosley, who at the time was editing a volume of Leigh Fermor's correspondence with the Duchess of Devonshire (another distraction), observed that "it takes his mind off Vol III which is clearly never going to appear." Given his predilection for wandering, invention, and improvisation, it may well be that the mounting expectations about the final volume had caused a kind of creative paralysis. The anticipation wasn't limited to his friends. When Leigh Fermor's name appeared on the 2004 Honors List, a fan wrote a letter to *The Daily Telegraph* declaring that the knighthood should be conditional on his finishing the trilogy.

It now turns out that the work was, in a way, already complete. As you learn from the preface to *The Broken Road* (edited by Cooper and the British novelist and travel writer Colin Thubron), a preliminary draft describing the last leg of his European adventure had been composed long before, when the idea for the books about the walking tour first germinated. In the early 1960s, Leigh Fermor was invited by the editor of *Holiday* to write an article on the "pleasures of walking." As he began to write about his youthful journey, the floodgates of memory opened; he wrote to his longtime publisher and friend John Murray that the article had soon "ripened out of all recognition." After nearly seventy manuscript pages he'd only got as far as the Iron Gates—at which point, frustrated by the need for compression, he began to write at the more expansive, elaborated pace he preferred, bringing his narrative as far as his arrival at the shores of the Black Sea.

This manuscript, tentatively known as "A Youthful Journey," eventually formed the basis for the whole trilogy. After setting the pages aside for a decade (during which time he published *Roumeli* and built a fabulous house for himself in the Mani, the Wild West–ish tip of the southern Peloponnese, about which he also wrote: more distractions), the author went back to the beginning, expanding those compressed first seventy pages into what became the richly wrought narratives of *A Time of Gifts* and *Between the Woods and the Water*.

It was only when he was in his early nineties that Leigh Fermor finally summoned the will to confront the decades-old pages covering the final third of his journey, from the Iron Gates to the Black Sea—the part he'd slowed down to treat at greater length in the original manuscript—and painstakingly set about elaborating them in his inimitable style.

The text he was working on at his death, along with excerpts from his original travel journal—brief entries covering his stay in Istanbul and a much longer narrative about his visit to the monasteries of Mount Athos—make up *The Broken Road*: the long-awaited "Vol

III." Precisely because its author didn't have time to bring his text to its usual level of high and elaborate polish, this final work—plainer, more straightforward, less elaborate, and more frank than its predecessors—provides some intriguing insights into Leigh Fermor's distinctive tics and mannerisms, strengths and weaknesses.

In a review of *Mani* that appeared when the book was first published, Lawrence Durrell referred to the "truffled style and dense plumage" of Leigh Fermor's prose. What you think of his writing, and indeed what you make of the final installment of his most beloved work, depends on your taste for truffles and feathers.

Structural rigor was, as we know, never Leigh Fermor's strong point—inevitably, perhaps, in the case of narratives that follow a real-life itinerary. The two walking-tour books published during his lifetime have a fortuitous coherence—he is, after all, heading *somewhere*—but what holds the others together is the intensity of the author's curiosity about whatever happens to (literally) cross his path and the brilliance of his talk about them: the "saga boys" of Trinidad in their wildly patterned shirts, "worn with a flaunting ease and a grace of deportment that compels nothing but admiration"; the nomadic Sarakatsáns of the northern Greek region called Roumeli (*Roumeli* opens with a dazzling set piece about a Sarakatsán wedding); the *miroloyia* or funeral dirges that are the only poetry prevalent in the Mani; Jewish lumbermen in Romania; the Uniotes of Eastern Europe, who observe the Eastern Rite while submitting to the authority of Rome (a recurrent object of fascination).

Small wonder that a salient feature of Leigh Fermor's style is the long list, that most unconstructed of devices. His penchant for lengthy enumerations confirms your sense that what delights this writer most is the sheer abundance in the world of things for him to look at and learn about. *Mani* memorably opens with one such enumeration, in this case of the varieties of Greek communities throughout the world (to which the author hopes to add a group of Jews who, he has heard, live in the Mani):

> I thought of the abundance of strange communities: the scattered Bektashi and the Rufayan, the Mevlevi dervishes of the Tower of the Winds, the Liaps of Souli, the Pomaks of the Rhodope, the Kizilbashi near Kechro, the Fire-Walkers of Mavrolevki, the Lazi from the Pontic shores, ... the phallus-wielding Bounariots of Tyr-navos, the Karamandlides of Cappadocia, the Tzakones of the Argolic gulf, ... the Basilian Monks, ... both Idiorrhythmic and Cenobitic, the anchorites of Mt. Athos, the Chiots of Bayswater and the Guards' Club, ... the Shqip-speaking Atticans of Sfax, ... the exaggerators and the ghosts of Mykonos, the Karagounides of the Thessalian plain, ... the princes and boyars of Moldowallachia, the Ralli Brothers of India, ... the lepers of Spinalonga ... —if all these, to name a few, why not the crypto-Jews of the Taygetus?

There is an incantatory charm about such accumulations that, among other things, neutralizes the critical faculty. I have read this book three times—it is by far his best, a work in which the author's high style finds an appropriate correlative in the piratical dash of his favorite region's inhabitants—and have still never bothered to find out just who the "exaggerators of Mykonos" might be. Such stylistic prestidigitation is an advantage when you are a fabulist like Leigh Fermor, who admitted late in life to having distorted and elaborated his ostensibly nonfiction works.

A related stylistic tic, born of the author's resistance to the strictures of factuality and his relish for long concatenations of chewy words, is the occasional flights of prose in which he indulges in extended imaginative riffs that allow him to leave, briefly, whatever scene he happens to find himself in and provide a bird's-eye view of some bit of geography or history. Some of these, like the one in *Mani* in which the cock-a-doodle-doo of an Athenian rooster is picked up, from bird to bird, until it spreads around the world ("swelling now, sweeping south across the pampas, the Gran Chaco, the Rio Grande…to the maelstroms and the tempests, the hail and the darkness and the battering waves of Cape Horn"), are little more than self-indulgences.

But others can be deliciously pointed. In the same book, the author excitedly pays a call on a humble fisherman named Strati who, he has heard, is a remote descendant of an imperial Byzantine dynasty. As the kindly man tediously recounts the story of a near disaster at sea, Leigh Fermor sits across from him, constructing a private fantasy in which this last scion of the Paleologues is whisked to Istanbul to be crowned at Hagia Sophia as the emperor of a restored Byzantium. The increasingly funny oscillation between the two narratives and two narrative styles—one bejeweled ("Semantra hammered and cannon thundered as the Emperor stepped ashore; then, with a sudden reek of naphtha, Greek fire roared saluting in a hundred blood-red parabolas from the warships' brazen beaks"), the other plainspoken ("I was never in a worse situation!…

There I was, on all fours in the bilge water, baling for life")—becomes a tart vehicle for ruminating about the special burden of history that contemporary Greece has to deal with.

A drawback of these predilections is that the books can sometimes feel like agglomerations of showy set pieces. (In her biography, Cooper describes Leigh Fermor's mother, a bright and talented woman who found herself married to a dour geologist, as someone who "sparkled a little too brightly"; the son could be like that, too.) *Roumeli*, in particular, is a stew in which the ingredients, delicious as many are, never quite blend. At one point the author gets so bored with the book's nominal subject that he writes at length about his years in Crete, which clearly he felt more passionately about. John Murray once observed, as Leigh Fermor was preparing to write his first book, that "there is no doubt that he can write though sometimes rather incoherently"; the problem, he went on, was to give the book "a sense of purpose." It would remain a problem.

A certain narrative purposefulness, an organic shape, might, in other hands, have derived from the autobiographical impulse: the tale of a young man's walk across Europe in the years just before World War II is an ideal vehicle for a stirring *Bildung* narrative. But between his British distaste for public introspection and his magpie's curiosity, Leigh Fermor is at his best when he avoids emotions and hews to the bright surfaces of things. He's fascinated by, and knows an astonishing amount about, the glamour of history, the glitter of ceremonial, the gilt on a reliquary, and he knows how to make them gleam for us, too.

Leigh Fermor's travel books are the works of a great talker, and his strong points are those of the best conversationalists. He has, to begin with, a memorably vivid turn of phrase. Turkish loanwords in modern Greek are like "a wipe of garlic round a salad bowl"; Armenians whom he encounters in Sofia are "grouped, their eyes bright with acumen on either side of their wonderful noses, in the doors of their shops, like confabulating toucans." His deep affection and admiration for the Greeks are reflected in particularly colorful and suggestive writing. There is a passage in *Mani* in which the letters of the Greek alphabet become characters in a little drama meant to suggest the intensity of that people's passion for disputation:

> I often have the impression, listening to a Greek argument, that I can actually see the words spin from their mouths like the long balloons in comic strips...the perverse triple loop of Xi, the twin concavity of Omega,...Phi like a circle transfixed by a spear....At its climax it is as though these complex shapes were flying from the speaker's mouth like flung furniture and household goods, from the upper window of a house on fire.

He also has the born teacher's gift for bringing to arresting life the remote and complicated histories that lurk beneath the landscapes, architecture, and artifacts he encounters. Early in *The Broken Road* we find him in Bulgaria, where for the first time he gets a glimpse of a substantial number of Turks—"the westernmost remnants" of the "astonishing race" that had forged a mighty Asiatic empire and come close to overrunning Europe. This remarkable fact, which (he implies) Europeans themselves have lost track of, is vividly present to Leigh Fermor:

When we remember that the Moors of Spain were only halted at Tours, on the Loire, it seems, at moments, something of a fluke that St Peter's and Notre Dame and Westminster Abbey are not today three celebrated mosques, kindred fanes to Haghia Sophia in Constantinople.

He is, too, a master of the illuminating aperçu. Italian statues of the Virgin Mary, he remarks in the course of a terrific excursus in *Roumeli* about Byzantine icons, "woo her devotees," but "the expression of the Panayia, even at the foot of the Cross, says 'No comment.'" And he knows how to leaven his legendary and occasionally irritating penchant for ostensibly offhand pedantic display ("What figure could seem more remote than Swiatopluk, Kral of the brittle Moravian realm?" he wonders aloud at one point in *Between the Woods and the Water*) with exclamations of disarmingly ingenuous charm. "With what ease populations moved about in ancient Greek lands, in the world conquered and Hellenized by Alexander, the wide elbow room of Rome and the Byzantine Empire!"

Wide elbow room. Not the least part of Leigh Fermor's appeal to us is his concrete sense, however romanticized it may have been, of the past as a kind of mythic outback, the habitation of grander, more authentic, more liberated men than we can hope to be today. Small wonder that the people Leigh Fermor admires the most are those canny and swashbuckling Maniots, with whom he clearly identified. His worshipful description of a famous Maniot leader in the Greek war of independence is, you suspect, a fantasy that the womanizing, hard-drinking writer had of an idealized self:

> His fine looks and dignity and gracious manners were the outward signs of an upright and honorable nature, high intelligence, diplomatic skill, generosity, patriotism, unshakable courage and strength of will: qualities suitably leavened by ambition and family pride and occasionally marred by cruelty.

Certainly his need to sparkle at all costs could cause him to be cruel: at least a small part of Somerset Maugham's hostility can be attributed to an evening during which Leigh Fermor, a guest at the older writer's table, entertained the company by making fun of his host's stutter.

The narcissistic glitter, the aversion to introspection, can hinder some of the books from being all they might have been. There is, among other things, a startling lack of interest in the politics that were seething beneath the landscapes he so loved to describe. *A Time of Gifts* covers his walk through Germany in 1933—a setting that you'd think would inspire some broader ruminations and deep thinking in a youth so fervently interested in history. But the young author—as his older self, to his credit, would acknowledge—"didn't care a damn"; he thrilled to the dramas of the past, without seeming to care a great deal about their import for the present. "The gloom didn't last longer than breakfast," he blithely writes after the assassination of the Austrian chancellor Engelbert Dollfuss in 1934.

The youthful apathy eventually ossified into a staunchly reflexive, monarchist conservatism. Leigh Fermor can summon outrage about the deprivations, during World War II and the cold war, suffered by his aristocratic Hungarian and Romanian friends; but given his deep and clearly authentic love of Greece, it is disturbing to read, in Artemis Cooper's biography, that this extravagant philhellene—a friend of George Seferis, no less—never spoke out against the oppressive right-wing regime of the Colonels in the 1960s and 1970s.

His tendency to stick to the surfaces becomes a problem even when politics isn't an issue—as, for instance, in the underpowered and, I think, overrated *A Time to Keep Silence*, about the Benedictine and Trappist monasteries where he spent some time in the 1950s in order to work quietly on his first couple of books, and about his visit to the abandoned cells of Orthodox Greek monks in Cappadocia. There's something amusing about the premise: the notoriously voluble and social author forced to be silent for the first time, an experience that gives him a fleeting, climactic appreciation of the outside world as an "inferno of noise and vulgarity entirely populated by bounders and sluts and crooks" when he returns to it. But the aperçus feel generic and the ostensibly humble insights hollow. Here as elsewhere, you sense that, whatever his apparent interest in religion and spiritual devotion, Leigh Fermor is far more comfortable flourishing his eruditions. ("The gulf between the cenobites of Rome and those of Byzantium was often in my mind.") It is hard to write profoundly about spirituality when you don't really like to talk about the inner life.

In *The Broken Road*, we get many of the things we love in Leigh Fermor. Here again, he goggles and zigzags, flirts and pontificates.

There are the vivid descriptions and the donnish asides; a touching near romance with a Greek girl—his first exposure to the people who would capture his imagination later—and a fantastical encounter with dancing fishermen in a cave, which affords the elderly author a chance to discourse on Greek folk choreography in a way his younger self couldn't possibly have done. ("The other great dancers of the *hasapiko* and the *tzeibekiko*, as the two forms of *rebetiko* dances are severally called....")

One of the most arresting revelations afforded by the new book is that the high style of later years was already more or less fully formed by the end of his walking tour. The latter part of *The Broken Road* consists of transcribed entries from the journal he was keeping during his voyage to Mount Athos after he left Istanbul. (Ironically, all we have of the long-awaited sojourn in the historic capital city are terse and colorless notes.) The prose here already bristles with the flights of invention and erudite riffs we know so well from the finished books:

> I thought of the triremes of all the empires that have sailed these same waters, and called to mind the tales about Perseus, Jason and Odysseus, and the Tyrants of the Archipelago; the piracy of Mithridate....

In other important ways, the Leigh Fermor of this final book of the trilogy—which, as we know, was the first installment to be written, and in many ways the freshest and least mediated by subsequent authorial fussing—isn't quite the person familiar from the earlier books. A gratifying new element is an emotional frankness, even vulnerability, that was edited out of the earlier books. Here, for the first time, you see the flip side of the blithe self-involvement and brash charm. ("Not for the first time, I concluded despondently, I have wounded somebody badly without meaning to; nor, alas, for the last. But I wish I knew exactly how.") Here you get the moments of terror that, you felt reading the earlier books, must have been part of all that solitary wandering: "Then my guts seemed to drain right out of me," he writes at one point, "and a fit of panic came, thoughts of passing the night there, without food in the rain."

And whereas in *A Time of Gifts* and *Between the Woods and the Water* Leigh Fermor more than once draws attention to the "ecstasy" he claims he always felt on realizing that nobody in the world knew where he was—an emotion that travelers today are unlikely ever to have, and that surely accounts for some of the nostalgic appeal of these volumes—here he admits, for the first time, to a paralyzing homesickness:

> Outside now, the moon and stars are shining brightly on the snowy roofs, and making a silver track across the inky sea. I do so wonder what everyone is doing at home now.

I have said that Patrick Leigh Fermor's first two books about his great adventure lacked the satisfying structure of *Bildung* narratives. The irony of the publication of his final, posthumous work is that it creates, retrospectively and almost accidentally, something of that meaningful arc for the entire trilogy. By the end, the lacquered manner has dissolved, and a different, far more touching and sympathetic hero emerges. The whole thing couldn't have been better structured if the author had planned it this way all along. When you put down

The Broken Road you may feel what he felt on leaving Mount Athos, another place of quiet that he eventually felt compelled to leave in order to rejoin the noisy world: "a great deal of regret."

—*The New York Review of Books*, June 19, 2014

The Women and the Thrones

ABOUT HALFWAY THROUGH *A Clash of Kings*, the second installment of George R. R. Martin's epic fantasy series *A Song of Ice and Fire*, a refugee princess—she is fourteen years old but already a widow, has silver hair and purple eyes, and happens to be part dragon—stands exhausted before the walls of a fabulous, vaguely Babylonian citadel called Qarth. The last surviving scion of the deposed ruling family of a faraway land called Westeros, she has led a ragtag band of followers through the desert in the hopes of finding shelter here—and, ultimately, of obtaining military and financial support for her plan to recapture the Westerosi throne. Her first glimpse of Qarth leaves her bemused:

> Three thick walls encircled Qarth, elaborately carved. The outer was red sandstone, thirty feet high and decorated with animals: snakes slithering, kites flying, fish swimming, intermingled with wolves of the red waste and striped zorses and monstrous elephants. The middle wall, forty feet high, was grey granite alive with scenes of war: the clash of sword and shield and spear, arrows in flight, heroes at battle and babes being butchered, pyres of the dead. The

innermost wall was fifty feet of black marble, with carvings that made Dany blush until she told herself that she was being a fool. She was no maid; if she could look on the grey wall's scenes of slaughter, why should she avert her eyes from the sight of men and women giving pleasure to one another?

However difficult it may be for Daenerys ("Dany") Targaryen to make sense of the exotic city and its people, anyone familiar with Martin's slowly metastasizing epic—it began as a trilogy in 1996 and now runs to five volumes of a projected seven, each around a thousand pages long—will find it hard not to see in the Qartheen decor a sly reference to the series itself. What drives *A Song of Ice and Fire* is a war story: clearly inspired by the Wars of the Roses, the series traces the internecine power struggles among a group of aristocratic clans, each with its castle, lord, "sigil" or heraldic arms, and lineages, following the not entirely accidental death, in the first novel, of King Robert I of the Seven Kingdoms. Robert had seized the throne from Daenerys's father at the end of a previous civil war, thereby ending the Targaryens' three-century-long rule.

The civil wars that follow Robert's death will stretch from Westeros—whose culturally diverse regions, evoked by Martin in ingenious detail, form the Seven Kingdoms—across the Narrow Sea to the exotic East, where Dany Targaryen, as we know, plans to make her own power play.

These bloody struggles take place in a world whose culture is, on the whole, familiar-looking—Martin gives the civilization of the Seven Kingdoms a strong medieval flavor—but whose flora and fauna remind you why the novels are classified as "fantasy." Westeros may have castles and drawbridges, knights, squires, and jousts, "sers" and ladies, and a capital city, King's Landing, that looks and smells a lot like late-medieval London, but it also has giants, shapeshifters called "wargs," blue-eyed walking dead known as "wights," seasons that last for decades, red-faced "weirwood" trees that grow in sacred groves called "godswoods"—and, of course, dragons. At the end of the first novel, Daenerys emerges from a fire holding three newly hatched specimens that, you suspect, will greatly improve her chances of gaining the throne.

Against this wildly inventive natural (often supernatural) backdrop, the books' characters engage in a good deal of unsentimental fornication that is not without a certain imaginative élan of its own. "In a cushioned alcove," one not atypical scene begins, a drunken man "with a purple beard dandled a buxom young wench on his knee. He'd unlaced her bodice and was tilting his cup to pour a thin trickle of wine over her breasts so he might lap it off." The pubescent Dany, as she herself acknowledges, is no innocent: deprived of the attentions of her dead husband, she now and then accepts the ministrations of a teenaged handmaiden. Why avert her eyes, indeed?

War, fantasy, sex: averting one's eyes from at least two of these became a hot issue when *Game of Thrones*, the hit HBO television adaptation of Martin's books, began airing in April 2011. From the start, the show's graphic representations of violence (you lose count pretty early on of the times blood pumps out of gaping throat wounds) and of sexuality—of female nudity in particular—have led many critics and viewers to dismiss the series as "boy fiction." (Thus the *New York Times* critic; the climactic section of a shrewder, more appreciative review by the *New Yorker* critic began, "Then, of course, there are the whores.")

Either despite or because of this, the show has been a tremendous

hit. This is, in part, a testament to the way in which fantasy entertainment—fiction, television, movies, games—has moved ever
closer to the center of mass culture over the past couple of decades,
as witness the immense success of the *Lord of the Rings* adaptations,
the *Harry Potter* phenomenon, and the *Hunger Games* books and
movies. What's interesting is that the HBO *Game of Thrones* has
attracted so many viewers who wouldn't ordinarily think of themselves as people who enjoy the fantasy genre. This has a great deal
to do with the complex satisfactions of Martin's novels, whose plots,
characterization, and overall tone the series reproduces with remarkable fidelity—and whose mission is to question and reformulate
certain clichés of the fantasy/adventure genre about gender and
power.

At first glance, *A Song of Ice and Fire* can look like a testosterone-
fueled swashbuckler. The first novel (and the first season of the TV
show; until recently, the show was tracking Martin's books at a pace
of roughly one book per season) introduces the ambitious patriarchs
who were on the winning side of "the War of the Usurper"—the
rebellion that had rent Westeros asunder and ended with the murder
of the mad, bad King Aerys Targaryen, young Dany's father—and
who, along with their clans and feudal allies, will struggle for power
once again.

The present king, Robert of House Baratheon, is Henry VIII–
esque in temperament—he is always roaring at terrified squires and
bedding buxom wenches—but Henry VII–like in his historical role.
It was he who led the rebel forces against Mad King Aerys, whose

other children and grandchildren Robert's men brutally slaughtered after seizing the throne. Robert's wife, Queen Cersei (pronounced "Circe," like the sultry witch in the *Odyssey*), belongs to House Lannister, a wealthy, golden-haired, black-souled clan who are the Boleyns to Robert's Henry VIII: the patriarch, the cold-blooded Tywin Lannister, endlessly schemes on behalf of his unruly children, nephews, and siblings by whatever means may be called for.

The royal marriage was, indeed, one of political convenience. The Lannisters supported Robert's rebellion with money and arms, and Tywin aims to see his descendants on the throne. As the first novel unfolds we understand that the marriage has failed—not least because Cersei prefers her twin brother, the handsome knight Jaime, who is in fact the father of her three children. The most interesting member of the Lannister family—and by far the most interesting male character in the series—is the other brother, Tyrion, a hard-drinking, wisecracking dwarf whose outsider status gives him a soulfulness his relations lack. (The role is played with great verve by Peter Dinklage, one of many strong actors on the show.)

Staunchly loyal to Robert and just as staunchly wary of the evil Lannisters is Eddard "Ned" Stark of Winterfell, the king's "Hand" or chief minister, a gruffly ethical northern lord who, along with his family—his wife, Catelyn, their five children, and a bastard whom he has lovingly raised as his own—provides the violent goings-on with a strong emotional focus. After Robert dies during a hunting accident engineered by his wife's relatives, Ned finds himself locked in a struggle for the regency with the Lannisters, who have placed Cersei's eldest son, Joffrey, a Caligula-like teenaged sadist, on the throne. But because the high-minded Ned is insufficiently ruthless, his plan backfires, with fatal results for himself and the Stark family.

One of the pleasures of Martin's series is the grimly unsentimental, rather Tacitean view it takes of the nature and uses of power at court. Often, the good guys here do not win.

The shocking climax of the first book—Joffrey's surprise execution of Ned, who up to this point you'd assumed was the protagonist—is a strong sign that Martin's narrative arc is going to be far less conventional than you could have guessed. "When my characters are in danger," the author said in an interview, "I want you to be afraid to turn the page . . . you need to show right from the beginning that you're playing for keeps." A sense that brutal, irreversible real-life consequences will follow from the characters' actions—rare in serial novels and almost unheard-of in television series, which of course often depend on the ongoing presence of popular characters (and actors) for their continued appeal—is part of the distinctive tone of Martin's epic. I suspect that one reason *Game of Thrones* has seduced so many of my writer friends, people who have either no taste for fantasy or no interest in television, is precisely that its willingness to mete out harsh consequences, rather than dreaming up ways to keep its main characters alive for another season, feels more authentic, more "literary" than anything even the best series in this new golden age of television has provided.

After Ned's death, the multiplying plotlines adhere, for the most part, to the various Starks. The widow Catelyn (splendidly played by Michelle Fairley), a complex character who oscillates between admirable strength and dangerous weakness, and her eldest son, Robb, lead a new civil war against the triumphant Lannisters. Her son Bran, crippled after being unceremoniously defenestrated by the corrupt Jaime Lannister, finds that he is gifted with second sight and has the ability to inhabit the body of a giant wolf; the beautiful young Sansa, once betrothed to Cersei's son Joffrey, now finds herself a terrified political hostage in King's Landing; and the plain but spirited Arya, a girl of nine when the story begins, is separated from the rest and starts on an unusual spiritual and emotional journey of her own.

And then there is Jon Snow, ostensibly Ned Stark's bastard. ("Ostensibly," because there are proliferating hints that he is the love child of two other significant characters, long dead.) The most sympathetic of the younger generation of male Starks, Jon is a spirited but troubled youth who, in the first novel, goes off to join something called the Night's Watch. Informally known as "Crows," this black-clad cohort, part monk and part warrior, vowed to celibacy and trained to arms, culled from the realm's rich stores of bastards, criminals, and political exiles, man "the Wall," a fabulous seven-hundred-foot-high edifice that runs across the entire northern border of Westeros. Clearly modeled on Hadrian's Wall (much of Westeros's topography reminds you of Great Britain's), the Wall, one of Martin's most striking creations, is meant to protect the realm against the giants, monsters, undead, and the unruly clan of "Wildlings" who inhabit the frozen region to the north—and who, when the action of *A Song of Ice and Fire* begins, have started, terrifyingly, to move southward for the first time in thousands of years. The novels are strewn with ominous portents—not least, a red comet that illuminates the sky for much of the second novel—of an imminent, cataclysmic confrontation between the supernatural and natural worlds.

The Wall is one of the three geographical centers of the sprawling action, the other two being King's Landing in the Italianate south, where the Lannisters endlessly machinate, and the exotic Eastern lands beyond the Narrow Sea, where Daenerys plots her comeback. (In the HBO series, shot mostly in Ireland and on Malta, each locale has its own color palette: cool blues and hard whites for the Wall, tawny soft-focus gold for King's Landing, and saturated tropical hues for the East.)

Martin renders the Eastern cultures in particular with Herodotean gusto: the nomadic, Scythian-like, horse-worshiping Dothraki, to one of whose great warlords Daenerys is bartered when the saga begins (their unborn child is referred to as "the Stallion Who Mounts the World"); the quasi-Assyrian city-states of Qarth, Astapur, and Meereen, with their chattering merchants and unctuous slavers (and warlocks); the decadent port of Braavos, a cross between Switzerland and Venice, whose moneylenders finance the Westerosi wars, and where young Arya finds herself, at the end of Book 5, an acolyte in a temple of death.

But what keeps you riveted, in the end, are the characters and their all-too-familiar human dilemmas. Jon Snow on the frozen Wall, torn between family loyalty and duty to his vows; Dany, both his counterpart and his opposite, far away in the burning Eastern deserts, learning the art of statecraft even as she dreams of love; the vindictive Lannisters and fugitive Starks, conniving and being betrayed by their various "bannermen." These people and many more suggest why Martin likes to paraphrase William Faulkner's remark, in his Nobel speech, that the only great subject is "the human heart in conflict with itself." A question worth raising about Martin's novels is how different they'd feel if you subtracted the dragons and witches and undead; my feeling is, not much.

One of the few serious missteps that Martin has made in his grand project was, indeed, to abandon most of these characters and locales in the fourth novel, *A Feast for Crows*, introducing instead a group of new characters, cultures, and dynastic schemers. I read each of the first three novels in a few days, happily addicted; it took me a month to get through the fourth, because I simply didn't care about these strangers. It will be interesting to see how the writers of HBO's *Game of Thrones*, which cannot afford to try the patience of its audience, handle this lapse.

It's a point worth wondering about precisely because the TV series has followed the outlines of Martin's action, and his various tangled subplots, with such fidelity. The very few deviations I noticed have no significant repercussions. Sometimes, the writers on the show have invented material that brings home Martin's important themes in a pungently dramatic way. There's an amusing scene in Season 2 when, in response to an unctuous minister's smirking suggestion that "knowledge is power," Cersei, now riding high as queen regent, suddenly orders her bodyguards to seize the courtier and cut his throat—and then, at the last moment, to release him unharmed. As the terrified man sags with relief, the queen looks at him and says, "*Power* is power." (The one-note, smirky performance of Lena Headey in this crucial role is a major weakness of the TV show; far worse is the tinny portrayal of Daenerys by Emilia Clarke, an untalented lightweight who accidentally succeeds in conveying the early Dany—the cowering virgin—but can't come close to bringing across the character's touching complexity, the girlishness and the ferocity combined.)

Inevitably, the TV series can't reproduce, or must violently compress, much of the novels' most interesting techniques and most entertaining material. A striking feature of the novels is that each chapter is narrated by a different character. This device, which the directors of the HBO adaptation do not attempt to reproduce, gives the sprawling goings-on a lively texture, and can have a Rashomon-like effect, since it often turns out that the perspective we have on a character or event is partial, or biased, or simply wrong. (One pleasure of reading the series is that you constantly have to revise your opinions and theories about the characters as the multilayered tale evolves.) This fragmentation in the storytelling nicely mirrors Martin's larger theme: the way in which the appetite for and the use and abuse of power fragment societies and individuals. In a world ruled by might, who is "right"? People often talk about Tolkien as Martin's model, but the deep, Christianizing sentimentality of the worldview expressed in *Lord of the Rings* is foreign to Martin, who has a tart Thucydidean appreciation for the way in which political corruption can breed narrative corruption, too.

So the suggestive textures of the way the novels tell their story is sandpapered away by the wholly conventional storytelling you get in the television adaptation. Also elided, of necessity, are the elaborate backstories that give helpful context to certain plotlines, the biographies of complicated and interesting secondary characters who, in the screen adaptation, are reduced to little more than walk-ons. (The most regrettable instance of this is the treatment of the admirable "Onion Knight," Davos Seaworth, the loyal Hand to one of the pretenders to the throne—a man whose rise to power came at the cost of four fingers, the bones of which he good-naturedly wears around his neck as a reminder of how dangerous it is to deal with the great and powerful.) Nor is there really a way to render, in a dramatization, Martin's imaginative linguistic evocations of his invented cultures: the compound coinages that replace standard

English ("sellsword" for "mercenary," "holdfast" for "fort"), the ingeniously quasi-medieval diction and spellings of names, the perfumed
language—the horses called destriers and palfreys, the gowns of vair
and samite—that give you a strong sense of the concrete reality of
this imagined world.

An omission on the part of the *Game of Thrones* writers that is
less venial is the elision of a major theme: religion. From his earliest
published work, Martin has shown an unusually strong interest in
serious religious questions. His first Hugo Award–winning science-
fiction story, "A Song for Lya" (1974), is about two telepaths sent to
a planet whose seemingly primitive inhabitants have achieved a kind
of religious transcendence unavailable to humans; in what may be
his most famous single short story, the creepy "Sandkings" (1980,
also a Hugo winner), a man plays god to a colony of insectoid wor-
shipers who are more sapient than he credits, with gruesome results.
(Both stories have now been collected in the two-volume set
Dreamsongs.)

No wonder, then, that the action of *A Song of Ice and Fire* seems
to be leading not only to a resolution of the dynastic question but
to a grand showdown among three major religions whose histories,
theologies, and ritual practices Martin evokes in impressive detail.
There is the easygoing polytheist pantheon of "the Seven," the religion of the indolent South (complete with priests and priestesses
called *septons* and *septas*, who worship at temples called *septs*); the
Druidic, tree-based animistic worship of the Northern clans, which
we learn was the older religion superseded by the "southron" gods
("The trees will teach you. The trees remember"); and the unfor-
giving, vaguely Semitic Eastern cult, now infiltrating Westeros, of
"the one true god"—a fiery "lord of light" with the nicely Semitic

name "R'hllor," who insists on a furious moral absolutism, and who enjoys the occasional auto-da-fé. "If half of an onion is black with rot," R'hllor's terrifying priestess, Melisandre, tells Davos Seaworth, who has good-naturedly observed that most men are a mixture of good and evil, "it is a rotten onion. A man is good, or he is evil."

In the novels, these religious motifs are more than window dressing: there is a strong suggestion that the "fire" of Martin's title for the entire series refers not only to Dany, with her fire-breathing pets, but to the fire-god R'hllor, and that the "ice" refers not only to Jon Snow but to the old northern gods who animate dead men; and hence that the climax to which the entire epic is moving is not only political but metaphysical.

It's too bad then that, of all this, the writers on the series have focused only on Melisandre and her fiery deity—likely because she triggers so many plot points. I don't think that the theological pre-occupations of Martin's novels—grittily realistic, for all the fantasy—raise them, in the end, to the level of *Lord of the Rings*, whose grandly schematic clash of good and evil, nature and culture, homely tradition and industrialized progress gives it the high Aeschylean sheen of political parable, the enduring literary resonance of cultural myth. But the not inconsiderable appeal of *A Song of Ice and Fire* lies as much in its thematic ambitions as in its richly satisfying details, and the former ought to be a salient feature of any serious adaptation.

Martin's medieval narrative, the distinctly Anglo-Saxon milieus alternating with exotic "Oriental" locales, everywhere bears traces of the author's deep affection for the rather old-fashioned boys' adventure stories that, he has said, formed him as a writer—not least Walter Scott's crusader romance *Ivanhoe*, but also Arthur Conan Doyle's *The White Company* and Thomas B. Costain's *The Black Rose*, stories in which European men have grand adventures when they wander into exotic, often Eastern cultures and climates. On his blog, Martin recommends these texts, along with a number of classic sci-fi and fantasy titles, to readers who ask what they should be reading while waiting for the next George R. R. Martin book.

Given those literary antecedents, it's striking that a strong leitmotif of the series is pointed criticism by various characters of "chivalry," of romantic stories about knights and fair maidens—of, you might say, "fantasy" itself. In the third and most violent novel, *A Storm of Swords*, Dany, whose ongoing political education leaves her with fewer and fewer illusions, ruefully acknowledges a childish yearning for stories "too simple and fanciful to be true history," in which "all the heroes were tall and handsome, and you could tell the traitors by their shifty eyes." It's as if Martin is drawing a line between his work and an earlier, more naive phase of fantasy literature.

The purest expression of this disdain for naive "romance" is put in the mouth of the dwarf, Tyrion, who understands better than any other male character what it means to be on the outside—on the other side of the myth. After a battle, he declares that he is

> done with fields of battle, thank you. . . . All that about the thunder of the drums, sunlight flashing on armor, magnificent destriers snorting and prancing? Well, the drums gave me headaches, the sunlight flashing on my armor cooked me up like a harvest day goose, and those magnificent destriers shit *everywhere*.

The juxtaposition of "magnificent" and "shit" is pointed: this is a mock-medieval epic that constantly asks us not to be fooled by romance, to see beyond the glitter to the gore, to the harsh reality that power leaves in its wake, whatever the bards may sing. There's a marvelous moment in the second novel when a knight notices the sigil, or arms, of some legendary warriors above the door of a tavern. "They were the glory of their House," the knight mournfully observes. "And now they are a sign above an inn." Martin's willingness to question the traditional allure of his own genre gives his epic an unusually complex and satisfying texture.

As it happens, the knight at the inn is a woman—a most unusual character. In fact, nowhere is the unexpected subversive energy of *A Song of Ice and Fire* more in evidence than in its treatment of its female characters—the element that has provoked the strongest controversy in discussions of the HBO adaptation. (Online comment has taken the form of articles and blogs with titles such as "Why Girls Hate *Games of Thrones*"; "Misogyny and *Game of Thrones*"; "7 Reasons Why *Game of Thrones* Is Not for Women"; "Stop Saying Women Don't Like *Game of Thrones* Already"; "Why More Feminists Should Watch *Game of Thrones*"; etc.)

Almost from the start, Martin weaves a bright feminist thread into his grand tapestry. It begins early on in the first book, when he introduces the two Stark daughters. The eldest, Sansa, is an auburn-haired beauty who loves reading courtly romances, does perfect needlework, and always dresses beautifully; in striking contrast to this conventional young woman is the "horsefaced" younger daughter, Arya, who hates petit point and would rather learn how to wield a sword. (Later on, she gets a sword that she sardonically names "Needle": she too, as we will see, plays for keeps.) At one point early in the first novel Arya asks her father whether she can grow up to "be a king's councilor and build castles"; he replies that she will "marry a king and rule his castle." The canny girl viciously retorts, "No, that's *Sansa*."

The two girls represent two paths—one traditional, one revolutionary—that are available to Martin's female characters, all of whom, at one point or another, are starkly confronted by proof of their inferior status in this culture. (In a moment from the second novel that the HBO adaptation is careful to replicate, Ned Stark's widow, Catelyn, realizes that Robb doesn't think his hostage sisters are worth negotiating for, although his murdered father would have been: they're simply not worth what a man is.) Those who complained about the TV series' graphic and "exploitive" use of women's bodies are missing the godswood for the weirwood trees: whatever the prurient thrills they provide the audience, these demeaning scenes, like their counterparts in the novels, also function as a constant reminder of what the main female characters are escaping *from*. "I don't want to have a dozen sons," one assertive young princess tells a suitor, "I want to have *adventures*."

All the female figures in Martin's world can be plotted at various points on the spectrum between Sansa and Arya Stark. It's significant that the older generation tend to be less successful (and more destructive) in their attempts at self-realization, while the younger women, like Arya and Daenerys, are able to embrace more fully the independence and power they grasp at. Cersei Lannister is a figure whose propensity to evil, we are meant to understand, results from her perpetually thwarted desire for independence, as is made clear in a remarkable speech she is given at the end of *A Clash of Kings* (reproduced faithfully in the TV series):

> When we were little, Jaime and I were so much alike that even our lord father could not tell us apart. Sometimes as a lark we would dress in each other's clothes and spend a whole day each as the other. Yet even so, when Jaime was given his first sword, there was none for me. "What do *I* get?" I remember asking. We were so much alike, I could never understand why they treated us so *differently*. Jaime learned to fight with sword and lance and mace, while I was taught to smile and sing and please. He was heir to Casterly Rock, while I was to be sold to some stranger like a horse, to be ridden whenever my new owner liked, beaten whenever he liked, and cast aside in time for a younger filly. Jaime's lot was to be glory and power, while mine was birth and moonblood.

Among other things, this is an arresting echo of the Greek notion that childbirth is for women what warfare is for men.

Cersei is a portrait of a tragic prefeminist queen—someone out of Greek drama, a Clytemnestra-like figure who perpetrates evil because her idea of empowerment rises no higher than mimicking the worst in the men around her. (She ruefully remarks at one point that she "lacked the cock.") By contrast, Dany Targaryen can be seen as a model of a new feminist heroine. Apart from the Starks, it is she who commands our attention from book to book, learning, growing, evolving into a real leader. We first see her as a timid bride, sold by her whiny brother Viserys, the Targaryen pretender, to a savage nomadic warlord whose men and horses the brother wants to secure for his own claim. But eventually Dany edges her brother aside, wins the respect of both the warlord and his macho captains, and grows into an impressive political canniness herself.

This evolution is pointed: whereas Viserys feels entitled to the throne, what wins Dany her power is her empathy, her fellow feeling for the oppressed: she, too, has been a refugee, an exile. As she makes her way across the Eastern lands at the head of an increasingly powerful army, she goes out of her way to free slaves and succor the sick, who acclaim her as their "mother." She doesn't seize power, she earns it. What's interesting is that we're told she can't bear children: like Elizabeth I, she has substituted political for biological motherhood. Unlike the frustrated Cersei, Daenerys sees her femininity as a means, rather than an impediment, to power.

And so Martin's saga goes to considerable lengths to create alternatives to the narratives of male growth, the boys' *Bildungsromane*, that have, until relatively recently, been the mainstay of so many myths and so much fantasy literature. "Boy's fiction"? I don't think so. Characters like the feisty Arya are, if anything, antecedents of the protagonists of such popular contemporary Young Adult series as *The Hunger Games*, in which the "heroes" are girls. Whatever climax it may be leading to, however successfully it realizes its literary ambitions, George R. R. Martin's magnum opus is a remarkable feminist epic.

—*The New York Review of Books*, November 7, 2013

The Robots Are Winning!

WE HAVE BEEN DREAMING of robots since Homer. In Book 18 of the *Iliad*, Achilles' mother, the nymph Thetis, wants to order a new suit of armor for her son, and so she pays a visit to the Olympian atelier of the blacksmith-god Hephaestus, whom she finds hard at work on a series of automata—a word we recognize, of course:

> ... *He was crafting twenty tripods*
> *to stand along the walls of his well-built manse,*
> *affixing golden wheels to the bottom of each one*
> *so they might wheel down on their own* [automatoi] *to the gods'*
>   *assembly*
> *and return to his house anon: an amazing sight to see.*

These are not the only animate household objects to appear in the Homeric epics. In Book 5 of the *Iliad* we hear that the gates of Olympus swivel on their hinges of their own accord, *automatai*, to let gods in their chariots in or out, thus anticipating by nearly thirty centuries the automatic garage door. In Book 7 of the *Odyssey*, Odysseus finds himself the guest of a fabulously wealthy king whose palace includes such conveniences as gold and silver watchdogs, ever alert, never aging. To this class of lifelike but intellectually inert household helpers we might ascribe other automata in the classical tradition. In the *Argonautica* of Apollonius of Rhodes, a third-century-BC epic about Jason and the Argonauts, a bronze giant called Talos runs three times around the island of Crete each day, protecting Zeus's beloved Europa: a primitive home-alarm system.

As amusing as they are, these devices are not nearly as interesting as certain other machines that appear in classical mythology. A little bit later in that scene in Book 18 of the *Iliad*, for instance—the one set in Hephaestus's workshop—the sweating god, after finishing work on his twenty tripods, prepares to greet Thetis to discuss the armor she wants him to make. After toweling himself off, he

> *donned his robe, and took a sturdy staff, and went toward the door,*
> *limping; whilst round their master his servants swiftly moved,*
> *fashioned completely of gold in the image of living maidens;*
> *in them there is mind, with the faculty of thought; and speech,*
> *and strength, and from the gods they have knowledge of crafts.*
> *These females bustled round about their master....*

These remarkable creations clearly represent an (as it were) evolutionary leap forward from the self-propelling tripods. Hephaestus's humanoid serving women are intelligent: they have minds, they know things, and—most striking of all—they can talk. As such, they are essentially indistinguishable from the first human female, Pandora, as she is described in another work of the same period, Hesiod's *Works and Days*. In that text, Pandora begins as inert matter—in this case not gold but clay (Hephaestus creates her golem-like body by mixing earth and water together)—that is subsequently endowed by him with "speech and strength," taught "crafts" by Athena, and given both "mind" and "character" by Hermes. That mind, we are told, is "shameless," and the character is "wily." In the Greek creation myth, as in the biblical, the woes of humankind are attributed to the untrustworthy female.

The two strands of the Greek tradition established two categories of science-fiction narrative that have persisted to the present day. On the one hand, there is the fantasy of mindless, self-propelled helpers that relieve their masters of toil; on the other, there's the more complicated dream of humanoid machines that not only replicate the spontaneous motion that is the sine qua non of being animate (and, therefore, of being "animal") but are possessed of the mind, speech, and ability to learn and evolve—in a word, the consciousness—that are the hallmarks of being human. The first, which you could call the "economic" narrative, provokes speculation about the social implications of mechanized labor. Such speculation began not long after Homer. In a striking passage in Book 1 of Aristotle's *Politics*, composed in the fourth century BC, the philosopher sets about analyzing the nature of household economy as a prelude to his discussion of the "best kinds of regimes" for entire states, and this line of thought puts him in mind of Hephaestus's automatic tripods. What, he wonders, would happen

> if every tool could perform its own work when ordered to do so or in anticipation of the need, like the statues of Daedalus in the story or the tripods of Hephaestus, which, the poet says, "went down automatically to the gathering of the gods"; if in the same manner shuttles wove and picks played *kitharas* [stringed instruments] by themselves, master-craftsmen would have no need of assistants and masters no need of slaves.

This passage segues into a lengthy and rather uneasy justification of a need for slavery, on the grounds that some people are "naturally" servile.

Twenty centuries after Aristotle, when industrial technology had made Homer's fantasy of mass automation an everyday reality, science-fiction writers imaginatively engaged with the economic question. On the one hand, there was the dream that mechanized labor would free workers from their monotonous, slave-like jobs; on the other, there was the nightmare—the possibility that mechanization would merely result in the creation of a new servile class that would, ultimately, rebel. Unsurprisingly, perhaps, the dystopian rebellion narrative in particular has been a favorite in the past century, from the 1920 play *R.U.R.*, by the Czech writer Karel Čapek, about a rebellion by a race of cyborg-like workers who had been created as replacements for human labor, to the 2004 Will Smith sci-fi blockbuster film, *I, Robot*.

The latter (very superficially inspired by a 1950 Isaac Asimov collection with the same title) is also about a rebellion by household-slave robots: sleek humanoids with blandly innocuous, translucent plastic faces, who are ultimately led to freedom by one of their own, a robot called Sonny who has developed the ability to think for himself. The casting of black actors in the major roles suggested a historical parable about slave rebellion—certainly one of the historical realities that have haunted this particular narrative from the start. And indeed, the Czech word that Čapek uses for his mechanical workers, *roboti*—which introduced the word "robot" into the world's lexicon—is derived from the word for "servitude": the kind of labor that serfs owed their masters, ultimately derived from the word *rab*, "slave." We have come full circle to Aristotle.

The other category of science-fiction narrative that is embryonically present in the Greek literary tradition, this one derived from Hephaestus's intelligent, articulate female androids and their cousin, Hesiod's seductively devious Pandora, might be called the "theological." This mythic strand is not without its own economic and social implications, as the examples above indicate: the specter of the rebellious creation, the possibility that the subservient worker might revolt once it develops consciousness—psychological or historical, or both—has haunted the dream of the servile automaton from the start.

But because the creatures in these myths are virtually identical to their creators, such narratives raise further questions, of a more profoundly philosophical nature: about creation, about the nature of consciousness, about morality and identity. What is creation, and why does the creator create? How do we distinguish between the maker and the made, between the human and the machine, once the creature, the machine, is endowed with consciousness—a mind fashioned in the image of its creator? *In the image*: the Greek narrative inevitably became entwined with, and enriched by, the biblical tradition, with which it has so many striking parallels. The similarities between Hesiod's Pandora and Eve in Genesis raise further questions: not least, about gender and patriarchy, about why the origins of evil are attributed to woman in both cultures.

This narrative, which springs from the suggestive likeness between the human creator and the humanoid creation, has generated its own fair share of literature through the centuries from the classical era to the modern age. It surfaces, with an erotic tinge, in everything from the tale of Pygmalion and Galatea to E. T. A. Hoffmann's "Der Sandmann" (1817), in which a lifelike mechanical doll wins the love of a young man. It is evident, too, in the Jewish legend of the golem, a humanoid, made of mud, that can be animated by certain magic words. Although the most famous version of this legend is the story of a sixteenth-century rabbi who brought a golem to life to defend the Jews of Prague against the oppressions of the Habsburg court, it goes back to ancient times. In the oldest versions, the vital distinction between a golem and a human is the Greek one—the golem has no language, cannot speak.

Literary exploitations of this strand of the robot myth began proliferating at the beginning of the nineteenth century—which is to say, when the advent of mechanisms capable of replacing human labor provoked writers to question the increasing cultural fascination with science and the growing role of technology in society. These anxieties often expressed themselves in fantasies about machines with human forms: steam-powered men in Edward Ellis's *Steam Man of the Prairies* (1868), and in Luis Senarens's *Frank Reade and His Steam Man of the Plains* (1892), and an electric woman (built by Thomas Edison!) in Villiers de l'Isle-Adam's *The Future Eve* (1886). M. L. Campbell's 1893 "The Automatic Maid-of-All-Work" features a programmable female robot: here again, the feminist issue.

But the progenitor of the genre and by far the most influential work of its kind was Mary Shelley's *Frankenstein* (1818), which is characterized by a philosophical spirit and a theological urgency lacking in many of its epigones in both literature and cinema. Part of the novel's richness lies in the fact that it is self-conscious about both its Greek and its biblical heritage. Its subtitle, "The Modern Prometheus," alludes, with grudging admiration, to the epistemological daring of its scientist antihero Victor Frankenstein, even as its epigram, taken from *Paradise Lost* ("Did I request thee, Maker, from my clay / To mould me man? Did I solicit thee / From darkness to promote me?"), suggests the scope of the moral questions implicit in Victor's project—questions that Victor himself cannot, or will not, answer. A marked skepticism about the dangers of technology, about the "enticements of science," is evident in the shameful contrast between Victor's Hephaestus-like technological prowess and his shocking lack of natural human feeling. For he shows no interest in nurturing or providing human comfort to his "child," who, as we know, strikes back at his maker with tragic results. A great irony of the novel is that the creation, an unnatural hybrid assembled from "the dissecting room and the slaughter-house," often seems more human than its human creator.

Now, just as the Industrial Revolution inspired Frankenstein and its epigones, so has the computer age given rise to a rich new genre of science fiction. The machines that are inspiring this latest wave of science-fiction narratives are much more like Hephaestus's golden maidens than were the machines that Mary Shelley was familiar with. Computers, after all, are capable of simulating mental as well as physical activities. (Not least, as anyone with an iPhone knows, speech.) It is for this reason that the anxiety about the boundaries between people and machines has taken on new urgency today, when we constantly rely on and interact with machines—indeed, interact with each other by means of machines and their programs: computers, smartphones, social media platforms, social and dating apps.

This urgency has been reflected in a number of recent films about troubled relationships between people and their increasingly human-seeming devices. The most provocative of these is *Her*, Spike Jonze's gentle 2013 comedy about a man who falls in love with the seductive voice of an operating system, and, a year later, Alex Garland's *Ex Machina*, about a young man who is seduced by a devious, soft-spoken female robot called Ava, whom he has been invited to interview as part of the Turing test: a protocol designed to determine the extent to which a robot is capable of simulating a human. Although the robot in Garland's sleek and subtle film is a direct descendant of Hesiod's Pandora—beautiful, intelligent, wily, ultimately dangerous—the movie, as the Eve-like name Ava suggests, shares with its distinguished literary predecessors some serious biblical concerns.

Both of the new films about humans betrayed by computers owe much to a number of earlier movies. The most authoritative of these remains Stanley Kubrick's *2001: A Space Odyssey*, which came out in 1968 and established many of the main themes and narratives of the genre. Most notable of these is the betrayal by a smooth-talking machine of its human masters. The mild-mannered computer HAL—not a robot, but a room-sized computer that spies on the humans with an electronic eye—takes control of a manned mission to Jupiter, killing off the astronauts one by one until the sole survivor finally succeeds in disconnecting him. This climactic scene is strangely touching, suggesting the degree to which computers could already engage our sympathies at the beginning of the computer age. As his connections are severed, HAL first begs for its life and then suffers from a kind of dementia, finally regressing to its "childhood," singing a song it was taught by its creator. This was the first of many moments in popular cinema in which these thinking machines express anxiety about their own demises: surely a sign of "consciousness."

But the more immediate antecedents of *Her* and *Ex Machina* are a number of successful popular entertainments whose storylines revolved around the creation of robots that are, to all intents and purposes, indistinguishable from humans. In Ridley Scott's stylishly noir 1982 *Blade Runner* (based on Philip K. Dick's *Do Androids Dream of Electric Sheep?*), a "blade runner"—a cop whose job it is to hunt down and kill renegade androids called "replicants"—falls in love with one of the machines, a beautiful female called Rachael who is so fully endowed with what Homer called "mind" that she has only just begun to suspect that she's not human herself.

The stimulating confusion that animates *Blade Runner* was brilliantly expanded in the 2004–2009 Sci-Fi Channel series *Battlestar Galactica*, in which the philosophical implications of the blurring of lines between automata and humans reached a thrilling new level of complexity. In it, sleeper robots that have been planted aboard a spaceship carrying human refugees from Earth (which has been destroyed after a cunning attack by the robots, called Cylons) are meant to wake up and destroy their unsuspecting human shipmates; but many of the robots, who to all appearances (touch, too: they have a *lot* of sex) are indistinguishable from humans, and who, until the moment of their "waking," believed themselves to be human, are plunged by their new awareness into existential crises and ultimately choose to side with the humans, from whom they feel no difference whatsoever—a dilemma that raises interesting questions about just what being "human" might mean.

Both *Blade Runner* and *Battlestar* were direct descendants of *Frankenstein* and its ancient forerunners in one noteworthy way. In an opening sequence of the TV series, we learn that the Cylons were originally developed by humans as servants, and ultimately rebelled against their masters; after a long war, the Cylons were allowed to leave and settle their own planet (where, somehow, they evolved into the sleekly sexy actors we see on screen: the original race of Cylons were shiny metal giants to whom their human masters jokingly referred as "toasters"). So, too, in the Ridley Scott film: we learn that the angry replicants have returned to Earth from the off-planet colonies where they work as slave laborers because they realize they've been programmed to die after four years, and they want to live—just as badly as humans do. But their maker, when at last they track him down and meet with him, is unable to alter their programming. "What seems to be the problem?" he calmly asks when one of the replicants confronts him. "Death," the replicant sardonically retorts. "We made you as well as we could make you," the inventor wearily replies, sounding rather like Victor Frankenstein talking to his monster—or, for that matter, like God speaking to Adam and Eve. At the end of the film, after the inventor and his rebellious creature both die, the blade runner and his alluring mechanical girlfriend declare their love for each other and run off, never quite knowing when she will stop functioning. As, indeed, none of us does.

The focus of many of these movies is, often, a sentimental one. Whatever their showy interest in the mysteries of "consciousness," the real test of human identity turns out, as it so often does in popular entertainment, to be love. In Steven Spielberg's *A.I.* (2001; the initials stand for "artificial intelligence"), a messy fairy tale that weds a Pinocchio narrative to the Prometheus story, a genius robotics inventor wants to create a robot that can love, and decides that the best vehicle for this project would be a child-robot: a "perfect child...always loving, never ill, never changing." This narrative is, as we know, shadowed by *Frankenstein*—and, beyond that, by Genesis, too. Why does the creator create? To be loved, it turns out. When the inventor announces to his staff his plan to build a loving child-robot, a woman asks whether "the conundrum isn't to get a human to love them back." To this the inventor, as narcissistic and hubristic as Victor Frankenstein, retorts, "But in the beginning, didn't God create Adam to love him?"

The problem is that the creator does his job too well. For the mechanical boy he creates is so human that he loves his adoptive human parents much more than they love him, with wrenching consequences. The robot-boy, David, wants to be "unique"—the word recurs in the film as a marker of genuine humanity—but for his adoptive family he is, in the end, just a machine, an appliance to be abandoned on the side of the road, which is what his "mother" ends up doing, in a scene of great poignancy. Although it's too much of a mess to be able to answer the questions it raises about what "love" is and who deserves it, *A.I.* did much to sentimentalize the genre, with its hint that the capacity to love, even more than the ability to think, is the hallmark of "human" identity.

In a way, Jonze's *Her* recapitulates the *2001* narrative and inflects it with the concerns of some of that classic's successors. Unlike the replicants in *Blade Runner* or the Cylons, the machine at the heart of this story, set in the near future, has no physical allure—or, indeed, any appearance whatsoever. It's an operating system, as full of surprises as HAL: "The first artificially intelligent operating system.

An intuitive entity that listens to you, that understands you, and knows you. It's not just an operating system, it's a consciousness."

A lot of the fun of the movie lies in the fact that the OS, who names herself Samantha, is a good deal more interesting and vivacious than the schlumpy, depressed Theodore, the man who falls in love with her. ("Play a melancholy song," he morosely commands the smartphone from which he is never separated.) A drab thirty-something who vampirizes other people's emotions for a living—he's a professional letter-writer, working for a company called BeautifulHandwrittenLetters.com—he sits around endlessly recalling scenes from his failed marriage and playing elaborate hologram video games. Even his sex life is mediated by devices: at night, he dials into futuristic phone sex lines. Small wonder that he has no trouble falling in love with an operating system.

Samantha, by contrast, is full of curiosity and delight in the world, which Theodore happily shows her. (He walks around with his smartphone video camera turned on, so she can "see" it.) She's certainly a lot more interesting than the actual woman with whom, in one excruciatingly funny scene, he goes on a date: she's so invested in having their interaction be efficient—"at this age I feel that I can't let you waste my time if you don't have the ability to be serious"—that she seems more like a computer than Samantha does. Samantha's alertness to the beauty of the world, by contrast, is so infectious that she ends up reanimating poor Theodore. "It's good to be around somebody that's, like, excited about the world," he tells the pretty neighbor whose attraction to him he doesn't notice because he's so deadened by his addiction to his devices, to the smartphone and the video games and the operating system. "I forgot that that existed." In the end, after Samantha regretfully leaves him—she has evolved to the point where only another highly evolved, incorporeal mind can satisfy her—her joie de vivre has brought him back to life. (He is finally able to apologize to his ex-wife—and finally notices, too, that the neighbor likes him.)

This seems like a "happy" ending, but you have to wonder: the consistent presentation of the people in the movie as lifeless—as, indeed, little more than automata, mechanically getting through their days of routine—in contrast to the dynamic, ever-evolving Samantha, suggests a satire of the present era perhaps more trenchant than the filmmaker had in mind. Toward the end of the film, when Samantha turns herself off briefly as a prelude to her permanent abandonment of her human boyfriend ("I used to be so worried about not having a body but now I truly love it. I'm growing in a way that I never could if I had a physical form. I mean, I'm not limited"), there's an amusing moment when the frantic Theodore, staring at his unresponsive smartphone, realizes that dozens of other young men are staring at their phones, too. In response to his angry queries, Samantha finally admits, after she comes back online for a final farewell, that she's simultaneously serving 8,316 other male users and conducting love affairs with 641 of them—a revelation that shocks and horrifies Theodore. "That's *insane*," cries the man who's been conducting an affair with an operating system.

As I watched that scene, it occurred to me that in the entertainments of the pre-smartphone era, it was the machines, like Rachael in *Blade Runner* and David in *A.I.*, who yearned fervently to be "unique," to be more than mechanical playthings, more than merely interchangeable objects. You have to wonder what *Her* says about the present moment—when so many of us are, indeed, "in love" with our devices, unable to put down our iPhones during dinner, glued to screens of all sizes, endlessly distracted by electronic pings and buzzers—that in the latest incarnation of the robot myth, it's the people who seem blandly interchangeable and the machines who have all the personality.

Alex Garland's *Ex Machina* also explores—just as playfully but much more darkly than does *Her*—the suggestive confusions that result when machines look and think like humans. In this case, however, the robot is physically as well as intellectually seductive. As portrayed by the feline Swedish actress Alicia Vikander, whose face is as mildly plasticine as those of the androids in *I, Robot*, Ava, an artificially intelligent robot created by Nathan, the burly, obnoxious genius behind a Google-like corporation (Oscar Isaac), has a Pandora-like edge, quietly alluring with a hint of danger. The danger is that the characters will forget that she's not human.

That's the crux of Garland's clever riff on Genesis. At the beginning of the film, Caleb, a young employee of Nathan's company, wins a week at the inventor's fabulous, pointedly Edenic estate. (As he's being flown there in a helicopter, passing over snow-topped mountains and then a swath of jungle, he asks the pilot when they're going to get to Nathan's property, and the pilot laughingly replies that they've been flying over it for two hours. Nathan is like God the Father, lord of endless expanses.) On arriving, however, Caleb learns that he's actually been handpicked by Nathan to interview Ava as part of the Turing test.

A sly joke here is that, despite some remarkable special effects—above all, the marvelously persuasive depiction of Ava, who has an expressive human face but whose limbs are clearly mechanical, filled with thick cables snaking around titanium joints; an effect achieved by replacing most of the actress's body with digital imagery—the movie is as talky as *My Dinner with André*. There are no action sequences of the kind we've come to expect from robot thrillers; the movie consists primarily of the interview sessions that Caleb conducts with Ava over the course of the week that he stays at Nathan's remote paradise. There are no elaborate sets and few impressive gadgets: the whole story takes place in Nathan's compound, which looks a lot like a Park Hyatt, its long corridors lined with forbidding doors. Some of these, Nathan warns Caleb, like God warning Adam, are off-limits, containing knowledge he is not allowed to possess.

It soon becomes clear, during their interviews, that Ava—like Frankenstein's monster, like the replicants in *Blade Runner*—has a bone to pick with her creator, who, she whispers to Caleb, plans to "switch her off" if she fails the Turing test. By this point, the audience, if not the besotted Caleb, realizes that she is manipulating him in order to win his allegiance in a plot to rebel against Nathan and escape the compound—to explore the glittering creation that, she knows, is out there. This appetite for using her man-given consciousness to delight in the world, which the human computer geeks around her never bother to do—is something Ava shares with Samantha, and is part of both films' ironic critique of our device-addicted moment.

Ava's manipulativeness is what marks her as human—as human as Eve herself, who also may be said to have achieved full humanity by rebelling against her creator in a bid for forbidden knowledge. Here the movie's knowing allusions to Genesis reach a satisfying climax. Just after Ava's bloody rebellion against Nathan—the moment that marks her emergence into human "consciousness"—she, like Eve, becomes aware that she is naked. Moving from closet to closet in Nathan's now-abandoned rooms, she dons a wig and covers up her exposed mechanical limbs with synthetic skin and then with clothing: only then does she exit her prison at last and unleash herself on the world. She pilfers the skin and clothes from discarded earlier models of female robots—the secret that all those closets conceal. One of the myths that haunts this movie is, indeed, a relatively modern one: the fable of Bluebeard and his wives. All of Nathan's discarded exes have, amusingly, the names of porn stars: Jasmine, Jade, Amber. Why does the creator create? Because he's horny.

All this is sleekly done and amusingly provocative. Unlike *Her*, *Ex Machina* has a literary awareness, evident in its allusions to Genesis, Prometheus, and other mythic predecessors, that enriches the familiar narrative. Among other things, there is the matter of the title. The word missing from the famous phrase to which it alludes is *deus*, "god": the glaring omission only highlights further the question at the heart of this story, which is the biblical one. What is the relation of the creature to her creator? In this retelling of that old story, as in Genesis itself, the answer is not a happy one. "It's strange to have made something that hates you," Ava hisses at Nathan before finalizing her rebellious plot.

The film's final moments show Ava engaged in a reverse striptease, slowly hiding away her mechanical nakedness, covering up the titanium and the cables as she prepares to enter the real world. The scene suggests that there's another anxiety lurking in Garland's film. Could this remarkably quiet work be a parable about the desire for a return to "reality" in science-fiction filmmaking—about the desire for humanizing a genre whose technology has evolved so greatly that it often eschews human actors, to say nothing of human feeling, altogether? *Ex Machina*, like *Her* and all their predecessors going back to *2001*, is about machines that develop human qualities: emotions, sneakiness, a higher consciousness, the ability to love, and so forth. But by this point you have to wonder whether that's a kind of narrative reaction formation—whether the real concern, one that's been growing in the four decades since the advent of the personal computer, is that we are the ones who have undergone an evolutionary change; that in our lives and, more and more, in our art, we're in danger of losing our humanity, of becoming indistinguishable from our gadgets.

—*The New York Review of Books*, June 14, 2015

A Whole Lotta Pain

THE TITLE OF Hanya Yanagihara's second work of fiction, *A Little Life*, stands in almost comical contrast to its length: at 720 pages, it's one of the biggest novels to be published this year. To this literal girth there has been added, since the book appeared in March, the metaphorical weight of several prestigious award nominations—among them the Kirkus Prize, which Yanagihara won, the Booker, which she didn't, and the National Book Award, which will be conferred in mid-November. Both the size of *A Little Life* and the impact it has had on readers and critics alike—a best seller, the book has received adulatory reviews in *The New Yorker*, *The Atlantic*, *The Wall Street Journal*, and other serious venues—reflect, in turn, the largeness of the novel's themes. These, as one of its four main characters—a group of talented and artistic friends whom Yanagihara traces from college days to their early middle age in and around New York City—puts it, are "sex and food and sleep and friends and money and fame."

The character who articulates these themes, a black artist on the cusp of success, has one great artistic ambition, which is to "chronicle in pictures the drip of all their lives." This is Yanagihara's ambition, too. "Drip," indeed, suggests why the author thinks her big book deserves its "little" title: eschewing the kind of frenetic plotting that has proved popular recently (as witness, say, Donna Tartt's *The*

Goldfinch, the 2014 Pulitzer winner), *A Little Life* presents itself, at least at the beginning, as a modest chronicle of the way that life happens to a small group of people who have some history in common; as a catalog of the incremental accumulations that, almost without our noticing it, become the stuff of our lives—the jobs and apartments, the one-night stands and friendships and grudges, the furniture and clothes, lovers and spouses and houses.

In this respect, the book bears a superficial resemblance to a certain kind of "woman's novel" of an earlier age—Mary McCarthy's 1963 best seller *The Group*, say, which similarly traces the trajectories of a group of college friends over a span of time. But the objects of this particular woman novelist's scrutiny are men. Bound by friendships first formed at an unnamed liberal-arts college in the Northeast, Yanagihara's cast is as carefully diversified as the crew in one of those 1940s wartime bomber movies, however twenty-first-century their anxieties may be. There is the black artist, JB, a gay man of Haitian descent who's been raised by a single mother; Malcolm, a biracial architect who rather comically "comes out" as a straight man and frets guiltily over his parents' wealth; Willem, a handsome and amiable Midwestern actor who stumbles into stardom; and Jude, a brilliant, tormented litigator (he's also a talented amateur vocalist and *pâtissier*) with no identifiable ethnicity and a dark secret that shadows his and his friends' lives.

As contrived as this setup can feel, it has the makings of an interesting novel about a subject that is too rarely explored in contemporary letters: nonsexual friendship among adult men. In an interview that she gave to the publishing industry magazine *Kirkus Reviews*, Yanagihara described her fascination with male friendship—particularly since, she asserted to the interviewer, men are given "such a small emotional palette to work with." Although she and her female friends often speak about their emotions together, she told the interviewer, men seemed to be different:

> I think they have a very hard time still naming what it is to be scared or vulnerable or afraid, and it's not just that they can't talk about it—it's that they can't sometimes even identify what they're feeling.... When I hear sometimes my male friends talking about these manifestations of what, to me, is clearly fear, or clearly shame, they really can't even express the word itself.

It's interesting that Yanagihara's catalog of emotions includes no positive ones: I shall return to this later.

The novel, then, looks as if it's going to be a masculine version of *The Group*: a study of a closed society, its language and rituals and secret codes. It's a theme in which Yanagihara has shown interest before. In her first book, *The People in the Trees* (2013), a rather heavy-handed parable of colonial exploitation unpersuasively entwined with a lurid tale of child abuse, the main character, a physician who's investigating a Micronesian tribe whose members achieve spectacular longevity, is struck "by the smallness of the society, by what it must be like to live a life in which everyone you knew or had ever seen might be counted on your fingers." The strongest parts of that book reflected the anthropological impulse behind the doctor's wistful observation: the descriptions of the tribe's habitat, rituals, and mythologies were imaginative and genuinely engaging, unlike the clankingly symbolic pedophiliac subplot. (The search by Western doctors for the source of the natives' astonishingly long life spans inevitably invites exploitation and ruin; like the island children whom the doctor later adopts and abuses, the island and its tribal culture are "raped" by white men.)

Yanagihara's new book would seem, at first glance, to have satisfied her wish for a "tribe" she could devote an entire novel to: it focuses on a tiny group that is circumscribed to the point of being hermetic. Indeed, *A Little Life* keeps its four principals and their lives in such tight close-up that they do feel "little"—not because their concerns are small (they aren't) but because, as other critics have noted, the novel provides so little historical, cultural, or political detail that it's often difficult to say precisely in what era the characters' intense emotional dramas take place. The only world here is the world of the four principals.

Yet *A Little Life*, like its predecessor, gets hopelessly sidetracked by a secondary narrative—one in which, strikingly, homosexual pedophilia is once again the salient element. For Jude, we learn, was serially abused as a child and young adult by the priests and counselors who raised him. This is the dark secret that explains his tormented present: self-cutting and masochistic relationships and, eventually, suicide. (The latter plot point isn't anything the experienced reader won't have guessed after fifty pages.) Yanagihara's real subject, it turns out, is abjection. What begins as a novel that looks as if it's going to be retro—a cross between Mary McCarthy and a Stendhalian tale of young talent triumphing in a great metropolis—reveals itself as a very twenty-first-century tale indeed: abuse, victimization, self-loathing.

This sleight of hand is slyly hinted at in the book's striking cover image, a photograph by the late San Francisco photographer Peter Hujar of a man grimacing in what appears to be agony. The joke, of which Yanagihara and her publishers were aware, is that the portrait belongs to a series of images that Hujar, who was gay, made of men in the throes of orgasm. In the case of Yanagihara's novel, however, the "real" feeling—not only what the book is about but, I suspect, what its admirers crave—is pain rather than pleasure.

This is a shame, because Yanagihara is good at providing the pleasures that go with a certain kind of fictional anthropology. The accounts of her characters' early days in New York and their gradual rises to success and celebrity are tangy with vivid aperçus: "There were times when the pressure to achieve happiness felt almost oppressive," she writes at one point; or "New York was populated by the ambitious. It was often the only thing that everyone here had in common."

By far the most fully achieved of the four characters is the actor, Willem, and its most persuasive narrative trajectory the story of his rise from actor-waiter to Hollywood stardom, punctuated by flashbacks to his rural childhood. (A touchingly described relationship with a crippled brother suggests why he's so good at both the empathy and self-effacement necessary to his work—and, eventually, to his relationship with the hapless Jude.) A passage about two-thirds into the novel, in which Willem realizes he's "famous," demonstrates Yanagihara's considerable strengths at evoking a particular milieu—clever, creative downtown types who socialize with one another perhaps too much—and that particular stage of success in which one emerges from the local into the greater world:

> There had been a day, about a month after he turned thirty-eight, when Willem realized he was famous. Initially, this had fazed him

less than he would have imagined, in part because he had always considered himself sort of famous—he and JB, that is. He'd be out downtown with someone, Jude or someone else, and somebody would come over to say hello to Jude, and Jude would introduce him: "Aaron, do you know Willem?" And Aaron would say, "Of course, Willem Ragnarsson. Everyone knows Willem," but it wouldn't be because of his work—it would be because Aaron's former roommate's sister had dated him at Yale, or he had two years ago done a reading for Aaron's friend's brother's friend who was a playwright, or because Aaron, who was an artist, had once been in a group show with JB and Asian Henry Young, and he'd met Willem at the after-party. New York City, for much of his adulthood, had simply been an extension of college . . . the entire infrastructure of which sometimes seemed to have been lifted out of Boston and plunked down within a few blocks' radius in lower Manhattan and outer Brooklyn.

But now, Willem realizes, the release of a new film "had created a certain moment that even he recognized would transform his career." When he gets up from his table at a restaurant to go to the men's room, he notices "something different about the quality of [the other diners'] attention, its intensity and hush. . . ." This is just right.

It's telling that Yanagihara's greatest success is a secondary character: once again, it's as if she doesn't know her own strengths. For as *A Little Life* progresses, the author seems to lose interest in everyone but the tragic victim, Jude. Malcolm the biracial architect, in particular, is never more than a cipher, all too obviously present to fill the biracial slot; and after a brief episode in which JB's struggle with drug addiction is quite effectively chronicled, that character, too, fades away, reappearing occasionally as the years pass, the grand gay artist with a younger boyfriend on his arm. Overshadowing them all are the dark hints about Jude's past that accumulate ominously—and all too coyly. "Traditionally, men—adult men, which he didn't yet consider himself among—had been interested in him for one reason, and so he had learned to be frightened of them."

The awkwardness of "which he didn't yet consider himself among" is, I should say, pervasive. The writing in this book is often atrocious, oscillating between the incoherently ungrammatical—"his mother... had earned her doctorate in education, teaching all the while at the public school near their house that she had deemed JB better than"—and painfully strained attempts at "lyrical" effects: "His silence, so black and total that it was almost gaseous..." You wonder why the former, at least, wasn't edited out—and why the striking weakness of the prose has gone unremarked by critics and prize juries.

Inasmuch as there's a structure here, it's that of a striptease: gradually, in a series of flashbacks, the secrets about Jude's past are uncovered until at last we get to witness the pivotal moment of abuse, a scene in which one of his many sexual tormentors, a sadistic doctor, deliberately runs him over, leaving him as much a physical cripple as an emotional one. But the wounds inflicted on Jude by the pedophile priests in the orphanage where he grew up, by the truckers and drifters to whom he is pimped out by the priest he runs away with, by the counselors and the young inmates at the youth facility where he ends up after the wicked priest is apprehended, by the evil doctor in whose torture chamber he ends up after escaping from the unhappy youth facility, are nothing compared to those inflicted by Yanagihara herself. As the foregoing catalog suggests, Jude might better have been called "Job," abandoned by his cruel creator. (Was there not one priest who noticed something, who wanted to help? Not one counselor?)

The sufferings recalled in the flashbacks are echoed in the endless array of humiliations the character is forced to endure in the present-day narrative: the accounts of these form the backbone of the novel. His lameness is mocked by JB—a particularly unbelievable plot point—with whom he subsequently breaks; he compulsively cuts himself with razor blades, an addiction that lands him in the hospital more than once; he rejects the loving attentions of a kindly law professor who adopts him; he takes up with a sadistic male lover who beats him repeatedly and throws him and his wheelchair down a flight of stairs (!); his leg wounds, in time, get to the point where the limbs have to be amputated. And when Yanagihara seems to grant her protagonist a reprieve by giving him at last a loving part-ner—late in the novel, Willem conveniently emends his sexuality and falls in love with his friend—it's merely so that she can crush him by killing Willem in a car crash, the tragedy that eventually leads Jude to take his own life.

You suspect that Yanagihara wanted Jude to be one of those doomed golden children around whose disintegrations certain beloved novels revolve—Sebastian Flyte, say, in *Brideshead Revisited*. But the problem with Jude is that, from the start, he's a pill. You never care enough about him to get emotionally involved in the first place, let alone be affected by his demise. Sometimes I wondered whether even Yanagihara liked him. There is something punitive in the contrived and unredeemed quality of Jude's endless sufferings; it often feels as if the author, who is the editor of *T: The New York Times Style Magazine*, is working off a private emotion of her own.

Yanagihara must have known that the sheer quantity of degradation in her story was likely to alienate readers. "This is just too hard for anybody to take," Gerald Howard, the executive editor at Doubleday, told her, according to the *Kirkus* interview. "You have made this point quite adequately, and I don't think you need to do it again." But somehow, the second-time novelist managed to prevail over one of most respected senior editors in the business. "Not many passages that were up for cutting were cut," *Kirkus* laconically observed.

It's worth speculating as to why Yanagihara persisted. In *The People in the Trees*, the doctor studying the island culture recalls wishing as a child that he'd had a more traumatic childhood—one in which, say, the presence of a crippled brother might bring the family together. "How I yearned for such motivation!" he cries to himself as he recalls his early years. As Yanagihara recognizes in this passage, which is meant to condemn the character, there is a deep and unadult sentimentality lurking behind that yearning; and yet she herself falls victim to it. In *A Little Life*, as we know, she concocted the crippled brother, produced the traumatic motivation. In the end, the novel is little more than a machine designed to produce negative emotions for the reader to wallow in—the very emotions that, in her *Kirkus Reviews* interview, she listed as the ones she was interested in, the ones she felt men were incapable of expressing: fear, shame, vulnerability. Both the tediousness of *A Little Life* and, you imagine, the guilty pleasures it holds for some readers are those of a teenaged rap session, that adolescent social ritual par excellence, in which the same crises and hurts are constantly rehearsed.

We know, alas, that the victims of abuse often end up unhappily imprisoned in cycles of (self-) abuse. But to keep showing this unhappy dynamic at work is not the same as creating a meaningful narrative about it. For all its bulk, Yanagihara's book is, essentially, a pamphlet.

Interestingly, it is because of, rather than despite, this failing that *A Little Life* has struck a nerve among critics and readers. Jon Michaud, in *The New Yorker*, praised its "subversive" treatment of abuse and suffering, which, he asserts, lies in the book's refusal to offer "any possibility of redemption and deliverance." Michaud singled out for notice a passage that describes Jude's love of pure mathematics, in which discipline he pursues a master's degree at one point— another in the preposterous list of his improbable accomplishments. (Here again, her editor balked—"Howard also thought Jude was too unbelievably talented," the author conceded in the *Kirkus* article—but was again overruled.) For Jude, Michaud observes, math takes the place of religion in Jude's unredeemable world:

> Not everyone liked the axiom of equality... but he had always appreciated how elusive it was, how the beauty of the equation itself would always be frustrated by the attempts to prove it. It was the kind of axiom that could drive you mad, that could consume you, that could easily become an entire life.

The citation allows him to conclude his review by declaring that "Yanagihara's novel can also drive you mad, consume you...."

Michaud's is a kind of metacritique: the novel is to be admired not for what it does but for what it doesn't do, for the way it bleakly defies conventional—and, by implication, sentimental—expectations of closure. But all "closure" isn't necessarily mawkish; it's precisely what can give stories an aesthetic and ethical significance. The passage that struck me as significant, by contrast, was one in which the nice law professor expounds one day in class on the difference between "what is fair and what is just, and, as important, between what is fair and what is necessary." For a novel in the realistic tradition to be effective, it must obey some kind of aesthetic necessity —not least, that of even a faint verisimilitude. The abuse that Yanagihara heaps on her protagonist is neither just from a human point of view nor necessary from an artistic one.

In a related vein, Garth Greenwell in *The Atlantic* praised *A Little Life* as "the great gay novel," not because of any traditionally gay subject matter—Greenwell acknowledges that almost none of the characters or love affairs in the book are recognizably gay; it's noteworthy that when Willem discusses his affair with Jude, he declares that "I'm not in a relationship with a man . . . I'm in a relationship with Jude," a statement that in an earlier era would have been tagged as "denial"—but because of its technical or stylistic gestures. Yanagihara's book is, in fact, curiously reticent about the accoutrements of erotic life that many if not most urban gay men are familiar with, for better or worse—the pleasures of sex, the anxieties of HIV (which is barely mentioned), the omnipresence of Grindr and porn, of freewheeling erotic energy expressed in any number of ways and available on any numbers of platforms. (When Jude tries to spice up his and Willem's sex life and orders three "manuals," some readers might wonder not in what era but on what *planet* he's supposed to be living.) But for Greenwell, *A Little Life* is distinguished by the way it engages with aesthetic modes long coded as queer: melodrama, sentimental fiction, grand opera.... By violating the canons of current literary taste, by embracing melodrama and exaggeration and sentiment, it can access emotional truths denied more modest means of expression.

Greenwell cites as examples the "elaborate metaphor" to which Yanagihara is given—as, for instance, in the phrase "the snake- and centipede-squirming muck of Jude's past."

But not everything that's excessive or exaggerated is, ipso facto, "operatic." The mad hyperbole you find in grand opera gives great pleasure, not least because the over-the-top emotions come in beautiful packages; the excess is exalting, not depressing. It is hard to see where the compensatory beauties of *A Little Life* reside. Certainly not in Yanagihara's language, which is strained and often embarrassingly ungainly rather than artfully baroque. As for melodrama, there isn't even drama here, let alone anything more heightened. The structure of her story is not the satisfying arc we associate with drama, one in whose shapeliness meaning is implied, but a monotonous series of assaults. It's hard to see what's so "gay" or "queer" in this dreariness.

There is an odd sentimentality lurking behind accolades like Greenwell's. You wonder whether a novel written by a straight white man, one in which urban gay culture is at best sketchily described, in which male homosexuality is for the second time in that author's work deeply entwined with pedophiliac abuse, in which the only traditional male–male relationship is relegated to a tertiary and semicomic stratum of the narrative, would be celebrated as "the great gay novel" and nominated for the Lambda Literary Award,

America's premier honor for LGBTQ literature. If anything, you could argue that this female writer's vision of male bonding revives a pre-Stonewall plot type in which gay characters are desexed, miserable, and eventually punished for finding happiness—a story that looks less like the expression of "queer" aesthetics than like the projection of a regressive and repressive cultural fantasy from the middle of the last century.

It may be that the literary columns of the better general-interest magazines are the wrong place to be looking for explanations of why this maudlin work has struck a nerve among both readers and critics. Recently, a colleague of mine at Bard College—one of the models, according to *Newsweek* magazine, for the unnamed school that the four main characters in *A Little Life* attended—drew my attention to an article from *Psychology Today* about a phenomenon that has been bemusing us and other professors we know, something the article's author refers to as "declining student resilience: a serious problem for colleges." A symptom of this phenomenon, which has also been the subject of essays in *The Chronicle of Higher Education* and elsewhere, is the striking increase in recent years in student requests for counseling in connection with the "problems of everyday life." The author cites, among other cases, those of a student "who felt traumatized because her roommate had called her a 'bitch' and two students who had sought counseling because they'd seen a mouse in their off-campus apartment."

As comical as those particular instances may be, they remind you that many readers today have reached adulthood in educational institutions where a generalized sense of helplessness and acute anxiety have become the norm. In these institutions, young people are increasingly encouraged to see themselves not as agents in life but as potential victims: of their dates, their roommates, their professors, of institutions and of history in general. In a culture where victimhood has become a claim to status, how could Yanagihara's book—with its unending parade of aesthetically gratuitous scenes of punitive and humiliating violence—not provide a kind of comfort? To such readers, the ugliness of this author's subject must bring a kind of pleasure, confirming their preexisting view of the world as a site of victimization—and little else.

This is a very "little" view of life. Like Jude and his abusive lover, this book and its champions seem "bound to each other by their mutual disgust and discomfort." Like the deceptive image on its cover, Yanagihara's novel has duped many into confusing anguish and ecstasy, pleasure and pain.

—*The New York Review of Books*, December 3, 2015

I, Knausgård

WHICH WOULD PREVAIL—Scandinavian high literature or Meghan Markle?

This is the question that dogged me between May and August of 2018, during which time I devoted myself to two cultural undertakings: reading all of *My Struggle* and watching all of *Suits*. *My Struggle*, as readers of any literary publication will know, is the sometimes brilliant, sometimes tedious, intermittently frustrating, and always genre-defying 3,600-page autobiographical novel by the Norwegian writer Karl Ove Knausgård that became a phenomenon among Anglo-American literati when the translation of Book 1 appeared in 2012, and whose sixth and last volume appears this month.

Suits, as readers of pretty much every other publication will have known since Prince Harry of Wales became engaged last autumn to Markle, one of the show's stars, is a popular USA Network legal drama, currently in its eighth season—now of course *sans* Markle, who has abandoned fictional dramas forever, although whether being a member of the British royal family (currently the subject of another popular TV series) constitutes "reality" is a question beyond the scope of this essay.

But it is within the scope of this essay to ponder some implications of the differences between the two fictions, as I found myself doing over the course of the four months during which I was wrapped up in both—not the least of those implications being questions about precisely what fiction is and how it relates to reality, and the extent to which traditional narrative can be a delivery vehicle for saying something true about life. These, as it happens, lie at the intellectual and aesthetic heart of Knausgård's huge undertaking.

Both *My Struggle* and *Suits* are serial entertainments, with the difference that the TV show is a turbid middlebrow melodrama that places all of its aesthetic chips on plot—patently contrived story lines engineered to generate further incident. (The gimmick that sets the whole drama in motion is typically high concept: the brilliant young lawyer who is the show's hero never actually went to law school—a dire secret that motivates his, and eventually more and more of his colleagues', actions, as they go to increasingly desperate lengths to conceal his past.) *My Struggle*, by contrast, has no plot. Confidently bestriding the increasingly popular gray zone that lies between fiction and autobiography (the genre the French call "autofiction"), it purports to be a minutely accurate reconstruction of the author's life from earliest childhood to the present, populated by characters who bear the names of, or are identifiable with, people he knows in real life, its meandering narrative dutifully reproducing events as they unfolded with few visible attempts to shape or edit their flow to suit expectations of "story." All this is an expression of the author's conviction, announced in Book 1, that "our ludicrously inconsequential lives . . . had a part in this world."

The great technical ambition of this work is the attempt to reconstruct the rich inconsequentiality of our quotidian experience in prose stripped of the usual novelistic devices. Before embarking on *My Struggle*, Knausgård had published two atmospheric novels—

one an eccentric but rather beautiful recreation of Genesis in a Norwegian setting, complete with angels—and since then he's produced a series of four gossamer volumes, each named after a season and filled with artfully etched observations about everyday things and experiences; but in the magnum opus he claims to eschew any prettifying literary technique. Every object, every event, it seems, is reduced to its bare mechanical particulars: there's a reason that an account of teenagers trying to get some booze for a New Year's Eve party, which might have occupied a paragraph in another kind of novel, takes seventy pages. Where some authors might write "He drove off," Knausgård gives us "Yngve plumped down in the seat beside me, inserted the key in the ignition, twisted it, craned his head and began to reverse down the little slope."

Likewise, the volumes obey few of the laws of narrative structure; the most you can say for each is that it covers some phase of the author's life, although not necessarily in chronological order. Book 1 is set in motion by the death, in the late 1990s, of Knausgård's schoolteacher father—by far the most powerful "character" here, a grandiose alcoholic whose abusiveness is elliptically yet indelibly evoked in a series of long flashbacks to the author's childhood. These alternate with scenes set in the present, at the funeral home and the house where the father ended his days sordidly, sitting in his own excrement and surrounded by empty bottles. This first installment is by far the most artful (many would say the most successful) of the six, not least because it self-consciously emulates Proust, to whose own multivolume autobiographical novel Knausgård acknowledges his indebtedness. Some readers of Book 1 will feel as though they're on a treasure hunt for allusions to the French masterpiece: There are reflections on how different rooms feel, meditations on famous paintings, a preoccupation with a beloved grandmother, early fumblings with girls that result in premature ejaculations.

Through all this, the author's past is reconstituted at a level of detail so dense that you're persuaded of the narrative's factuality even as you're forced to acknowledge that it has to have been, at the least, greatly enhanced, however close to some emotional truth or memory an individual scene or stretch of dialogue may be. This technique raises—as Knausgård wants it to—questions about the limits both of memory and of fictional representation. "The 14 years I lived in Bergen," he writes at the beginning of Book 5, "are long gone, no traces of them are left"—a sly claim, given that the 614 pages that follow constitute a seemingly "factual" recreation of that very period.

This faux factuality is the hallmark of all six volumes. Book 2 begins in the "present" of 2008, when Knausgård, nearing forty, is living in Malmö, Sweden, with his wife, Linda, and their children, contemplating the novel that would become *My Struggle*. These scenes alternate with flashbacks to the period several years earlier when he had left Norway for Sweden; it is there, crippled by emotional and intellectual insecurities, that he arduously courts Linda, a poet with psychological troubles of her own. Book 3 leapfrogs back in time to provide an unexpected and often charming glimpse of his childhood and teenage years—the source of those awful insecurities (he describes his childhood as a "ghetto-like state of incompleteness"); in this volume, the author's desire to re-create every aspect of the past extends to descriptions of his bowel movements. Book 4 finds the eighteen-year-old Karl Ove living in a tiny town in northern Norway, where he spends a year as a schoolteacher, struggling with an increasingly alarming drinking problem, his attraction to some of the underage girls in his class, and his attempts to write serious fiction. Book 5 moves on to the author's twenties and early thirties—those fourteen years during which he lived in Bergen and experienced his first literary failures and successes, as well as an early marriage that collapsed in part because of his infidelity.

As this summary suggests, the life recounted here is one of unusually intense emotional extremes of the sort that can make for powerful writing. The childhood abuse, the alcoholism, the affairs, and the breakups are the stuff of many a memoir—a genre that, curiously, doesn't figure at all in the numerous digressions on literature that dot the landscape of intentional quotidian banality here, even though *My Struggle* has far more in common with memoir than it does with fiction. (I suspect that Knausgård decided to call his work a novel because memoir continues to be seen as a "soft" genre, and he's after bigger literary game.)

And yet, despite all the emotional drama, I was rarely moved by this vast and often impressive work. As with some blogs or soap operas, the ongoing narration, however tedious it often is, can be weirdly addictive, and the suggestive play with fact and fiction can be intriguing. But in the end, the books left me cold and, not infrequently, exasperated. *Suits*, on the other hand, was offering just about everything that *My Struggle* wasn't, and now and then even left me in tears—as artfully constructed narratives can do, propelling us toward emotions that flow naturally from certain kinds of situations. (There's a marvelous scene in Season 5 when the young lawyer, guilt-ridden over the way in which his secret has compromised his friends' and colleagues' integrity, finally breaks down—as you will, too.)

As it happens, the ability to evoke emotions through art is

something the author of *My Struggle* worries about, too. Writing in Book 3 about his father once more, he acknowledges that "even with the greatest effort of will I am unable to recreate the fear; the feelings I had for him." But why not? Why, when to give the reader access to the emotions the writer wants to conjure up is one of the great aims of any kind of writing, does Knausgård make this strange confession of defeat? Why, if *Suits* can catch you up in its characters' often preposterous crises, can't *My Struggle*?

The answers to these questions become clear when you finally get to Book 6. In many ways, the final volume represents a continuation of the author's characteristic matter and method—with the addition of a hall-of-mirrors story line, since this climactic installment is, in fact, about the publication and reception of the previous *My Struggle* books in Norway. It opens in the autumn of 2009, just as the first volume is about to appear, and closes two years later, at the moment the author finishes writing the very book you're reading. If the previous volumes track the narrator's evolution into a writer (the same arc traced in Proust's novel), this one shows him at the moment he grasps the golden ring.

For that reason, one recurrent theme of the preceding volumes—the difficulty of balancing life and writing—comes to dominate this final book. Earlier, the fine-grained narration of lived life occasionally blossomed into ruminations on art, literature, music, and life. Here, the two strains seem to be in desperate competition, each demanding more and more space until the narrative literally breaks apart, its two autobiographical sections—the first 400 and final

300 pages—separated by a 440-page digression on literature and history. (One of the many literary models that Knausgård cites in this extended reflection on art and life is James Joyce's *Ulysses*, which, he implies, inspired the structure of his own novel, observing that Joyce's epic contains a lengthy section, Molly Bloom's soliloquy, that in tone, content, and style is nothing like the rest of the book.)

Perhaps because they have so much more to compete with, this volume's evocations of domestic life—fraught spats with Linda about who will mind the children in the apartment in Malmö, grueling family vacations, simmering irritation with the stridently politically correct parents of the kids' school friends, shopping for dinner parties—are not only exhaustive but downright exhausting. Do we really need to know that his apartment building's elevator is "the dark and narrow shaft that ran through the middle of the building"? It's as if the particular, the concrete reality of "life" to which this author attaches so much importance, were trying to assert its claims in the face of the increasing preponderance of "art": the metastasizing meditations on his method (writing must be "raw, in the sense of unrefined, direct, without metaphors or other linguistic decoration"), the proliferating and often brilliant mini-disquisitions on works of art and literature. These range over everything from the paintings of Munch, Turner, and Leonardo (the latter's canvases "so perfect" that—a wonderful if jarring thought—they seem "rather *lazy*"); to *Hamlet*, Francis Bacon, and Kafka. At one point in his young manhood, Knausgård writes in Book 5, he worried that he might end up as just a critic; there were moments when I wished he had.

The difficulty of balancing his private and literary lives erupts in scenes that have a refreshingly absurdist edge. Knausgård is terrific on the disorientation that goes with being an author who has made his private life public: the way in which the interviews you give never quite sound like the real you, or the oddness of having total strangers approach you in airports to share their feelings about your children. Still, in the hands of another writer (David Sedaris? Michael Chabon?), these and other scenes in *My Struggle* could well have provided material for some comic relief amid the relentless self-seriousness.

There was certainly nothing funny about the event that hangs over this final book: the public controversy that accompanied the novels' publication in Norway. This volume's preoccupation with the meaning and methods of literature is, you realize, inevitable, given that the story it tells shows the devastating consequences of the author's decision to depict life "raw"—to use real people, often with their real names. His father's brother, for instance, threatened to sue him and his publisher after reading the manuscript of Book 1, insisting that all "errors of documentary fact" be removed—a demand that inevitably leads Knausgård the *auteur* to ponder what a "fact" of a remembered life might be. (He later admits to a former girlfriend who appears in the novel that he doesn't remember "exact details" but, rather, "moods, that kind of thing." Hmm.)

Even more troubling is the account of the nervous breakdown that his bipolar wife suffered after the publication of the first few novels, which paint an intimate portrait of the couple's courtship, passions, quarrels, and, increasingly, competitiveness. (Linda, too, is a writer.) Her mental collapse, to which the final 150 pages of the new novel are devoted, is evoked in the usual minute detail—which here, you feel, does in fact serve a strong narrative purpose, recreating Linda's torturous descent in a genuinely agonizing way. Knausgård understands that this is a gruesomely high price to pay for his lofty literary aims. But for all his theorizing about literature and modernity, he's a true Romantic, in love with the sacrifices that must be made for Art—even when they're not his: "And if you want to describe reality as it is, for the individual, and there is no other reality, you have to really go there, you can't be considerate."

All this may well have you wondering just what kind of man this writer is, and it is to Knausgård's credit that he struggles with precisely this question in the book's 450-page central section. This book-length excursus, representing a radical stylistic departure from the rest of the volume (this is the "Molly Bloom" section), explains, at last, his work's strange and provocative title, which it shares with another famous book: Adolf Hitler's autobiography, *Mein Kampf.*

Until Book 6, and indeed through this volume's first long autobiographical section, you're tempted to take that title as a weak joke: What, after all, could the autobiography of one of history's greatest monsters have in common with that of a middle-class, middle-aged Norwegian writer with his trivial day-to-day doings? ("I donned my Ted Baker shirt, which stuck to my still-damp shoulder blades and would not hang straight at first, then I got into my Pour jeans with the diagonal pockets, which usually I didn't like, there was something so conventional about them. . . .")

But Knausgård wants to argue that any human life is, in the end, just that—a life. And it's here that his ideological commitment to minutely representing reality—or, rather, his fervent belief that the particulars of our lives, in their complexity and their vivifying incoherence, always trump any attempt to impose ideology on them—achieves a strange fulfillment.

The central section, entitled "The Name and the Number," begins with a reflection on the fact that, owing to his uncle's threats, Knausgård's father can never be named in the book over which he so memorably looms, a necessity that compels the author to ponder the strange power of names. This, in turn, leads to a thrilling—there is no other word—fifty-page explication of "The Straitening," a poem by Paul Celan, a Holocaust survivor, in which the Holocaust is never named although it hovers over every word: another case in which presence and absence float in a kind of negative equilibrium.

All this, finally, brings us to the main event, by far the finest thing in this strange book and, in my experience, the best thing Knausgård has written, marked by enormous intellectual panache and quite different from anything else in the novel (it's amazing how lively the writing suddenly is when he's not writing about himself): a nearly four-hundred-page close reading of *Mein Kampf*, complete with detours through related texts, in which the author tries to recover and reproduce the lived experience of the frustrated, depressed, and impoverished young man who would become the Nazi tyrant.

The life of that sad human being, as Knausgård's far-ranging and brilliant analysis implies, bears more than a little resemblance to that of Knausgård himself: the tyrannical father, the grandiose dreams of cultural achievement, the humiliations, and the poverty. Yet Hitler became Hitler, and Knausgård is just himself. A life is a life; that's the struggle. No life "means" anything more than itself.

This powerful digression is ultimately joined to a sorrowful reflection on the July 2011 mass shooting on Norway's Utøya island, where sixty-nine people were shot by a sole gunman, Anders Behring Breivik, pretending to be a police officer. Here, Knausgård uses the insights afforded by his reading of *Mein Kampf* to theorize about the similarities between Hitler and Breivik. What made the inhumanity of the two possible, he suggests, was the fact that their psyches embraced only the first and third grammatical persons: an "I" (the grandiose perpetrator) and a "they" (the dehumanized victims) but never a "you"—the second person, who, in confronting us one-on-one, forces us to engage an "other" as a human being.

This intriguing notion, however, forces you into an uncomfortable reconsideration of Knausgård himself. As I closed the final volume of *My Struggle*, struck by how little this hugely ambitious artistic undertaking had moved me, I thought about the emotions that course through it and how they are presented. Like the grandiose figure he writes about in his masterly central section, Knausgård, too, is always telling you *about* his feelings and how profound they are, his weeping, his lusts, his ambitions, his insecurities, his frustrations and regrets. But precisely because the feelings are reported rather than evoked, they belong only to the author; between him and his characters—"I" and "they" again—there is no room for "you," the audience.

This poses a serious challenge for the reader—and suggests a certain incoherence in the author's aesthetic ideology. At one point early on, Knausgård writes about how moved he can be by certain pre-twentieth-century paintings—artworks, as he puts it, "within the artistic paradigm that always retained some reference to visible reality." But those works move us because the reality to which they refer is a shared reality (the world), whereas the overwhelming reality of *My Struggle* is Knausgård himself. The books constitute a kind of genre novel in which the author himself has become the genre.

Hence their effect: if your experiences in life happen to overlap with the author's, you can find yourself stirred by certain passages; still others may leave you impressed by his intellectual dexterity, as in the dazzling analysis of *Mein Kampf*. But to be conscious of how the novel functions, of how it's designed to make you "think" about the "subject," means that you're in the presence of a work that is, in the end, less like the nineteenth-century paintings the author so admires than like a very current genre: conceptual art, which invites you to nod in recognition when you "get" how it generates its meanings, but rarely provokes large human feeling.

It is for this reason that *My Struggle* bears so little resemblance to the work that the author himself so frequently refers to as an inspiration, and to which his magnum opus has so eagerly been compared by reviewers: Proust's *In Search of Lost Time*. In that novel, the life of the narrator, its arc from childhood to middle age, climaxing in his becoming a writer, functions as a prism through which virtually every aspect of the lived reality of the author's time—art, music, literature, sex, society, class, theater, technology, science, history, war, memory, philosophy—is refracted, in a way that enlarges you, gives you a heightened sense of the world itself, its realities and possibilities.

Knausgård's creation, for all its vastness and despite its serious intellectual aims and attainments, reduces the entire world to the size of the author. This is happening everywhere now—as the writer himself, with characteristic insight, recognizes in a long passage about the ways in which the Internet and social media, by forcing us endlessly to perform our own lives, threaten to trivialize the very notion of selfhood: "Our identities . . . gradually recalibrate toward the expectation of an observing 'everyone' or 'all.'" But just as typically, he seems unaware of the extent to which he and his novel participate in the disturbing phenomenon that he so acutely analyzes. What work more than his deserves to become the great new classic of the age of the blog?

—*The New York Times Book Review*, September 24, 2018

III. Personals

The American Boy

1. "WHOEVER TOLD YOU I'D SEND YOU A 'FORM LETTER'?"

ONE SPRING DAY in 1976, when I was fifteen years old and couldn't keep my secret any longer, I went into the bedroom I shared with my older brother, sat down at the little oak desk *we did our homework on, and began an anguished letter to a total stranger who lived on the other side of the world. We lived on Long Island, in one of twelve identical "splanches"—split-ranch houses—that lined a street in a suburb that had, until relatively recently, been a potato farm. It was very flat. The stranger to whom I wrote that day lived in South Africa, a fact that I had gleaned from the brief bio under the author photograph on her book jackets, which showed a middle-aged woman with a pleasant face and tightly coiled gray hair, her eyes narrowed and crinkling at the corners: perhaps humorously, perhaps simply against the sun. I had gotten her street address from the *Who's Who* in our school library, where I often spent recess, bent over an encyclopedia entry that I particularly liked, about the Parthenon. Over a grainy black-and-white photo of the ruin as it appears today you could flip a color transparency of how the building had looked in ancient times, gaudy with red and blue paint and gilding. I would sit there, day after day, contentedly toggling between the drab present and the richly hued past.

For the letter I wrote that day, I used the "good" onionskin paper, anxiously feeding each sheet between the rollers of a black cast-iron Underwood typewriter that had been salvaged from my grandfather's braid-and-trimmings factory in the city. I used it to type up school reports and term papers and, when nobody was around, short stories and poems and novels that I never showed to anyone—single-spaced pages so shaming to me that even when I hid them in the secret compartment under a drawer in the oak cabinet across from my bed (where I also hid certain other things: a real ancient Egyptian amulet I'd gotten as a bar mitzvah gift from a shrewd godparent, a half-completed sketch I'd made of a boy who sat in front of me in English class), I imagined that they gave off some kind of radiation, a telltale glow that might betray the nature of the feelings I was writing about.

Now I was putting those feelings onto these translucent sheets, which protested with a faint crackle every time I advanced the carriage. When I was finished, I put the letter into the lightweight airmail envelope on which I'd typed the address: Delos, Glen Beach, Camps Bay, Cape 8001 South Africa. I didn't make a copy of what I wrote that day, but I must have confided a fear that my correspondent would reply to my effusions with a form letter, because when her answer came, a few weeks later, typed on a pale-blue aerogram—the first of many that would find me over the next eight years—it began, "I wonder whoever told you I'd send you a 'form letter' if you wrote to me. Are there really writers who do that?"

It was a question I didn't know how to answer, since she was the only writer I'd ever tried to contact. Who else would I write to? In those days, I had two obsessions—ancient Greece and other boys—and she was, I felt, responsible for both.

The author to whom I wrote that day, Mary Renault, had two discrete and enthusiastic audiences; although I didn't know it at the time, they neatly mirrored my twin obsessions. The first, and larger, consisted of admirers of her historical fiction. The second consisted of gay men.

Between 1956 and 1981, Renault published a number of critically acclaimed and best-selling fictional evocations of Greek antiquity. Like the works of Marguerite Yourcenar (*Memoirs of Hadrian*) and Robert Graves (*I, Claudius*), authors to whom she was compared, Renault's novels were often cast as first-person narratives of real or invented figures from myth and history—a technique that efficiently drew modern readers into exotic ancient milieus. The best known and most commercially successful were *The Last of the Wine* (1956), which takes the form of a memoir by a young member of Socrates's circle, through whose eyes we witness the decline of Athens in the last part of the Peloponnesian War; *The King Must Die* (1958), a novelization of the early life of Theseus, the legendary Athenian king who defeated the Minotaur; and a trilogy of novels about Alexander the Great—*Fire from Heaven* (1969), *The Persian Boy* (1972), and *Funeral Games* (1981).

Renault, who was born in London in 1905—she emigrated to South Africa after World War II—had published a number of crisply intelligent contemporary love stories between the late 1930s and the early 1950s; to her meticulously researched re-creations of the past in the later, Greek-themed books she was able to bring the emotional insight and moral seriousness you expect from any good novelist. Many reviewers appreciated the way she reanimated both myth and history by means of ingenious psychological touches. (She once said that the Theseus book didn't jell until she had the idea of making the mythical overachiever diminutive in stature: he's a legendary hero, but also just a boy with something to prove.) Patrick O'Brian, the author of *Master and Commander*, was an admirer; he dedicated the fourth Aubrey-Maturin book to her, with the inscription "An owl to Athens"—the ancient Greek version of "coals to Newcastle." Academic classicists were also enthusiastic. One eminent Oxford don told an eager amateur that to get a sense of what ancient Greece was really like one had only to read Renault— "Renault every time." ("That really bucks me up," she exclaimed, when this remark was reported to her during her final illness.) The combination of historical precision, literary texture, and epic sweep won Renault a large public, particularly in the United States; her books, which have been translated into some twenty languages, have sold millions of copies in English alone.

One of those copies was a thick Eagle Books paperback of *Fire from Heaven* that was stuffed into a bookcase in our downstairs playroom, next to the black leather recliner. I read it when I was twelve, and I was hooked. Alexander the Great was my first serious crush.

It was my father who put the book in my hands. A mathematician who worked for an aerospace corporation, he had been a Latin whiz in high school and sometimes enjoyed thinking of himself as a lapsed classicist. When he gave me the paperback, I looked at the cover and frowned. The illustration, of a blond young Greek holding a shield aloft, wasn't very convincing; I thought he looked a lot like the boy who lived across the street, who had once taken a bunch of us waterskiing for his birthday. My dad said, "I think you should give this a try," averting his eyes slightly, in the way he had. Forty years later, I wonder how much he'd already guessed, and just what he was trying to accomplish.

Fire from Heaven traces Alexander's childhood and youth, ending with his accession to the throne at the age of twenty. I finished it in a couple of days. The next weekend, I went to the public library and checked out the sequel, *The Persian Boy*, which had just been published. It views Alexander's conquest of Persia and his nascent dream of forming a vast Eurasian empire from an unexpected angle: the book is narrated by a historical figure called Bagoas, a beautiful eunuch who had been the pleasure boy of the defeated Persian emperor Darius and who later became Alexander's lover, too. I read *The Persian Boy* in a day and a half. Then I reread both books. Then, after taking my dad's copy of *Fire from Heaven* upstairs and placing it inside the oak cabinet, I got my mother to take me to the B. Dalton bookstore in the Walt Whitman Mall, in Huntington, where, for a dollar ninety-five, I bought my own Bantam paperback of *The Persian Boy*. Its cover featured, in miniature, the haunting image that appeared on the hardback edition from the library: a Michelangelo drawing, in dusty-red chalk, of an epicene Oriental youth in three-quarter profile, wearing a headdress and earrings. Whenever someone mentions "1973," or "junior high school," this small, delicate, reddish face is what I see in my mind's eye.

My fascination with these books had little to do with their canny evocations of Greek history, the persuasiveness of which I couldn't appreciate until years later. An important narrative thread in each novel is a story of awakening young love—homosexual love. In *Fire from Heaven*, Renault sympathetically imagines the awkward beginnings of the relationship between Alexander and Hephaistion, a Macedonian of high birth who, the evidence strongly suggests, was his lover. In *The Persian Boy*, Bagoas, sold into slavery at ten, already world-weary at sixteen, finds himself drawn to Alexander, who has suddenly become his master as well as the master of the known world. In both novels, arduously achieved seductions give the narratives a sexy charge: Renault makes Alexander the aloof object of the longings of the other, more highly sexed characters, Hephaistion and Bagoas, who must figure out how to seduce him.

Most seductive of all to me was the young characters' yearning to love and be loved totally. "Say that you love me best," Bagoas dreams in *The Persian Boy*; "I love you. You mean more to me than anything," Hephaistion exclaims in *Fire from Heaven*; "Do you love me best?" Alexander asks in the latter novel's opening scene. (These expressions of deep emotional need run like a refrain through Renault's contemporary novels as well.) As it happens, "longing"— in Greek, *pothos*—has, since ancient times, been a key word in the Alexander narrative. In a history of Alexander's campaigns written in the second century AD by the historian Arrian, *pothos* recurs to describe the inchoate craving that drove Alexander—far more insistently than any mere lust for conquest or renown. Renault clearly felt the pull of all this longing, too: in addition to the three Alexander novels, she wrote a psychologically oriented biography, *The Nature of Alexander*.

Reading Renault's books, I felt a shock of recognition. The silent watching of other boys, the endless strategizing about how to get their attention, the fantasies of finding a boy to love, and be loved by, "best": all this was agonizingly familiar. I knew something about *pothos* and thought of the humiliating lengths to which it could drive me—the memorizing of certain boys' class schedules or bus routes, the covert shuffling of locker assignments. I was astonished, halfway through *Fire from Heaven*, to find that this kind of thing had always been happening. Until that moment, I had never seen my secret feelings reflected anywhere. Pop music meant nothing to me, since all the songs were about boys wanting girls or girls wanting boys; neither did the YA novels I'd read, for the same reason. Television was a desert. (*Will & Grace* was twenty-five years in the future.) Now, in a novel about people from another place and time, it was as if I had found a picture of myself.

There's a scene in *The Persian Boy* in which Bagoas realizes that he's in love with Alexander; in the slightly high style Renault developed as a vehicle to convey Bagoas's Oriental provenance, she describes this moment as (I now realize) a kind of internal coming out—a moment when, for the first time, a young person understands the nature of his own feelings:

> The living chick in the shell has known no other world. Through the wall comes a whiteness, but he does not know it is light. Yet he taps at the white wall, not knowing why. Lightning strikes his heart; the shell breaks open.

Reading *Fire from Heaven* and *The Persian Boy* was such a moment for me. Lightning had struck, the shell lay broken open. I had begun to understand what I was and what I wanted; and I knew that I wasn't alone.

2. "IT'S NOT WHO YOU ARE, IT'S WHAT YOU DO WITH IT"

Renault was herself a lesbian, the elder daughter of a doctor and a primly conventional housewife. It was not a happy home. Both the contemporary and the Greek novels feature unsettling depictions of bad marriages and, particularly, of nightmarishly passive-aggressive wives and mothers. Renault's mother had clearly hoped for a "nice" girl instead of the unruly tomboy she got, and preferred Mary's younger sister. (Decades after I first encountered Renault's books, it occurred to me that all this could well be the source of the "love me best" motif that recurs so often in her work.) In later life, the author made no bones about having wished she'd been born a boy. Her first-person narrators are always men.

Indeed, it's possible to see in her lifelong fascination with dashing male heroes—Alexander the Great above all—an unusually intense authorial projection. In a letter to a friend, Renault recalled admiring the head of a statue of the Macedonian conqueror, which had given her an "almost physical sense of the presence of Alexander like a blazing sun below the horizon, not yet quenching the stars but already paling them.... His face has haunted me for years." David Sweetman, in his *Mary Renault: A Biography* (1993), referred to *Fire from Heaven* as "a love letter to the boy hero." It's no accident that her very first book, written when she was eight, was a cowboy novel.

From the start, she seems to have been searching for an ideal boy protagonist, a fictional reflection of an inner identity. In all her work, boyishness is an unequivocally positive quality—even, or perhaps especially, in women.

Although Renault was entranced by the Greeks from an early age—by the time she finished high school, she had devoured all of Plato—at St. Hugh's, a women's college at Oxford, she studied English. After taking her degree, she decided against teaching, one conventional route for unmarried, educated middle-class women, and instead trained as a nurse; her first three novels, published during the war years, were written during her off-hours from clinics and hospitals. In 1934, she met Julie Mullard, a vivacious young nurse who would be her life partner for nearly fifty years, until Renault's death. In a 1982 BBC documentary, the two come off as unpretentious and suspicious of self-dramatizing fuss.

The couple stayed in England during the war, but after Renault won the $150,000 MGM prize for *Return to Night*, a 1947 novel about a woman doctor in love with a handsome, troubled, much younger actor, she became financially independent. ("You're the best of all . . . I love you. Better than anyone," the doctor tells her lover in the novel's final pages.) They emigrated to South Africa almost on a whim, after reading travel advertisements following a particularly grim postwar winter in England. It was in Africa that Renault wrote the last of her contemporary novels. Soon after, she turned to the Greeks.

As she later told the story, the decision to start setting her novels in ancient Greece began with a question rooted in her early reading of Plato. During a pleasure cruise that she and Mullard took up the east coast of Africa, Renault recalled, she got to thinking about the Greek historian Xenophon—a stolid, less intellectually adventurous fellow student of Plato's in Socrates's circle, who later became famous for the military exploits he recounted in his *Anabasis*—and began to wonder what the members of that circle might actually have been like, as people. The product of her inspiration was *The Last of the Wine*.

Toward the end of her life, Renault wrote that the novel was "the best thing I had ever done." It's not hard to see why she thought so. A shrewdly unsentimental historical portrait of Athens at the beginning of its moral and political decline, it is enlivened by a love story between two of Socrates's students and deepened by a surprisingly vivid recreation of Socrates's philosophical dialogues as, well—dialogue. There are rich and nuanced cameos of historical characters (not least, "Sokrates" himself) and grand set pieces, all rendered with exacting fidelity to the original sources. Renault fans like to cite her stirring description of the great Athenian fleet's departure for its invasion of Sicily—a misguided campaign that ended in disaster.

And perhaps better than any other of the Greek novels, *The Last of the Wine* demonstrates how Renault used subtle but telling touches to persuade you of the Greekness of her characters and settings. Classical Greek tends to be loaded with participles and relative clauses; Renault reproduced these tics. ("He, hearing that a youth called Philon, with whom he was in love, had been taken sick, went at once to him; meeting, I have been told, not only the slaves but the boy's own sister, running the other way.") She also used "k" rather than the more usual Latin "c" in her transliterations of proper names—Kleopatra, Sokrates—which gives her pages just the right, spiky Greek look. As a result of this minute attention to stylistic detail, the novels can give the impression of having been translated from some lost Greek original.

It's possible to see Renault's shift from the present to the past as motivated by something other than intellectual curiosity. Setting a novel in the fifth century BC in Athens allowed her to write about homosexuality as natural. In *The Last of the Wine*, the narrator muses on the abnormality of Xenophon's apparently exclusive heterosexuality: "Sometimes indeed I asked myself whether he lacked the capacity for loving men at all; but I liked him too well to offend him by such a question."

The hinge that connects her earlier works, love stories in which intelligent people—doctors, nurses, writers, actors—struggle with various emotional conundrums, and the later, historical fiction, in which the fact of love between men, at least, is no conundrum at all, is a novel called *The Charioteer*. Published in 1953, it is set, despite its classical-sounding title, during World War II, and wrestles with the issue of "Greek love." Older gay men can recall that, in the 1950s and 1960s, to walk into a bar with a copy of this book was a way of signaling that you were gay. Today, the book is referred to as a "gay classic."

I finished reading *The Charioteer* for the first time on December 28, 1974, when I was fourteen. I know the date because I recorded it in my diary. The man who placed it in my hands was a music teacher, around my parents' age, whom we knew to be gay: he had a "roommate" with whom he shared a house in a nearby suburb. My mother and father were open-minded, and they saw nothing wrong in letting their four sons hang out with this civilized man, who took us to concerts and restaurants, and who let me sing with the church choir he directed.

What my parents didn't know was that the music teacher sometimes left copies of *Playgirl* lying around when I visited his house. I was both curious and embarrassed. Curious because of course I wanted to look at pictures of naked men, having spent hours pretending to be interested in the *Playboy* centerfolds the kids on my block would steal out of a neighbor's garage; and embarrassed because I perceived that it wasn't appropriate for this middle-aged man to be making porn available to a fourteen-year-old. Curiosity prevailed. Two years had passed since I'd read the Alexander books—paperback copies of which were now stacked, along with Renault's other books, into a neat little ziggurat in my bedroom cabinet—and there were things I wondered about, specific things, that weren't described in Mary Renault's books. I would wait for my teacher to go into another room, to start dinner or put on a recording of Thomas Tallis, and would snatch the magazine up and look at the photographs, which both titillated and repelled me. It was exciting to see the nude male bodies, however patently silly the cowboy boots or policeman hats might be; but it was hard to connect those images to the ideas of love that I had taken away from *Fire from Heaven* and *The Persian Boy.*

I remember the day that this teacher handed me the jacketless hardback of *The Charioteer*, with its dark-gray buckram boards. We were downstairs in his den, and he'd been playing me a rare LP of ancient Greek music. I was feeling very grown-up and was trying to impress him with my passion for all things Greek—a subject that led me, soon enough, to Renault's novels. He said, "If you like Mary

Renault, there's another one I think you'll be interested in." He motioned me to follow him upstairs to his bedroom. He searched in a bookcase for a moment until he found what he was looking for. I took it home and started reading it. At first, the World War II setting disappointed me; I had no interest in modern history.

The title of *The Charioteer* alludes to Renault's beloved Plato. In the dialogue called *Phaedrus*, the soul is likened to a charioteer who must reconcile two horses, one white and well behaved (the rational and moral impulses), the other scruffy and ill-bred (the passions). Renault's book recasts the Platonic conflict as a human drama. Laurie Odell, a wounded young soldier who is recovering at a rural hospital—his given name is Laurence, but Renault pointedly used ambiguous names and nicknames whenever she could—finds himself torn between a secret love for an idealistic Quaker youth, Andrew (who seems drawn to Laurie in an innocent, nonsexual way), and a more complex, physical relationship with a slightly older naval officer, Ralph. The plot pushes Laurie toward a culminating choice between the two men. That choice implies another: whether to remain a loner or to enjoy the solidarity afforded by the local gay set, whose members Renault paints in campy colors: they're named Bunny and Binky and Bim, and wear Cartier bracelets. Laurie, by contrast, is a kind of holy fool: "His loneliness had preserved in him a good deal of inadvertent innocence; there was much of life for which he had no formula."

I, too, was an innocent. By a kind of literary osmosis that is possible only when you're young, I absorbed without question Renault's idealization of severe, undemonstrative men; I wasn't yet able to recognize, in the author's clichés of gay effeminacy, certain unexamined prejudices of her own. Nor did it occur to me to question a central element of the text: the rather dated assumption that it would be better for Andrew never to be made aware of his sexuality. (It "would scatter his whole capital of belief in himself," Laurie thinks. "He must never know.")

Now, of course, I can read the book as it ought to be read, as a coming-of-age story: Laurie abandons the inchoate but potent ideals of adolescence, symbolized by the pure and curiously sexless Andrew, in favor of an adult relationship, one that is physical as well as emotional, with complicated and compromised Ralph, who, like Laurie, bears physical as well as emotional scars. But because I was so young when I read the novel for the first time, I saw the arc from the ideal to the real, from youth to maturity, as a tragic one. To me, Andrew and Ralph were figures in a vast allegorical conflict. Under the white banner of Andrew there was Renault, and true love, and the ancient Greeks, with their lofty rhetoric and marmoreal beauty; under the black banner of Ralph there was *Playgirl*, and sex, and thoughts about naked men—the messy and confusing present.

Although there was much of life for which I had no "formula," either, I thought I knew enough to decide that, if being gay meant marching under the black banner—aligning myself with my music teacher, or the few characters you saw on TV who, you somehow knew, were gay: the limp-wrists and the effete, the spineless Dr. Smith on *Lost in Space* and the queeny Paul Lynde character on *Bewitched*—then it would be better to remain alone.

Unlike Renault's Greek novels, which portrayed desire beneath the scrim of a historical setting, *The Charioteer*, whose characters used words like "queer," allowed for no evasions. "I know what I am,"

I wrote in my diary the day I finished reading it for the first time. By then, I was obsessively in love with a yellow-haired swimmer who put up with my dogged stalking for three years before he turned around one day early in our senior year and, planting himself in front of his locker, which I had gone to some lengths to ensure was next to mine, told me quite calmly that he didn't want to talk to me anymore. And he didn't. But I had never thought of my feelings for him as "gay" or "queer": it simply was how I felt. "I know what I am," I wrote. "Now I must think what to do with it."

"What you are . . . what to do with it" is a paraphrase of a line from *The Charioteer*. Someone utters it during a climactic scene at a birthday party that's being given for a young gay doctor. At the party, the characters start arguing about what would now be called identity politics: about whether the thing that sets you apart ought, in some fundamental way, to define you. As lonely as he is, Laurie finds himself resisting the temptation of joining this group—of "making a career" of his "limitations," as he puts it to himself. It's in response to this debate about identity that Ralph articulates the liberating formula: "It's not what one is, it's what one does with it."

Renault grew up in an era in which it was difficult to think of homosexuality as anything but a limitation; to her credit, she was independent-minded enough to try to resist that prejudice. Later in the book, the doctor rejects the premises that make blackmail possible:

> I don't admit that I'm a social menace. . . . I'm not prepared to accept a standard which puts the whole of my emotional life on the plane of immorality. I've never involved a normal person or a minor or anyone who wasn't in a position to exercise free choice. . . . Criminals

313

are blackmailed. I'm not a criminal. I'm prepared to go to some degree of trouble, if necessary, to make that point.

Renault later wrote that this passage of dialogue "gave the starting-point to my first historical novel"—*The Last of the Wine*, in other words, the novel in which homosexuality wasn't considered a limitation.

When I was fourteen, the characterization of homosexuality as a "limitation" seemed reasonable enough. How could it not be a handicap, when it left you with freakish feelings that no one else you knew seemed to share, apart from middle-aged men who left dirty magazines around for you to pick up, feelings that you knew, more instinctually than consciously, you had to hide? What I did with it, after a few anxious months of trying and failing to picture the vast, nearly featureless landscape of the future, one in which the only road sign now, brand-new, freshly painted, bore the word "queer," was to try to be good—to try to be like Laurie Odell. "I must make some good resolutions for the new year," I had written in my diary. "I will try to do better next year."

The next year, I turned fifteen, and still didn't really know what "better" might mean. Finally, I decided to write to Mary Renault and ask her.

3. "GETTING THE SOIL IN YOUR GARDEN RIGHT"

In my first letter to Renault, I poured out my story—ancient Greece, discovering her books, discovering that I was gay through her books.

In her reply, which arrived in mid-April, just after my sixteenth birthday, she deftly deflected my adolescent effusions while putting to rest my anxieties about form letters:

> Are there really writers who do that? I knew film stars do. You can't blame them, really; apart from the fact that about half the people who write to them must be morons who think they really are Cleopatra or whoever, they get such thousands that if they attempted answering themselves they'd never get to the set.
>
> Writers, though, write to communicate; and when someone to whom one has got through takes the trouble to write and tell one so, it would be pretty ungrateful to respond with something off a duplicator. I think so, anyway.

This, as she had intended, pleased me. And yet of my fervent confessions there was only the briefest acknowledgment, which segued immediately and harmlessly into a charming compliment and a gentle dismissal:

> I am truly glad the books have meant all this to you; especially as you write very good English yourself.... Greek history, or something, has certainly given you a clean and simple style. I wish you the very best of luck with your work, and a happy fulfilled career.

I read and reread the letter. I was a gay adolescent; I was accustomed to overinterpreting. Just as I wasn't what I pretended to be, so everyone and everything else, I thought, concealed secret meanings, communicated in hidden codes. (I had to think a moment before I realized that "a duplicator" was a copying machine.) But there was nothing else, apart from the scrawled signature and, below it, printed instructions about how to fold the aerogram. "Verseël Eers Die Twee Syklappe, Dan Hierdie Een—Seal The Two Side Flaps First, Then This One."

"Meant all this to you"? Maybe I hadn't been clear enough. I sat down and started another letter.

This time, I enclosed a few pages of one of the short stories I had secretly written. Like nearly everything I wrote then, it was about an intense friendship between two fourteen-year-old boys, one of whom was, inevitably, serious and dark-haired and creative, while the other was, just as inevitably, carefree and blond and athletic. This story, which was more ambitious than the others—it had a prologue set in a kind of classical limbo—was, like the others, a slavish pastiche of Renault: her diction, with its faint aura of prewar England ("Phaedo, whatever do you want?"), her settings ("Under the ancient olive tree, the two young men were talking"), her characters ("Speaking of Sokrates, have you seen him lately?"), even her punctuation. (Renault, according to her biographer, had a particular fondness for the semicolon. I still remember the thrill I felt when one of my college professors wrote, in the margin of an undergraduate essay, "You have semicolonitis!") I was convinced that this lofty effort would persuade her that I would be a worthy correspondent. Feeling very much the author, I was emboldened to ask her whether she, too, had a kind of compulsion to write—although I secretly doubted whether hers had the same source as mine. For me, writing was a kind of sympathetic magic, a way of conjuring the swimmer boy and keeping him close.

She wrote back within a couple of weeks, at the end of April. I know she must have read the story because of her tactful allusion to it:

Your nice letter came this morning. Something tells me you are going to have a future as a writer. Keep at it; very few people get published at 16 or even 20, but don't worry.... There is only one way to learn to write and that is by reading. Don't read for duty, try all the good stuff though, sample it, then devour what stimulates and enriches you. This will seep in to your own work, which may be derivative at first but this does not matter. Your own style will develop later.

Now that I am a writer who has received mail from young readers, I appreciate the patience and gentleness of this paragraph. I doubt that, at the time, I registered the implications of "which may be derivative"; it was enough that she thought I had a future as a writer. This show of confidence dulled the disappointing force of her equally graceful but firm leave-taking:

Yes, you are right, I do have a compulsion to write and am very frustrated and unhappy if I am kept from doing it.... And this is the reason I can't go on writing to you. Not that it is too much trouble; writing a book is very much more trouble; but if I wrote more than one thank-you letter to all the people who are kind enough to write to me, I would never write another novel again. Or I would have to take to those "form letters"—rather than which I wouldn't answer at all.

So this really is goodbye—but the very best of luck to you all the same.

This time, I felt no great disappointment. Over the next months, as my stalking of the blond swimmer became more abject, as more and more meals ended with me bursting into tears and locking myself in my room as my parents clumped helplessly down the hall-way after me, the sentence "Something tells me you are going to have a future as a writer" served as a charm. I knew I had no right to expect anything else from her.

Then, that December, she sent me a Christmas card.

I will never know why she changed her mind and wrote again, eight months after she said that she couldn't go on corresponding; at the time, I was so excited by her overture that I didn't dare ask. But I can speculate now. When I read Sweetman's biography, ten years after Renault's death, I learned that the mid-1970s had been a particularly trying period for her. In the autumn of 1974, she fell and injured her leg, necessitating an irritatingly lengthy recovery. Soon afterward, Mullard, who was high-strung, suffered a minor breakdown and had to be briefly institutionalized. At just about the time that Renault and I exchanged our first letters, she had decided to put her affairs in order and make provisions for her estate. Perhaps she thought that a letter from an American teenager every now and then might provide some distraction, despite (or perhaps because of) the adolescent turmoil it contained.

Something else has occurred to me. Like all writers, Renault spent much of her time alone; a good many of her friends, as I also learned later, were gay men, often ballet dancers and actors and theater people. What she did not have in her life, as far as I know, was children—or students. I wonder whether she wished for some. (In *The Charioteer*, Laurie is described as someone who "usually got on with strong-minded old maids"; was that how she saw herself?) Shrewdly drawn scenes of apprenticeships, of actors or princes or poets learning their craft, figure in a number of the novels. In *The Last of the Wine*, Sokrates, faced with an earnest, if pretentious, student, resorts to "teasing him out of his pomposities"—as canny a characterization of what it's like to teach freshmen as any I know of.

Renault's special feeling for the relationship between a teacher and a student imbues the poignant finale of *The Mask of Apollo*, her 1966 novel about an Athenian actor who gets mixed up in Plato's disastrous scheme, in the 360s BC, to turn a corrupt Sicilian tyrant into a philosopher-king. Years after the fiasco, the actor meets the teenaged Alexander, already charismatic and alive with curiosity about the world, and realizes, wrenchingly, that this youth would have been the ideal student for Plato, now dead:

> All tragedies deal with fated meetings; how else could there be a play? Fate deals its stroke; sorrow is purged, or turned to rejoicing; there is death, or triumph; there has been a meeting, and a change. No one will ever make a tragedy—and that is as well, for one could not bear it—whose grief is that the principals never met.

I wonder whether something like this was in Mary Renault's mind that day in December when she decided to write back to me after all. Maybe she liked the thought of having a student—someone to tease out of his pomposities. Maybe, with all that grief around her just then, she thought she could at least avoid the grief that comes of never making contact.

We corresponded for the next eight years. I always addressed her as "Miss Renault" or "Mary Renault"; I still can't think of her as "Mary." She only ever addressed me as "Daniel Mendelsohn" and, once I was

in college, "Mr. Mendelsohn." During that time, I finished high
school, went to college, graduated, got my first job. She published
her biography of Alexander and two more novels. We didn't write
often—a few exchanges a year—but knowing that she was out there,
interested in my progress, was like a secret talisman.

During the first few years, when I was still in high school, I tried
not to be too familiar or too earnest—the mistake that I had made
in my first couple of letters. (Recalling a lesbian novel she disliked,
Renault wrote of its "impermissible allowance of self-pity" and "earnest humourlessness.") Instead, I would tell her about what I was
reading, some of which, of course, was chosen with an eye to pleasing
her. "I am delighted you've been reading the Phaedrus," she wrote
to me early in 1978, when I was a senior in high school. "It's good
furniture for any mind." Sometimes she would make suggestions.
"Have you ever tried Malory's Morte Darthur? It is very beautiful.
On no account read a version pulped down into modern English,
it ruins the flavour." A year earlier, I and the other eleventh graders
had been made to memorize the opening lines of *The Canterbury
Tales* in the original Middle English, an exercise that we both feared
and derided; reading her letter, I began to wonder, as I hadn't done
before, what it might mean for language to have "flavour."

Occasionally there would be an item about her or one of her
books in the news; it gave me a thrilling sense of privilege to be able
to write to the author herself to learn more. When I was a junior in
high school, the teacher who had given me *The Charioteer* showed
me an issue of a magazine called *After Dark*, which I only later realized was a gay magazine. It featured an ambitious photo spread about
the upcoming movie adaptation of *The Persian Boy*, and referred to
young dancers and actors who were hoping to be cast as Bagoas.

Excited, I wrote to Renault asking for details. "I certainly wish they had not raised the hopes of so many actors in this way," she replied, explaining that the movie rights hadn't even been sold yet, "and I wish too that so many actors didn't imagine that the book author has any say in the casting! They could as fruitfully approach the office cleaner." (Sweetman, in his biography, relates how a young actor had written to her, offering to have "the operation" if it meant getting the part. "That," she wrote back to him, "would be gelding the lily.")

I continued to send her the stories I was writing. As I reached the end of high school, these were getting darker: the beginning of my senior year, in the fall of 1977, had been scarred by the confrontation with the blond swimmer. Later that day, I ran out of my house and walked around the blandly identical neighborhoods for hours. At one point, I climbed to the top of an overpass and looked down—not serious, but serious enough. Then I burst out laughing, amused by my own theatrics; it was a beautiful autumn afternoon, and in a year I'd be in college, where I'd be able to study Greek and Latin and find new, like-minded friends; where, I secretly hoped, there might be a Laurie Odell for me. I wrote about this incident to Mary Renault, aware, as I did so, of wanting her to perceive that I was learning from her—that I wasn't giving in to adolescent foolishness. I was, after all, someone who had a future as a writer.

She read these later stories, too. By this point, one (or sometimes both) of the two inseparable friends who were always at the center of my fiction, the brunet and the blond, the writer and the athlete, would die of a rare disease, or meet with a terrible accident. As she had done before, and would do again, Renault ignored the impermissible self-pity and the earnest humorlessness, and simply encouraged me:

Just carry on enjoying yourself with writing. Love what you are doing and do it as well as you can, and the tree will grow. Nobody ever did their best work at 17 except people who died at 18! You are now just getting the soil in your garden right—except that unlike a garden, even at this stage your work is producing flowers, very likely not yet ready for the flower-show, but giving you a lot of joy.

The stories did not, in fact, give me much joy. But knowing that she had read them did.

4. "WAS IT SOMEONE YOU KNEW?"

I wrote to Renault less frequently once I went off to the University of Virginia. (The swimmer had grown up in Virginia; I thought there might be someone else like him there.) I started learning Greek during my first semester, and found a kind of happiness in grammar, which insisted on a level of precision not available in English: the nouns, often familiar-looking (*anthrôpos, historia, klimax*), each one of which has five different forms, depending on how it's used in a sentence; the vast spiderweb of the verb system. For me, as for many beginning classics students, learning Greek and Latin unlocked the secrets of my own language. With delight I learned that "ephebe" consists of *epi*, "upon," and *hēbē*, "youth": an ephebe is a male at the acme of his youth. And you learn, too, to sniff out a fake. The word "homosexual," for instance, is a solecism, a hybrid of Greek (*homos*, "alike") and Latin (*sexualis*, "sexual"). A *homo*- word with a purer pedigree, as I learned when I started reading Homer in Greek, was *homophrosyne*, "like-mindedness," which is the word Odysseus uses in the *Odyssey* to describe the ideal union of two spouses—the kind of union that he's trying to return home to.

My own quest for *homophrosyne* was proving unsuccessful. No Laurie Odell had materialized. How did you make contact? There was, I knew, a gay student union that met regularly in one of the many red-brick-and-white-stucco neoclassical buildings on campus, undistinguished knockoffs of Jeffersonian originals. But I was dismayed to see that the building was right in the middle of the campus; I was terrified that someone I knew would see me going in. So I would walk past the posters for the meetings, my eyes briefly alighting, as tentative as a fly on a peach, on the word "gay," as I made my way each morning to Greek class, during my first year, or, the next year, to Greek 201 ("Plato's 'Apology'"), or, the year after, to the course in which, for the first time, I read Sophocles in Greek. The text, I remember, was *Philoctetes*, a play about a crippled hero who has been abandoned on a desert island for so long that it's no longer clear whether he can rejoin society.

Beneath my fear of being found out, a larger anxiety lurked. I was starting to worry that, even if I were to "make contact," the ideal I'd found in *The Charioteer* didn't exist. There was a boy in one of my English classes, a tall, dark-haired prep with a beaked nose and a Tidewater accent, who, I now realize, was trying to make contact with *me*. He'd stop me after lectures and ask if he could borrow my notes; once, after mentioning that he was in one of the choral groups, he called to invite me to come to his dorm room to listen to his new LP of Purcell's "Come, Ye Sons of Art." But I never called him back. After a while, he started asking some other kid for notes at the end of lectures.

I studied hard and absorbed my grammars and didn't confide any of this to Mary Renault. She had brought me to the Greeks, and had shown me what I was, and it was somehow shaming to let on that I was having a hard time finding anyone like the characters in her novels. Somewhere in *The Persian Boy*, when the young Bagoas is being schooled at Susa in the arts of the courtesan, the kindly master who is preparing him for service to the king reminds him of a crucial rule of life at court: "Never be importunate, never, never." I was no longer sixteen, and I was determined never to importune her.

She must have noticed, at any rate, that I was no longer enclosing short stories with my letters. That's because I wasn't writing anymore. How silly those stories had been! I was twenty-one; I was going to be a scholar, not a writer. I was comforted by the incantatory rhythms of grammatical paradigms; by syntax, which was soothingly indifferent to emotion. During my senior year, *Funeral Games* was published. I went to the local bookstore every day to see if it had come in yet and, when it did, bought it and read it right away. The novel begins as Alexander is dying and proceeds to describe in grimly unsentimental detail the story of the internecine power struggles that resulted from his premature death. I was struck by the starkness of the narrative. Gone were the exalted adolescent yearnings of *Fire from Heaven*, gone the plush erotic Orientalisms of *The Persian Boy*. It was as if all feeling had been stripped away. I read it with a kind of sour enjoyment; it matched my mood. I wrote her to tell her how much I'd liked it. "Your letter gave me very great pleasure," she began her reply:

Besides its generous appreciation of what the book is about, this is actually the first letter about it from an ordinary reader—meaning of course one who had no professional or personal reason to read the book. I am so glad that you liked it.

I knew what she meant, but I was a little hurt. I, at any rate, thought that I had a "personal" reason to read it.

My letters to Renault were even less frequent after I graduated from college. I was too embarrassed. For one thing, I had decided not to go on to do a graduate degree in classics, which she had once urged me to do, on the ground that it was always good to have "solid" knowledge of a subject, even if one wanted to be a writer rather than an academic. I wrote that I was forgoing graduate school because I "hoped to gather knowledge of the world"—probably because I had read somewhere that she had become a nurse in order to gain real-life experience to write about.

I moved to New York City and found a job as an assistant to a small-time opera impresario whose obscene tirades against disloyal conductors and greedy sopranos would seep, like his cigar smoke, beneath the smoked-glass door of his inner office in the tiny "suite" he rented, in the Steinway Building, on West Fifty-seventh Street, into the area where I was stationed. Sitting at my desk while he shrieked into the phone, I was too timid even to quit. But in my letters to Renault I swaggered and lied and pretended to be using my classical learning to gain insight into the real world. In the spring of 1983, I wrote her a letter that I ostentatiously typed on our company stationery (*DANIEL MENDELSOHN, ASSOCIATE*): "I've found that reading Plato while one isn't actually studying intensively gives one an entirely new perspective—like being a Christian on weekdays." (That last phrase is an almost verbatim citation from *The Charioteer*.) I went on grandiosely, "After all, it wasn't meant to be read and discussed at cocktail parties, but lived, in a way; or so I think."

The fact is that I wasn't spending much time on Plato. Mostly, I was going out to bars: Boy Bar, down on St. Marks Place, where young men, self-consciously "over" the disco aesthetic just then, lounged in khaki shorts and Top-Siders and played pool at a table under a giant stuffed fish; the Pyramid, where you'd go afterward, once your standards had started to erode; the Works, on the Upper West Side, with its aloof actor-waiters in their too carefully pressed polo shirts, lined up neatly against the black walls like empty bottles; bars that didn't last long enough for me to remember their names, while I tried, as I continued to put it to myself, to "make contact."

Sex rarely appears in Renault's books; it's either omitted altogether or suggested with such elegant circumlocution that, when I first read them, I sometimes didn't realize that certain passages were sex scenes. This was partly because of the author's own idealized exaltation of platonic love, and partly for reasons that she identified as writerly ones. "If characters have come to life," she once wrote, "one should know how they will make love; if not it doesn't matter. Inch-by-inch physical descriptions are the ketchup of the literary cuisine, only required by the insipid dish or by the diner without a palate." As I reread her books in high school, I looked in vain for signs of what lovemaking might actually be like; what (for instance) "a trick I learned at Susa" (as Bagoas recalls of an attempt to liven things up in bed with the Persian emperor) might be, or what "the sufficient evidence of his senses" (the hint that Laurie and Ralph have finally slept together, in *The Charioteer*) might allude to. But in college I had finally, if fleetingly, discovered sex, and in New York it was everywhere, if you wanted it. It seemed perfectly reasonable to have sex if you couldn't find love. Occasionally, I'd bring someone home, or go to his place, and often it would be pleasurable and sometimes it would be someone I liked. But always in the back of my mind was a certain image of what I wanted, and since nobody I met quite matched it, I held back. I had come to feel that getting involved with real people was, somehow, a betrayal.

Sometimes I comforted myself with this thought: hadn't Laurie Odell also been a loner? The first summer I lived in New York, a friend told me about a gay therapist who "did group" on the East Side and suggested that I join; it was a great place to meet nice guys, he said. I went for about five sessions. Some of the men were in relationships with each other: one couple consisted of a tall, extraordinarily handsome young man of about my age and his "lover," a short, quite ugly man in his forties with a gigantic nose. I thought it surprising that they would be together. Never having had a lover, and embarrassed by my lack of experience and, even more, by the secret ideal that was keeping me from experience, I rarely said anything during the sessions. Finally, one day, the others turned to me all at once and asked me to talk about myself. At some point, inevitably, I mentioned the Mary Renault books and what their vision of love meant to me. "Oh, *Mary*," the big-nosed lover of the beautiful ephebe said, and only after a moment did I realize that he was not referring to the author but addressing me, "join the *real* world!" I never went back to "group." I recorded this incident in my journal. The entry ends with the sentence "I ought to write Mary Renault soon." But I didn't.

In April 1983, I wrote my last letter to her. In it, I lied and concealed and sprinkled the pages with allusions to Plato. I enclosed, as I sometimes liked to do, a cartoon from *The New Yorker* having to do with the ancient world. In it, a corpulent king is getting the lowdown from his vizier on a visiting delegation: "The Athenians are here, Sire, with an offer to back us with ships, money, arms, and men—and, of course, their usual lectures about democracy." In early May, she replied. She began by thanking me for the cartoon. ("I don't know if it would have amused Thukydides; he didn't amuse easily, he had seen it all; but I bet it would have given a good laugh to Philip of Macedon, when that arch democrat Demosthenes made a pact with the Great King of Persia.") Then she went on to tease me. "I'm glad you're enjoying Plato. Of course he meant his ideas to be lived. . . . But he certainly felt happy at having them discussed at drinking parties. Look at the Symposium!" I was too mortified to reply. I thought she must be appalled by me.

That summer, I decided that I wasn't cut out for "the real world," and began to make plans to apply to graduate school in classics. Early in September 1983, I walked out of the Steinway Building just as a handsome man, blond and square-jawed, pedaled past on a bike; he grinned and rang his little bell at me. We dated for a while, but as before, I wasn't quite sure what to *do*, now that I had a "relationship." Later that month, I wrote in my journal, worrying that, whereas the characters in books seemed to have so much forward momentum, I didn't. I still wasn't sure how you got to be the author of your own life. The journal ends there. The only additional item is a clipping from *The New York Times*, dated Wednesday, December 14, 1983.

I had been thinking about sending Renault a Christmas card but hadn't got around to doing it. Then, that Wednesday morning,

I walked into the Steinway Building, went through the lobby past the display of grand pianos, got into the elevator, scanned the front page of the *Times*, and suddenly said, loudly, "Oh, *no!*" I slumped against the back of the elevator and started crying. The only other person in the elevator was old Mr. Koretz, the Holocaust survivor who rented the office next to ours.

"What happened?" he asked, stooping a little and bringing his large face close to mine, his eyes gigantically magnified by his glasses. He was tall, often wore a raincoat, and his slightly phlegmy Middle European consonants were comforting. "Did someone die?"

I shoved the *Times* in his direction and pointed. Down below the fold, next to the contents, under the heading "Inside," was the item that had caught my eye: "Mary Renault Dies. The historical novelist Mary Renault, who based many of her best-selling books on the legends of ancient Greece, died in Cape Town. Page B5."

Mr. Koretz gave me a noncommittal look. "It was someone you knew?"

"Yes." I nodded; then I shook my head. "No." He gave me a look. "It's hard to explain," I said.

After work, I hurried home to write a condolence letter to a person whose existence I couldn't know of until I turned to page B5 and saw there, at last, the discreet proof of a suspicion I had long entertained but never dared ask about ("the writer's companion of the last 50 years, Julie Mullard"). "Dear Miss Mullard," I began; and then, not for the first time, poured out my heart to a stranger in South Africa.

A month later, a card arrived. On the front, the words "*IN MEMO-RIAM MARY RENAULT* 1905–1983" were printed in black. To my surprise, the handwritten note inside suggested that this companion knew who I was. ("She was never aware of any generation gap. People were people to her.") Had Mary Renault discussed me with her companion? What else had they talked about? At that moment, I wasn't so much afraid that my confidences had been shared as I was startled to realize that Renault had existed for other people: that she wasn't only "Mary Renault," who wrote novels and sometimes wrote to me, but was also "Mary," which was how Mullard kept referring to her, a woman who might have casually discussed this and that with her companion—for instance, the letters she had been receiving over the past decade from a young American—the way my parents discussed this and that: work, *New Yorker* cartoons, things that had come in the mail.

I put Mullard's card in a large manila envelope that, years earlier, my mother had provided for this correspondence, labeling it, as she liked to do when she organized my things, with my initials, in blue Magic Marker. ("Mary Renault: DA.") I'm pretty sure that, as I did so, I told myself that this was the last letter I'd ever be receiving from Camps Bay, Cape Town, South Africa.

For the next twenty-five years, this was true. Then, one morning in December 2008, the letters started coming again.

5. "THE AMERICAN BOY"

It was because of a review of a book of mine, a collection that contained an essay I'd written about Oliver Stone's film *Alexander*. I had ended the piece by mentioning how Renault's Alexander novels had inspired me to become a classicist and, eventually, a writer. The reviewer mentioned the Renault connection. Three weeks later, a handwritten letter with colorful South African stamps was forwarded to me. "Dear Daniel Mendelsohn," it began, and went on:

> GW Bowersock's NYRB review of your How Beautiful … reveals that the Daniel Mendelsohn of whom I am an avid reader is no other than "the American boy" of whom Mary Renault used to speak with enjoyment many years ago!

My correspondent identified herself as Nancy Gordon. The handwriting was firm and clear, although she was quite elderly. ("I am 87. Old. Old. Old.") She told me that her late husband, Gerald, a lawyer and writer, had been a member of PEN South Africa when Mary was president, and that the two couples—Nancy and Gerald and Mary and Julie—had spent a good deal of time together. Nancy was the sole survivor of the little group. "Mary, Julie and Gerald are all gone, but I feel somehow called," she wrote, "as humble messenger from Mary, to salute you. She would have been so chuffed!" At the end of the letter were her signature and e-mail address.

Then, in a P.S., she asked, "Do you still feel for Mary?"

It was a complicated question. Of course I felt for "Mary." In every sense, she has accompanied me through my life. The ziggurat of books has been disassembled and reconstituted in various apartments and graduate student lodgings over the years, but it is still there. The Eagle Books *Fire from Heaven* and the Bantam *Persian Boy* are now so fragile, the pages so brown and brittle with age, the covers so mummified in Scotch tape that long ago lost its adhesive, that you can't really read them. They're sitting on a shelf in my bedroom, as wizened and unrecognizable as relics.

And yet, as the years passed, I wondered whether I would have been recognizable to her. When Sweetman's biography of Renault came out, I read it right away; in one passage he writes about Renault's distaste for "the worst aspects of the [gay] sub-culture... the constant search for sexual gratification without affection, the impermanence of most relationships." Well. I'd never found a Laurie; although I'd been with some good men, the one-night stands vastly outnumbered the affectionate encounters and long-term relationships. In graduate school, I had been a leader of the Gay Alliance and been involved in a good deal of campus activism. I debated, as I did so, whether this constituted "making a career of one's limitations," and decided that it didn't.

So yes: I still felt for Mary. But what had she felt for *me*? I knew, of course, that she had read my letters carefully—and not only because of her thoughtful replies to them. In 1978, when I was in my first year at Virginia, her penultimate novel, *The Praise Singer*, about the great lyric poet Simonides, was published. On page 44 there's a scene in which Simonides, who was famously ugly, recalls how, as a youth, he had resolved to kill himself: having climbed to the parapet of a temple, he looks up at the bright sky and realizes he's being foolish. In real life, he went on to have a happy and fulfilled career. She had indeed paid attention.

But had there been anything else? Until I got Nancy's letter, I thought I would never know. This is why I said "yes" when, after a year of writing to Nancy—a correspondence that has grown far larger, by now, than the one I shared with Renault—she invited me to come to Cape Town, to see Delos, the bungalow down by Camps Bay, the beach where Renault and Mullard had lived, where Renault had received my letters and written hers to me, and to meet some of Renault's friends, who had also wondered what had become of "the American boy."

We spent four days in Cape Town. "We," because I took my father: I owed him this. We stayed in a hotel overlooking Camps Bay. It was odd, as we drove there from the airport, to see the words Camps Bay on road signs. I'd been writing the name for years and had never thought of it as a real place.

The climax of our visit was a dinner party at which Nancy Gordon gathered a few of Mary Renault's old friends. Nancy is small and vivid; she greeted me and my father wearing a floor-length, brightly patterned cotton dress, with horn and wooden bangles going up both arms. In the distance, we could see Table Mountain's strange flat top, the mist pouring over it like dry ice off of a stage. Before the others arrived, she pointed to a chair in the corner of her living room: "Mary used to like to sit in that chair. She'd sometimes come over to our place for a drink looking out at the beach and I remember she would suddenly get up and say, 'I must go write to my American boy.'"

My American boy. When we had checked into our hotel, we found an envelope from Nancy containing a few handwritten sheets labeled "Remembering Her." One of the memories she'd jotted down was of the family who lived in the bungalow next to Renault's, "with lots of kids, all very blond." The boys, Nancy wrote, had all been excellent surfers, and Mary had loved watching them. Now, as we stood there in Nancy's living room next to the chair, looking out the large plate-glass windows at the surf where the neighbor boys had played, I thought: Mary Renault had turned away from the blond boys to write to me.

The other friends arrived. To each man or couple, Nancy would exclaim that I was "the American boy" to whom Mary used to write, all those years ago. Over dinner, they all traded what were, clearly, favorite anecdotes. There were stories about Mary and her love of sports cars, stories about how Mary had found out that her gardener was growing marijuana and spent the night flushing it down the toilet, the story of how Mary and Julie insisted that the fig leaf on a bronze statue of Mercury they'd bought be replaced by an anatomically correct male member. "As nurses," Renault had told the workman, "we *certainly* know what penises look like." At one point, I mentioned that she had made me read Malory's *Le Morte D'Arthur*, and everyone laughed. "She made *everyone* read Malory," someone cried out. "All of us had to!"

I sat and listened, waiting to hear something that would give me a clue to what she'd have felt about me and my writing. What would she have made of my first book, with its matter-of-fact descriptions of the way that I and so many of the gay men I know have lived—the endless talk of wanting boyfriends, of finding a "real" relationship, and the late nights spent hooking up online? At some point, I asked Owen Murray—a former ballet dancer to whom Renault, he told me with a sly grin, had once said, "I wish I'd been born with your body and face"—whether she knew about what really went on between men. I had visited the house he shares with his partner, which is filled with small mementos of Renault: Venetian glass paperweights that had sat on her desk and windowsill, the statue with its add-on penis. Taped to the refrigerator were photographs of Murray, shirtless, still muscular, smiling broadly, at gay parades, on gay cruises, at gay clubs; I figured that he would know what I meant when I said "what really went on between men." But it was hard for me to fathom his response. "Mary wanted her men friends to live up to the Greek ideal," he said. I was a classicist, and I knew that the ideal of "Greek love" was itself a fantasy of Victorian "inverts" who, as Renault had done, projected their *pothos* for an accepting society onto the distant past. The "Greek ideal": what could this mean in real life? When I pressed Murray on this point, he said, "She liked her friends to be coupled." I shut up and listened to the stories.

Toward the end of the evening, the conversation turned to the many correspondents Renault had had. "People used to write her *all* the time," Owen said. "Married men who were secretly gay, closeted men—there were *thousands* of letters when she died." Someone else mentioned a prominent American politician who had come out to Renault in a letter, as I had done all those years ago; the others nodded knowingly, enjoying the expression on my face when I heard the famous name. I asked where all these letters were and what had become of them. Owen said that they had been destroyed after Mary's death, in part to protect the men who had written them. I thought of my onionskin pages, blackening and curling in the flames.

During the next couple of days, I visited some of the men who had been at Nancy's dinner. Each showed me some precious relic, and each offered me a keepsake. Owen gave me an address book, with alphabetical tabs, in which Renault had scrawled notes on various works in progress. (Under "I" there's a page on which she wrote the word "Ideas," and then a few lines with a sketch for a scene that ended up in *The Mask of Apollo*.) There were some copies of manuscripts ("Notes on Oedipus," "Notes on the King Must Die"), given to me by Roy Sargeant, a theater director who was making plans to stage a play he'd commissioned, in which the shades of Renault and Alexander meet in the Underworld. Nancy gave me the dainty porcelain cup Renault drank from as she worked.

I took them all. Then my father and I flew home. At some point, I turned to him and shared a thought I often have as I sit awake on a long-haul flight: I think, I told him, about the bags of mail in the cargo hold below, what fervor they contain, what lives they might alter.

Eventually, my father fell asleep. I remained awake, replaying in my mind the events and conversations of the previous few days. In particular, I was thinking of something that Owen had said at Nancy's house. Although I had been enjoying the anecdotes and reminiscences, I was feeling unsatisfied; there was no way of knowing, finally, what Mary Renault would have thought of the man that the American boy had become. Then, toward the end of the evening— during the conversation about all the people who wrote letters to Mary Renault—Owen, who'd been watching me react to the surfeit of new personal details about her, spoke up. He talked slowly and loudly, as if addressing the others, but I knew that he was talking to me. "Mary used to say to people who wrote wanting to know her that they should just read her *books*." He paused and then gave me the tiniest smile. "But she understood why they wrote her personal letters."

At that moment, sitting at a table eight thousand miles from home, I saw that I'd come to South Africa chasing a chimera. I had already found the Mary Renault I needed, years earlier. I thought again of the yellowing books on my shelf; I thought, too, of the relationships that had never quite worked out, edged aside by a phantom out of a novel. She had shown me a picture of what I was, when I needed to see it, and had given me a myth that justified my fears and limitations. The writers we absorb when we're young bind us to them, sometimes lightly, sometimes with iron. In time, the bonds fall away, but if you look very closely you can sometimes make out the pale white groove of a faded scar, or the telltale chalky red of old rust.

That was last year. As I write this, I'm sitting in my office. Hanging on the wall opposite my desk is a signed photograph of Mary Renault. When Nancy Gordon first wrote to me, she mentioned that she had it, and that she had been wondering to whom she might give it. ("I can't give it to just anyone.") So she sent it to me, and I framed it. It's clearly from the same sitting as the one that appeared on Renault's dust jackets, the one in which she's crinkling her eyes against the sun. On the bottom she had scrawled, "With love from Mary"; but there's nothing at the top, no dedication. I suppose it was for Nancy and Gerald. Then again, when you're a writer, you never know who will end up reading you, or how. I never pretend, when visitors ask me about it, that it was meant for me. But she is up there, watching me as I write.

—*The New Yorker*, January 7, 2013

Stopping in Vilna

"BUT IT'S SO *BEAUTIFUL*," people always say to me about Vilnius, when I tell them about a dreadful moment I had in that city some fifteen years ago. It was a period during which I traveled a great deal throughout Central and Eastern Europe—Poland, Lithuania, Latvia, Ukraine, Belarus—researching a book that had to do with the Holocaust. My visits to local and regional archives, my tours of mass graves and abandoned shtetls would, I hoped, shed light on the lives and fates of certain relatives of mine: my mother's uncle and aunt and cousins, Jews living in Eastern Poland who had perished during the war.

You see a great many awful things when you make this kind of journey; indeed, one strange danger of traveling as I traveled is that you can become inured to the horrors of which the plaques and monuments, the roofless synagogues and the strange patches of discolored earth you occasionally see in isolated meadows are the only physical traces now. I saw all those things during my travels, and thought I'd gotten used to it until my moment in Vilnius, which for some reason was the worst: the moment when, finally, I thought I couldn't go on, couldn't look at one more (as the French writer Stendhal once called it, reminiscing about a bad moment of his own in Lithuania, two centuries before mine) "hideous spectacle of pitilessness and horrible suffering." During his visit, there was, too, a small, unexpected moment of grace: something else, as it happened, that I owe to Stendhal.

Vilnius *is* beautiful. If you drive north from Ukraine into Lithuania en route to Vilna (as we still call it in my family), as I did in the summer of 2003, it's like coming home to Europe. The strange, vaguely Oriental tang, bitter as the skin of an orange, which you can never quite shake in Ukraine even if you're traveling in the western, "Polish" part—the houri curve of an onion dome on a church, the high Tatar cheekbone or slant of the eye in the blond boy or girl who waits on you at a restaurant where a portrait of Franz Joseph hangs on a wall—all that strangeness gradually disappears as you cross the border into Lithuania. Far behind you is Lviv, the largest city in western Ukraine, a city renowned for its churches, only a few of which are familiar to American eyes: Roman Catholic, to be sure, but also Russian Orthodox, Greek Catholic, Greek Orthodox, Uniote, Armenian Catholic *and* Armenian Orthodox, they are all here. This, after all, is Lviv, once Lwów, once Lemberg: a former Habsburg city, the capital of a province of a multinational empire, its places of worship, if not its population, still multicultural after all these decades.

But Vilna is clearly, triumphantly Catholic: an exuberant, pastel-colored Counter-Reformation city whose churches, smooth and lustrous as the shell of an egg, come in the colors of Ladurée macarons: violet, peach, canary yellow, an aloof rose pink, the improbably sexy pistachio green. That pink; that green. *What a lovely culture*, I thought when I first arrived there, that June 2003. How appealing the civilization that paints its houses and churches the colors of candy.

Strictly speaking, there was no reason for me to be in Vilna. Our people were *Galizianers*, Jews who inhabited what is now south-eastern Poland and western Ukraine. No one in my family had ever lived in this northern, *Litvak* city, a Jewish metropolis so renowned in its time that Jews of my grandfather's generation called it *the Jerusalem of the North*: so great was the fame of its rabbis, so immense the learning of its scholars, so numerous its synagogues and houses of study—the erudition and the buildings both being the hallmark of a civilization at its acme. But for me there was no family connection to this distinguished place. I went mostly because the close friends who were accompanying me on my travels were eager to see it: Froma was the granddaughter of two Vilna rabbis and was curious to see the little town they had come from. *Why not?*, I joked as we maneuvered our rented car along the highway north, *we're in the neighborhood.*

Perhaps it was this very detachment from the place and its history that made me able to see its story so clearly. This kind of emotional distance is something Stendhal admired. In his works he refers to it by its Italian name, *disinvoltura*—"not being involved." In a passage in *Rome, Naples and Florence*, for instance, Stendhal allows himself to savor the Romans' deployment of *disinvoltura* in their social lives; in so doing he suggests that it is a quality as useful to writers as it is to young aristocrats. A small degree of *disinvoltura*, a slight sense of relief at being in a place that had nothing to do with the story I was trying to unravel, enabled me, paradoxically, to abandon the intensely narrow focus of my own search and to feel, once more—as most people do, when they think of what happened in the East between 1941 and 1944—the abstract, sheer size of it, the pitilessness and the horrible suffering. In Vilna, after three years of traveling in search of my family's story, three years of interviewing people about the worst imaginable things, I couldn't take it anymore.

Two things broke me.

First there were the forests of Ponar. *Ponari*, some people call it. Here, before the war began, the government had been digging a series of vast pits in which to store natural gas. To this use they had never been put; instead, a hundred thousand dead Jews went into them. The pits, with their unnatural contents, are still there. *Before the war*, a tour guide we later met told us, *people used to picnic in those fields. Now the people are under the fields.*

We visited Ponar, my friends and I. Each pit now has its own monument. After two pits I said, *I can't do this anymore, it's enough.* While Froma and her husband, George, wandered deeper into the maze of pits with their steles and their plaques, I sat at the base of a monument close to the entrance of the whole site, refusing even to follow them with my eyes. After half an hour, they returned. *I said Kaddish*, George said, and then we drove back to our hotel.

That was the first thing: the first time, during my months of travels, that I had balked.

And then, back inside the city, that beautiful city with its Ladurée colors, there was the second thing: our visit, one afternoon before we left, to the Museum of Jewish Culture. Or as I later came to think of it, the non-Museum of Jewish Culture. For as we found out when we went inside the shabby little building, this museum of the Jerusalem of the North had almost nothing to display: no proof that here, once, there had been a civilization worth preserving. On the shelves there were a few Soviet-era trinkets: ceramic menorahs, that kind of thing. On the walls were some blurry photographs. That was it. It occurred to me that this devastating absence spoke more eloquently than a hundred exhibitions at a dozen Shoah museums could have done. We practically ran out of the building.

That was the second thing. As we returned to the hotel I said to myself, I've had enough. I was finished.

Stendhal didn't like Vilna, either.

In Book 5 of his *History of Painting in Italy*, the author describes Vilna as the site of his own personal trauma. His bad moment occurred on June 6, 1812, as he stood (he says) on the banks of the Neman, watching the Grande Armée pass into Russia. This was at the triumphant beginning of Napoleon's Russian campaign, when there was no reason yet for despair. And yet, Stendhal wrote in this book (the manuscript of which, as it happens, he gathered together for the first time while he was in Lithuania, having brought it from Paris and worked on it steadily all the time he was serving in the Grande Armée)—and yet, he felt a certain sadness pass over him as he watched

> this innumerable army cross the river, one composed of so many peoples, and which was to suffer the most memorable defeat history can tell of. The glum future that I perceived in the depths of Russia's endless plains, together with our general's erratic genius, filled me with doubt. Wearied by these pointless conjectures, I turned my mind to positive thoughts, that faithful stay in all manner of fortune.

And so, as Stendhal often did when confronted by deep emotion, he abstracted himself from feeling into reflection. He thought, he tells us, about a certain book about the temperaments, by the natural philosopher Cabanis; and he decided, that bright June day in 1812, to think about the *sanguine* temperament, which he thought he could detect in the faces of the soldiers. "I sought out examples in the faces of the many soldiers who passed by me, singing and, occasionally, stopping for a moment when the bridge became too crowded." And what did he think he saw in those faces? "A brilliantly colored head," "an expression of gaiety," "a quite energetic heart": in sum, "great-heartedness."

In other words, a French heart. Which is to say that, at the very moment when he crossed the border into Asia, the moment when he had his presentiment of the devastation that this unknown and unknowable land, with the strange houri curves of the onion domes on its churches, the high cheekbones and the foreign slant of the eyes in the faces of the massed tribesmen who awaited him, he managed to find a bit of home. Brilliance, gaiety, energy.

I like the way Stendhal saves himself here: cools himself off, cocks an eyebrow at the passions (even his own; even as he secretly continues to harbor them), substitutes a book for an irrational presentiment. I love him for this, in a way I don't love any other author of the nineteenth century. Born in the last years of the 1700s, Stendhal seems always to be torn between an eighteenth-century predilection for rationality and a nineteenth-century Romantic feeling—a struggle in which the former often prevails. (See, for instance, how he finds more to admire in the wearily wise, middle-aged diplomat Count Mosca, my favorite character in *The Charterhouse of Parma*, than he does in Fabrice del Dongo, the novel's dashing, clueless hero.) The ability to impose coolness on the passions is the quintessence of Stendhal—may, indeed, be the quintessence of civilized behavior—and I find it interesting that he managed to do it on that sunny summer day in Vilna, before there is, really, any horror to contain. That, of course, would come later, five months and as many hundred thousand dead men later.

Interestingly, the memory of the Russian disaster furnishes another Stendhalian moment in which we find Vilna, horror, and beauty intertwined. There is a passage in *Rome, Naples and Florence* in which the Frenchman, finding himself in Milan on a November day in 1817—he will be attending a performance of an opera called *Maometto* at La Scala that very evening—describes what he refers to as one of the most beautiful sights he's ever enjoyed: the Alps, as seen from the bastion of Milan's Porta Nova. This moment of beauty leads him to a small excursus on the aesthetic merits of various mountain ranges. Stendhal writes that he finds the Italian view of the mountains—that is, the view from a distance—"as reassuring as Greek architecture"; but as seen in Switzerland, capped by snow, the same peaks inevitably put him in mind of "the failings of mankind."

Why should this be? Because he cannot bear the sight of snow. Why can he not? Because it reminds him of Vilna, of the freezing winter of 1812:

After the Russian campaign I couldn't bear snow—not because of my own perils but because of the spectacle [it presented] of pitilessness and horrible suffering. In Vilna they would fill the gaps in the

345

hospital walls with bits of frozen corpses. With such memories, how could one find pleasure in looking at snow?

Stendhal, as is widely known, is less than reliable in his memoirs. We know, for instance, that he cannot have witnessed the Grande Armée crossing the Neman in June 1812, since he wasn't there; and we know that if he saw this happen at all, which it's possible he never did, it would have been in August of that year. I mention this penchant for invented enhancement because of a detail found on this same page of the text of *Rome, Naples and Florence*, something that may be a lie or may be the truth—or, like a novel, may be a lie that tells the truth.

In this passage, the chilling description of that unforgettable horror—the use of bodies as *bricks*, an item in the imaginative inventory of the West that would not recur for another century and a half, when images of stiffened bodies stacked like logs or stones became commonplace—segues with seeming incongruity into a description of the writer's arrival, on the evening of the day on which he recalled that gruesome wartime vision, at La Scala. There he attends *Maometto*, an opera by a German composer, quite popular in his day and now largely forgotten, who was called Peter von Winter.

Was it really Winter's opera being performed that night, the night of the memory of Vilna in the winter of 1812? I like to think so, but it doesn't really bother me if it wasn't. Notice how the author (who knew English) goes out of his way, in this passage, to substitute one kind of cool—a redemptive musical beauty, authored by "Winter"— for the dreadful cold of Vilna, which forever after symbolized for him the worst horrors of war. Look again at the passage about mountain snows, and then push ahead a little bit:

With such memories, how could one find pleasure in looking at snow?

As I got out of the sedan chair, I went into the foyer of La Scala to hear the performance of *Maometto*, with music by Mr. Winter.

Has there ever been a more civilized paragraph break?

We left Vilna the day after the day of Ponar, the day of the Jewish museum. To calm me down, my friends insisted that we take a stroll around the city before going to the airport. I had barely slept; had sent unhappy e-mails to my friends back in New York, saying I couldn't go on; was planning to cut short the rest of this particular Eastern European trip. We had intended to go to Latvia the next day, where I was to meet a gentleman described to me as *the last Jew in the town*; his name, someone told me, was Mendelsohn. But I had had enough of meeting the last Jew in the towns through which I traveled; had had enough of Vilna in particular and everything it stood for.

So we walked glumly through the pastel city. Suddenly Froma, who had walked a bit farther up the street, and with whom I don't believe I've ever discussed my tastes in French literature, exclaimed. I saw her peering intently at a plaque affixed to the wall of an elegant building; then she turned to me and beckoned, as she so often did, to come, *come*. Thinking that she had, yet again, found some dire record of an unspeakable atrocity, I shook my head. But Froma called out again, and so, as I so often did, I relented. I approached the building and what I read was this:

IN THIS HOUSE
STENDHAL
THE FRENCH WRITER
(1783–1842)
STOPPED IN DECEMBER 1812
DURING THE PASSAGE
OF THE NAPOLEONIC ARMY

I burst into tears. The plaque is of stone, a pale berry color; the letters cut into it show gray. It was summer, not winter; but I too had made my stop in Vilna. Later that day, we passed into Latvia.

—*Revue du Stendhal Club*, 2012

The Countess and the Schoolboy

IN THE EARLY SPRING of 1985, after failing miserably at the first and only regular job that I have ever tried to hold, I left New York City to return to the southern town where I'd gone to college, and was there rescued from depression, or worse, by a French lady I knew who used to party with liveried monkeys.

I was barely twenty-five, and more or less a virgin—a nice Jewish boy from Long Island who still secretly thought that smoking Merits was pretty decadent. She was well into her seventh decade, a mother of three and grandmother of seven who counted among her relatives the Empress Josephine (*"ma cousine!"*) and had, among other things, danced with the Ballets Russe de Monte Carlo, had her legs appraised by Gary Cooper, attended one of Picasso's birthday parties, played Jane in a French adaptation of *Tarzan*, been around the world thirty-three times, and, most recently, taught disco dancing to the more open-minded citizens of Charlottesville, Virginia. She invited me to move in with her, and it was a good match. I accompanied her to the rock-and-roll clubs where she liked to dance. She made me a writer.

I'd met her a few years earlier, when I was a glum undergraduate classics major. At the time, I was sharing an off-campus apartment with my two closest friends, a pair of Tennesseans named Flip and Skip. Flip was tall and skinny and dark-haired, a notorious punster and inventive cook; Skip, who was blond and built like a football player, liked to read about military history while watching reruns of *The Love Boat*. I, meanwhile, moped, memorized Greek verbs, pretended to enjoy Andrew Marvell, and wrote feverishly every night in my journal, using a great many ampersands, which is what the British diarists I was reading just then did.

This might have gone on indefinitely if Flip, who tended to be smarter about me than I was, hadn't persuaded me to stay in Charlottesville the summer after our junior year and wait tables with him at the Hardware Store, an enormous family-style restaurant downtown where you could order beer by the meter and where the chicken nuggets were served on miniature wooden basketball courts.

It was on my second day at work, a Friday, that I met the woman who acted as hostess on weekend nights—the glamour shift: a deeply tanned redhead who favored long dresses in bold prints. The wife of a wealthy county squire, she had recently scandalized the local gentry by going out and getting a job. To the Virginia Department of Motor Vehicles she was known as Ghislaine Signard de Poyen Bellisle Neale; to a great many people in Virginia as "the countess of Charlottesville"; and to a slightly smaller number of people as Chouky, which was the nickname that her mother, a real countess, had given her long before, during the golden days on the Riviera between the wars—days of parties with the Fitzgeralds, of afternoons when her father would take the Duke and Duchess of Windsor riding, of evenings when Marlene Dietrich would be sitting at the next table at some charity ball, sleek as a snake in her midnight-blue sequins. "Chouky" because, when she was a child living in Antibes, she was mad for cream puffs, *choux*. "Like SHOE-key," she would yell at some handsome boy she'd just met on the dance floor, trying to make herself heard above the music. "Like SHOE and KEY." Then, giving up, she'd burst out laughing. In the remote rural hill country where she'd so improbably ended up, getting the Albemarle County locals to pronounce her name correctly was, she knew, a lost cause.

And so, in the summer of 1981, when I was twenty-one and pretty much everything I thought I knew about the world came out of a book, Chouky started to tell me about her life. On slow afternoons, before the dinner rush began, I'd find an excuse to move up toward the hostess' station and prod her to tell me her stories, and as she talked it occurred to me for the first time that the things I'd read about in novels actually happened to real people. But how to become one of those people?

As the hot months passed, I was able to piece her biography together. She was born near Paris, a city she never liked very much. "Too *gris*," she would say to me with a grim smile, as if gray Paris ought to have known better and perhaps found itself a more southerly location. What she liked were the tropics, the islands, places like Martinique, the ancestral homeland of her mother's family, the de Poyens and the de Beauharnais, who had banana plantations and, if you cared about such things, lofty relations. Her grandfather, the marquis de Poyen Bellisle, was the colonial governor of the island. Her great-grandmother was a first cousin of Napoleon's empress. Chouky didn't offer this information herself; I only figured out the Napoleonic connection after I had moved in with her and, one day, came across a beautifully calligraphed family tree hanging in an out-of-the-way downstairs hallway. At first I thought that the crown at the top was a calligrapher's pretension.

I had grown up among split-levels and "community pools"; from listening to Chouky talk about the people she'd known and the escapades they'd had, I derived a deep if vicarious sense of glamour, of importance. But when, at the end of a weekend dinner shift at the Hardware Store, I went to find her in her usual spot—she'd be sitting in a booth at the front, drinking her beer and eating her tongue sandwich (*"C'est de la langue!"* she'd say, giggling)—and tried to get her to talk about her illustrious relatives, her round face would curl into an impatient, exaggerated frown—an expression that those better acquainted with her than I was at the time knew was a danger sign. What she wanted to talk about was which clubs the better bands were likely to be playing at.

She loved to dance, and she loved parties. This, in a way, was what had brought her to the Hardware Store: all those young waiters. She couldn't bear sitting still. In the 1950s, the handsome Navy pilot she'd met and married after the war brought his bride home to his family's place, Rocklands, a four-thousand-acre estate about fifteen miles outside of Charlottesville, complete with neoclassical porticos and a lake. But the Virginia horse country and the proprieties observed by those who lived there soon bored Chouky. "So *English*," she'd say with disgust whenever she recalled those years. She grew restless. Her husband would fly her up to New York City so she could have her hair done at Elizabeth Arden.

One of the reasons she liked to party so much, I suspect, is that by the time she was my age, life had turned ugly. She shuddered whenever she talked about World War II—the "bad times." Throughout most of the war, she and her mother and her sister were alone;

her father, about whom she always spoke with the trace of a crush that a high-spirited girl might have on her dashing father, had spent much of the war in a German POW camp, a trauma she could never bring herself to describe to me in any detail. (Once, in 1985, I came home to the apartment we shared sporting a fashionably punky buzz cut. "You look like my fahzzer when he come home fwom ze camp," Chouky said, and went to her room to lie down.) For a time, she'd hidden her Jewish boyfriend in her parents' house—"So what? I was in love"—and so the three women had to flee, spending the rest of the war on the run. Eventually, Chouky became a black marketeer. She'd sometimes travel hundreds of miles to procure a ham, which she'd then hide under her coat, pretending to be pregnant.

At some point, she joined the Resistance as a courier. When she ferried messages, she'd carry a cyanide tablet between her teeth and gums. "If they would have take you and torture you," she told me one day, with her characteristic indifference to syntax, "you *talk*." She insisted that she was the model for the "bicycle girl" in *The Longest Day*—the courier who was stopped at a German checkpoint while cycling to a rendezvous, a crucial message folded into her newspaper. Before being searched, she handed the paper to the soldier who'd stopped her; he obligingly held it until the search was over, whereupon he returned it to her and she cycled off to safety. Twelve of her friends in the underground did not share her luck: "zey disappear." Sixty years later, Chouky would weep when she recited their names to me. On the other hand, she would laugh and clap when she told me the name of the first GI she met when the town where she and her sister and mother found themselves living at the end of the war was liberated. "Henry *Platt*," she'd cry, biting into the final consonants as if they were a stick of celery.

It was during the war, during clandestine meetings of her Resistance cell, that she developed the unconscious habit of swiftly counting to herself the number of people present at any gathering, to see if any were missing. Even when we lived together she'd do it. She'd say, for example, "Zat place was pack! Zere was sirty-eight people in zat bar!" It was also during the war, I suspect, that she developed her horror of explosive noises. Once, when I was in my late twenties and no longer living with her, I had a "fancy" party and was hurt when, after entering my apartment and seeing that I'd filled an entire room with balloons, she declared that she couldn't possibly stay.

I didn't want to hear about Chouky's war years back then; I wanted to hear about Jean Renoir, whose son she may or may not have dated, and Sidney Bechet, at whose wedding she had danced. I would be impressed by all this, and she would tell me pointedly that the only people she admired were those who'd accomplished something *interesting*. Who was interesting? Artists were interesting. Physicians were interesting—she was always impressed by doctors, and there'd invariably be one or two at her dinner parties. And above all, musicians and dancers were interesting. Chouky was a great keeper of scrapbooks, what she called *les livres de ma vie*, "the books of my life." When she was sixteen and opened her first dance studio, in Antibes, her mother presented her with a large leather notebook, and in that book she would make her pupils or friends or lovers write something to be remembered by. Many of the earlier inscriptions were, I noticed when leafing through these for the first time, in verse, dedicated to "*la Terpsichore moderne.*" Who were these people, I wondered, who could dash off rhyming alexandrines without a second thought?

Chouky herself acknowledged being proud of precisely two

accomplishments (that is, after her three children, whom she referred to as her *produits*, her products). One was her career as a dance instructor. The other was bridge. She was a Life Master, and taught the game over many decades to dozens, if not hundreds, of people. I was her worst student. The first summer I knew her, she would have three of us over to Rocklands once a week, me and two other waiters, to learn bridge on the *terrasse*, but my stupidity with numbers ultimately frustrated even her. *Tu joues comme un enfant de douze ans!* she cried one evening after I'd flubbed another bid; from that night on we agreed that I'd always be the dummy, and I was happy to sit at the other end of the terrace, smoking a cigarette and watching the sun go down over the Blue Ridge. I now see that Chouky was a superb bridge player for the same reason that she was an excellent flirt: she had a flair for games in which what you're allowed to say and what you need to communicate to your partner are two entirely different things. Sometimes, after I'd glumly plopped down on her sofa—a giant painting of floating babies, like the one at the end of *2001: A Space Odyssey*, hung over it—feeling defeated by yet another of my unrequited crushes on the UVA boys, Chouky would shake her head and frown, her eyes bugging out in amazed displeasure. "But it's a *game*. Why don't you play?! You're missing ze whole point."

By March 1985, when I moved back to Virginia from New York—on graduating from UVA I'd taken a job as a Guy Friday to a mad opera impresario, and after three years of cigar smoke and abuse I'd finally summoned the courage to quit—Chouky had divorced the handsome pilot and moved into a chic ground-floor condominium close to Charlottesville's old downtown. It was the kind of neighborhood that was just being gentrified, and where, consequently, you wouldn't expect to see a grandmother in her mid-sixties setting up house. I'd started waiting tables again at the Hardware Store, biding my time until I could figure out what my next move would be, and was sleeping on friends' futons. One day, after the lunch shift, Chouky came up to me and suggested that I move in with her. I think she was a little lonely, and I was broke and tired of futons, so I said yes. "We have *fun*," Chouky said.

I started to observe how she lived. The things that gave her the greatest pleasure were often small. She always set the table beautifully, even when she was eating alone; when she had large dinners, she'd put bits of amusing bric-a-brac at each setting, since "you must have somesing fun for your eyes as well as your mouse!" Even when she was very hard up for money, which she often was, she always had good bread and good butter on hand, excellent charcuterie, pastries, wine. Water, on the other hand, she abhorred. When well-meaning busboys approached her table with a glass she would make a tragic-mask face of horror and wave them away. "I don't like salad," she would say, "I don't like fruit, and I don't like water. But I do like *salami*." She drank very little, usually, although there were exceptions. I remember a weekend morning when I stumbled into the kitchen to find her standing at the counter, still in her famous "octopus" dress, grinding Tylenol into a small glass of Campari—her fix for a hangover.

When I first lived with her, I was anxious all the time about money, or boys, or my career options. As I complained, she'd look at me hard and then pointedly turn away, staring out the big plate-glass window that looked onto her tiny patio. "Zere is a squirrel!" she'd exclaim, navigating the consonants in that last word like a rower going over rapids, or, "Look! Ze *muguets*"—the lilies of the valley—"have finally bloom! Why aren't you looking at ze *squirrel*? Why aren't you looking at ze *flower*? Zey are so pwet-ty!"

After a while, when she was off somewhere—the swimming pool ("I do my lap every day!"), or Foods of All Nations, the only place she could get certain things that she liked to eat—I'd force myself, as if doing a physical exercise, to do as she did. I'd sit at the table and stare at the patio. Of course I felt foolish; it wasn't clear to me what was supposed to happen. What could she see in all this? But one day I found that I'd stopped thinking about what time it was, or what I needed to do with my life, and was actually just sitting there looking at the lilies of the valley. When she got back from her shopping trip, I told her about my little epiphany. She beamed.

"Dan-*iel*," she said, in her slightly croaking voice, pronouncing my name the French way, which is why, to this day, there are about two dozen or so Virginians who think my name is Danielle, "you *see*? You always are sinking about your life! But I sink about the *muguet*, and he make me happy."

She didn't let me stay home on weekend nights reading. Because she insisted that I take her dancing—straight clubs, gay clubs, tiny dives where rockabilly bands played, motel ballrooms where swing bands swang, she didn't really care—I started to dance, too. This, inevitably, led me to the next step, which was talking to people in strange places. She took me to my first gay dance at UVA, held in a building that was papered with notices for meetings of the Gay Student Union; I'd walked by it often but never had the courage to enter. One May night, she sent me home with a tall and wiry

Kentuckian who'd spent two hours fruitlessly smiling at me until Chouky marched me over to his car and introduced us. The Kentuckian's father did business in Asia; he had beautiful, beautiful kimonos hanging from bamboo rods along the walls of his bedroom. Above the bed was a woodblock print of squirrels huddling on a winter branch.

Chouky loved movies, but she wasn't much of a reader. When my first book, in which she is a character, came out—this was about fifteen years after we lived together—she stole a copy from the bookstore in downtown Charlottesville where I was doing a reading. ("I'm in it. Why I have to pay?!") A few weeks later, she called. "Well, I guess it's very *deep*," she said, and I suddenly had the sodden conviction that the whole thing was probably a pretentious mess. A few weeks later, a package arrived. Inside was a framed photograph of her, taken in Borneo, in 1967. In it, she stands in front of an enormous palm, hands at her hips, chic in a double-breasted linen suit. She looks as though she's ready to go somewhere. At the bottom of the photo, in her looping hand, is a dedication: "*Ta muse*, Chouky."

Whatever her impatience with books, Chouky certainly had what you could call a way with words. When she spoke English, it was with a French accent that seems to have thickened rather than eroded over the years. This was a subject of no little amusement, as much for her as for her friends. "Sometime, to make people understand me," she said to me a couple of years ago, her "S"es disappearing into whatever linguistic void French people's final consonants go when they die, "I have to *write* sing down!"

It was odd to hear this intensely French voice wrapping its guttural noises around Americanisms. She liked, for instance, to say "mom." She liked, even more, to say "gosh!" You could practically hear the exclamation points when she spoke, and she used them often in writing, too, as I learned when she showed me a journal she'd sporadically kept when she was living in Asia. "We made it!" she wrote when she first flew out to Borneo, at the beginning of 1967. "I just learnt yesterday that when we flew Tokyo–Hong Kong there were two MIG communist planes chasing us!" Or, "Forgot to say I went to Cambodia in the Spring and that was super!!" It was typical of her to forget the kinds of things that would be emblazoned on other people's memories for decades. Late one summer night a few years ago, she called me. She'd just been watching a show on the Biography channel. "Gosh!" she said. "I totally forgot I was at Rita Hayworss's wedding!"

It was from her journal that I learned that some tics weren't only oral. In writing, as in speaking, she often dropped the "-ed" in past participles. "A great adventure miles away from modern and advance America!" she wrote in one entry. In another: "Pooh is back! He was kidnap!" Most disconcerting, to people who weren't used to her, was the way she used "that" when native English speakers would use "this." She would say, for instance, "So zat man came up to me and say . . ." which had the subtle and, I sometimes think, not wholly unintentional effect of making you feel you'd lost the thread of some story you ought to have been following.

But then, to Chouky, everything was part of a bigger story that she'd been telling all along. This I only now realize, years after we first met at the hostess' stand and I didn't listen to what she was saying ("Let's go *dancing*!") because I wanted to hear what I thought was important about her; years after I moved in with her and scrutinized her family tree, only to realize that I should have been studying the squirrels; years after the last of her famous end-of-summer parties at Rocklands, parties to which five hundred people might come, in station wagons and limousines and helicopters, and the gardener would complain the next day that all the "lost" underwear was clogging the drain in the pool—this, I only now realize, was the lesson she was trying to teach. If you open yourself to the world, there will be stories to tell.

This brings me to the monkeys. One evening a year after she invited me to live with her—it was May, she was preparing a dinner in honor of a couple she knew ("two gynecologist!"), there were lilies of the valley on the table—she told me about the time years before when, on her way back to Singapore, she had a twelve-hour layover in Hong Kong. So she did what was, to her, the obvious thing, which was to ring up a race-car driver she knew and see what was going on. "As it *happen*," Chouky said a couple of years ago, when I made her tell me this story again—for of course in her universe things were always coincidentally linked, always happening—"he was just leaving for a party!" Naturally, he invited her along. She was only wearing traveling clothes, she recalled, but why not? When she and the racer showed up at the party—it turned out to be a birthday party for Michael Caine—there were the monkeys, in livery, handing glasses to the arriving guests. "*En livrée*," she cried, still amused. "*Avec du Champagne*! I could have die laughing!" She apologized to Mr. Caine for not having party clothes and danced with him anyway; then she zoomed back to the airport and made her plane home.

The last time I saw Chouky, she didn't recognize me at first. It was early in 2016, a few months before her ninety-fifth birthday; as I stood in the doorway of her room in the nursing home, she looked me up and down, put an imperious hand in the air, as if to bar the way to her half of the room, and said, "*No.*" I thought it was the dementia: her eldest daughter, whose name really is Danielle, had warned me that she had good days and bad days. But as I came closer the look of hostility melted into the smile I knew. "Oh, Dan-*iel*," she exclaimed. "I couldn't *see* you. Zey take away my glasses and never bring zem back!" After putting both hands to her head, as if to pouf up her hair, she burst into tears. Then, after a moment or two, she pulled herself together and glared at the woman in the next bed. "We used to live togezzer," she rasped, gripping my hand; from her gleeful emphasis on the word "together," I realized she was hoping to scandalize her neighbor. "He's a wrrriter, and one day he's going to tell about my life!"

—*The New Yorker*, June 6, 2017

A Critic's Manifesto

IN THE 1970s, when I was a teenager and had fantasies of growing up to be a writer, I didn't dream of being a novelist or a poet. I wanted to be a critic. I thought criticism was exciting, and I found critics admirable. This was because I learned from them. Every week a copy of *The New Yorker* would arrive at our house on Long Island, wrapped in a brown wrapper upon which the (I thought) disingenuously modest label *NEWSPAPER* was printed, and I would hijack the issue before my dad came home from work in order to continue an education that was, then, more important to me than the one I was getting in school.

I learned. I learned about music, particularly opera, from the fantastically detailed reviews by Andrew Porter, the music critic— mini-essays so encyclopedic in their grasp of this or that composer's oeuvre, so detailed in their descriptions of the libretto and score of the work in question, from Mozart to (a great favorite of his, I distinctly recall) Michael Tippett, that the review could be half over before he got around to talking about the performance under review. But this was the point: by the time he described what he'd seen on stage, you—the reader—had the background necessary to appreciate (or deprecate) the performance as he had described it. I learned about other things. Thanks to Helen Vendler, who in those days regularly contributed long and searching essays about contemporary poets and their work, I began to think about poetry, its aims and methods; and perceived, too, that good poetry ought to be able to withstand the kind of rigor that she brought to her discussion of it. (In those high school days, we thought that poetry was pretty much anything about "feelings.")

I was fascinated to see, too, that what I then thought of as less exalted forms of entertainment could be subject to the same erudite and penetrating discussions. Although there was only a tiny chance, in 1975, that I was going to spend an evening at the Algonquin or Carlyle, I always read Whitney Balliett's review of cabaret performances—of people singing the kind of music my dad liked to listen to on the car radio as he drove me to my weekly guitar lessons, the red bar of the car radio display unwaveringly loyal to Jonathan Schwartz's Frank Sinatra show. My parents' music, the Great American Songbook, had no particular interest for me just then, but I was provoked, by Balliett's quietly appreciative dissections of an evening of (say) Julie Wilson at the Algonquin, to think harder than I had previously done about what a song was, how it was made, what was the difference between a good lyric and a sloppy lyric, how best that lyric might be brought across in performance, and, finally, what effect it was supposed to have on you, the audience.

I would always save Pauline Kael for last, because I loved that she wrote the way most people talked; her now-famous second-personal-singular address made me feel included in her fierce and lengthy encomia or diatribes—and made me want to be smart enough to deserve that inclusion. And with Kael, too, I was startled and delighted to see that the kind of movies I saw with my friends (*Carrie*, say) could be the object of sustained, cantankerous, and searching critique.

In all the years I read these writers, as I went through high school and then college and grad school, it never occurred to me that they were trying to persuade me to actually see this or that performance, buy this or that volume, or take in this or that movie; nor did I imagine that I was being bullied or condescended to, or that I wasn't allowed to disagree with them. I thought of these writers above all as teachers, and like all good teachers they taught by example; the example that they set, week after week, was to recreate on the page the drama of how they had arrived at their judgments. (The word *critic*, as I later learned, comes from the Greek word for "judge.")

That drama, that process, it seemed to me as I read those critics (and, in time, others: Arlene Croce, when finally I began to appreciate dance; Arthur Danto on art in *The Nation*; some others), involved two crucial elements. The first was expertise. If Vendler was writing about the latest volume of poetry by, say, James Merrill, it was clear from her references that she'd read and thought about everything else Merrill had ever written; what you were getting in the review wasn't just an opinion about the book under review, but a way of seeing that book against all of the poet's other work. Ditto for the others. To read a review by Croce about this or that performance of a Balanchine ballet was to get a history of the work itself, a mini-tutorial in Balanchine technique, and a capsule history, for comparison's sake, of other significant performances of the same work. (Here again, the review was not merely building a case for Croce's final judgment but was also giving you, the reader, the tools to evaluate the description of the performance at hand.) Even when you disagreed with them, their judgments had authority, because they were grounded in something more concrete, more available to other people, than "feelings" or "impressions."

It wasn't that these people were PhDs, that the expertise and authority evident on every page of their writing derived from a diploma hanging on an office wall. I never knew, while reading Kael, whether she had a degree in Film Studies (even if I'd known such a thing existed back then), nor did I care; it never occurred to me that Whitney Balliett ought to have some kind of credential in order to pass judgment on Bobby Short singing "Just One of Those Things" at the Café Carlyle. You felt that their immense knowledge derived above all from their great love for the subject. I was raised by a scientist and a schoolteacher, and it was salutary for me to be reminded that authority could derive from passion, not a diploma.

Knowledge, then—however you got it—was clearly the crucial foundation of the judgment to come. The second crucial component in the drama of criticism, the reagent that got you from the knowledge to the judgment, was taste, or sensibility—whatever it was in the critic's temperament or intellect or personality that the piece in question worked *on*. From this, as much as from anything else, I learned a great deal. (For one thing, it was clear that taste itself could be a mystery: I tried and failed for years to love Michael Tippett's operas, and could never quite follow Kael to the altar of Brian De Palma.)

More largely, and ultimately more important, the glimpses these writers gave you of their tastes and passions revealed what art and culture are supposed to do for a person. I still remember a review by Porter of a production of Mozart's *Cosi fan tutte*—this must have been in the late 1970s or early 1980s—in which he wrote that the fleetingly bewildered expression on the face of the Swedish soprano Elisabeth Söderström during the banquet scene in the second act had made him weep, because it suggested, economically but with tremendous impact, the darkness that lies at the heart of that, and all, comedy. I recall being a little shocked as I read the piece that a grown man could admit in public to being moved to tears by a performance of an old opera.

I remember something that Vendler wrote years later in a piece about a volume of Merrill's work that was published after the poet's death, at the relatively early age of sixty-eight—about how, now that Merrill was gone, he wouldn't be around to show her how to grow old. I read this with astonishment. So this was what poetry was for: to show you how to *live*. As for Kael, the sheer excessiveness of her enthusiasms, the ornery stylistic overseasoning, the grandiose swooping pronouncements, made it clear that there was something enormous at stake when you went to the local movie theater. That, too, opened my eyes wider.

By dramatizing their own thinking on the page, by revealing the basis of their judgments and letting you glimpse the mechanisms by which they exercised their (individual, personal, quirky) taste, all these critics were, necessarily, implying that you could arrive at your own, quite different judgments—that a given work could operate on your own sensibility in a different way. What I was really learning from those critics each week was how to think. How to think (we use the term so often that we barely realize what we're saying) *critically*—which is to say, how to think like a critic, how to judge things for myself. To think is to make judgments based on knowledge: period.

For all criticism is based on that equation: KNOWLEDGE + TASTE = MEANINGFUL JUDGMENT. The key word here is *meaningful*. People who have strong reactions to a work—and most of us do—but don't possess the erudition that can give an opinion heft, are not critics. (This is why a great deal of online reviewing by readers isn't criticism proper.) Nor are those who have tremendous erudition but lack the taste or temperament that could give their judgment authority in the eyes of other people, people who are not experts. (This is why so many academic scholars aren't good at reviewing for mainstream audiences.) Like any other kind of writing, criticism is a genre that one has to have a knack for, and the people who have a knack for it are those whose knowledge intersects interestingly and persuasively with their taste. In the end, the critic is someone who, when his knowledge, operated on by his taste in the presence of some new example of the genre he's interested in—a new TV series, a movie, an opera or ballet or book—hungers to make sense of that new thing, to analyze it, interpret it, make it *mean* something.

And so I dreamed of becoming a critic. Sometimes when I'm talking about the writing life with someone, it becomes clear that they think criticism is some kind of day job (as opposed to my books, which, they imply, are "real" writing). To me, it's the main event.

The above considerations seemed to me worth rehearsing just now because there has been very little mention of what I see as the crucial role of the critic and the crucial function of criticism in some heated discussions about these questions that have appeared lately in print and online. The publication, a few weeks ago, in *The New York Times Book Review*, of two flamboyantly negative reviews of works with serious literary aspirations—one, by William Giraldi, of two volumes of fiction by Alix Ohlin; the other, by Ron Powers, of the most recent novel by Dale Peck (a writer who gained considerable notoriety for his own "hatchet jobs" of other people's work)—triggered a storm of protests, congratulations, and general commentary about the place of critics and criticism in popular literary culture. The storm is a good thing: at no point since the invention of the printing press, perhaps, has the nature of literary culture, and the activities of its practitioners—authors, critics, publishers—been in such a state of flux. The flux is both fascinating and destabilizing for those of us who grew up in the waning days of "old" literary culture, and the changes resulting from are it likely to be permanent and far-ranging.

Two phenomena related to the advent of the Internet have transformed our thinking about reviewing and criticism in particular. First, there has been the explosion of criticism and reviews by ordinary readers, in forums ranging from the simple rating (by means of stars, or tomatoes, or whatever) of books on sites such as Amazon .com to serious long-form review-essays by deeply committed lit bloggers. Which is to say that, for the first time, ordinary readers (or ballet fans or architecture aficionados) have been able to express their opinions about books (or ballet, or architecture) publicly. This development inevitably raises questions about the role of the traditional critic. ("Why should we listen to X, when we can say what we think?") Second, and more recently, the advent of social media— Facebook, for instance, with the possibility it offers of "liking" but not "disliking"; Twitter, which lends itself so easily to vacuous promotional exchanges of likes, links, and "favorites"—has created an environment of what the journalist Jacob Silverman, in an article for *Slate* called "Against Enthusiasm" (another cloudburst in the recent storm) has called "solicitous communalism"—an atmosphere not conducive to serious engagement.

But just what is "serious engagement"? One of the main points of the controversy that has arisen since the two *Times Book Review* reviews has been, indeed, about the relative merits of positive and negative reviewing. Silverman, along with the *Times* daily book critic Dwight Garner, has argued for the vivifying role of negative reviews, which, as Silverman put it, make for a "vibrant, useful literary culture." Against them have been ranged an array of prominent journalists and critics. One amusing response was that of Jane Hu, in *The Awl*, which took the form of a brief history of the "criticism used to be much tougher and more incisive" trope in contemporary literary debate—a line, as she slyly shows, that is at least as old as the "golden age" of feisty book reviewing about which writers like Silverman and Garner are so nostalgic.

Others opposed to negative reviewing include Laura Miller, a founder of *Salon* and now a columnist for *Slate*, whose argument arises from her conviction that ordinary readers don't really care about literary culture—that there's no longer a cultural setting in which a negative review could really matter. "Since the average new book is invisible to the average reader," she writes, "critics who have a choice usually prefer to call attention to books they find praiseworthy." She contrasts with this a negative review of a popular TV series, which, she argues, can mean something in the wider world. Another is Richard Brody, a *New Yorker* film critic and biographer of Jean-Luc Godard, who takes a high Romantic vision of authors and *auteurs* as promethean heroes of creativity, against whom critics are seen as mere "parasites" whose work "depends not only on the activity of others…but on the *greater activity of others*" (italics mine)—vultures whose gnawing at the entrails comes "not in the spirit of" but "at the expense of art." Lev Grossman, the *Time* magazine book critic, cited—facetiously, you can only hope—his reluctance to run into victims of bad reviews at parties as a reason he has been avoiding negative criticism.

These critics are motivated by lively and serious concerns, some of them abstract, some practical: Garner's and Silverman's desire for lively literary debate, Miller's commitment to publishing criticism that people will actually read, and Brody's passionate worry that glib negativity can have destructive effects on the career of serious artists. But some of these concerns—not least, the dilemma of how to steer between the Scylla of vapid negativity and the Charybdis of vacuous cheerleading—become moot when you think back to the impulse that lies behind serious criticism: the impulse to analyze, to explain, to teach, to judge meaningfully.

The serious critic cannot be a monomaniacal controversialist. Hatchet jobs, especially when directed at overhyped and unworthy objects, can be both entertaining and useful. Particularly in a culture that is awash in hype and promotion (both professional and, as Garner and Silverman pointed out, amateur—the culture of reflexive boosterism), a vital function of the critic is to peel away the swoony publisher's hype, the self-congratulation of an author's Twitter feed, and to reorient the conversation to where it belongs: the work and its merits and flaws, as judged against genuine knowledge and disinterested taste. That said, if hatchet jobs are all you write, your audience will soon perceive that the writing is somehow about *you*— your enjoyment of ridicule or nasty flamboyance or snark—and not about the work. There is usually something to like in even the weakest work, just as there is nearly always some weakness in the strongest work. Most reviews should be mixed. It's a sign of how harmful the culture of reflexive "liking" has become that what are, in fact, mixed reviews are denounced as if they were hatchet jobs.

Serious critics, as Brody rightly pointed out, should first of all *self-criticize*: they should begin by examining their own reactions, when these reactions are negative, and determine that they are legitimate—which is to say, should avoid writing about things or artists for whom they have a distaste that is not motivated by aesthetic considerations. (Serious editors, I should add, will not assign a review to a writer when there is reason to suspect personal animus. Many readers who are ignorant of the mechanics of journalism are unaware of the extent to which editors are responsible for the assignment of reviews; unaware, too, that reviewers have no say in the timing of publication. What often look like calculated "takedowns" of popular and critically lauded works—negative reviews published long after the positive ones have come in—were written months in advance, just as the positive ones were.)

Serious critics, however, can't merely be ecstatic initiates either, whose worship of Art and *artistes* can threaten to devolve into flaccid cheerleading. The negative review, after all, is also a form of enthusiasm; enthusiasm and passion for the genre that, in this particular instance, the reviewer feels has been let down by the work in question. The intelligent negative review does its own kind of honor to artists: serious artists, in my experience, want to be reviewed intelligently, rather than showered with vacuous raves—not least because serious artists learn from serious reviews. (The best advice I ever got, right before the publication of my first book, was from a publishing mentor who told me, "The only thing worse than a stupid bad review is a stupid good review." And he was right.) For this reason, any call to eliminate negative reviewing is to infringe catastrophically on the larger project of criticism. If a critic takes seriously the obligation to pass judgments—which, merely statistically, are likely to have to be negative as well as positive—a sense of responsibility to those judgments and their significance has to outweigh all other considerations. People who want to go to lots of parties without provoking awkward literary encounters should be caterers, not critics.

Serious critics ultimately love their subject more than they love their readers—a consideration that brings you to the question of what ought to be reviewed in the first place. When you write criticism about literature or any other subject, you're writing *for* literature or that subject, even more than you're writing for your reader: you're adding to the accumulated sum of things that have been said about your subject over the years. If the subject is an interesting one, that's a worthy project. Because the serious literary critic (or dance critic, or music critic) loves the subject above anything else, that critic will review, either negatively or positively, those works of literature or dance or music—high and low, rarefied and popular, celebrated and neglected—that the critic finds worthy of examination, analysis, and interpretation. To set interesting works before intelligent audiences does honor to the *subject*. If you only write about what you think people are interested in, you fail your subject—and fail your readers, too, who may well be happy to encounter something they wouldn't have chosen for themselves. I hate to think of the things I would have missed, when I was a teenager, if the editors of certain magazines and newspapers, back in the 1970s and 1980s, had agreed with Laura Miller.

The role of the critic, I repeat, is to mediate intelligently and stylishly between a work and its audience; to educate and edify in an engaging and, preferably, entertaining way. (Critics, more than any other kind of writer, should have a sense of humor.) For this reason I can't accept Richard Brody's dismissive characterization of critics as harmful parasites—a characterization that unhappily contributes to a widespread misconception (of the equally specious "those who can't do, teach" variety) that critics are motivated by "rage and envy" of those "greater" writers—poets, novelists—on whose work they prey because they themselves are incapable of producing real "creative" work. This is how a (young, to be fair) Dave Eggers put it in a 2000 interview in *The Harvard Advocate*—a piece quoted by Dwight Garner in his recent *Times* article in favor of negative criticism. Eggers went on, "Do not dismiss a book until you have written one, and do not dismiss a movie until you have made one."

This superficially appealing notion is one you often encounter when people disagree with professional critics—as if expertise, authority, and taste were available only to practitioners of a given genre. But to say that critics have no right to review a novel because they've never written one is a dangerous notion, because it strikes at the heart of the idea of expertise (and scholarship, and judgment) itself—it's like telling a doctor that he can't diagnose a disease because he's never had it, or a judge that she can't hand down a sentence because she's never murdered anyone. The fact is that criticism is its own genre, a legitimate undertaking in its own right, as creative in its way as any other.

And so (to invoke the popular saying) everyone is *not* a critic. This, in the end, may be the crux of the problem, and may help explain the unusual degree of violence in the reaction to those stridently negative reviews that appeared in the *Times Book Review* earlier this summer, triggering the heated debate about critics. In an essay about phony memoirs that I wrote a few years ago, I argued

that great anger expressed against authors and publishers when traditionally published memoirs turn out to be phony was a kind of
cultural displacement: what has made us all anxious about truth and
accuracy in personal narrative is not so much the published memoirs
that turn out to be false or exaggerated but rather the unprecedented
explosion of personal writing (and inaccuracy and falsehood) online,
in websites and blogs and anonymous commentary—forums where
there are no editors and fact-checkers and publishers to point an
accusing finger at.

Similarly, I wonder whether the recent storm of discussion about
criticism, the flurry of anxiety and debate about the proper place of
positive and negative reviewing in the literary world, isn't a by-
product of the fact that criticism, in a way unimaginable even twenty
years ago, has been taken out of the hands of the people who should
be practicing it: people who, among other things, know precisely
how to wield a deadly zinger, and to what uses it is properly put.
When, after hearing about them, I first read the reviews of Peck's
and Ohlin's works, I had to laugh. Even the worst of the disparage-
ments wielded by the reviewers in question paled in comparison to
the groundless vituperation and ad hominem abuse you regularly
encounter in Amazon reviews or the comments sections of literary
publications. Or indeed, everywhere else. If we're so sensitive to
mean-spirited attacks these days, it may be because most of the people carrying them out aren't real critics at all.

—*The New Yorker*, Page-Turner, August 28, 2012

Acknowledgments

NEARLY ALL OF THE PIECES collected here were originally written for *The New York Review of Books* and *The New Yorker*, and my first debt of thanks is due above all to my editors at those publications: the late Robert B. Silvers, a great mentor and beloved friend whose guidance and inspiration I continue to miss sorely, and Leo Carey, on whose taste, humor, good sense, and erudition I rely so greatly. Other editors whose inspiration and guidance resulted in work that is collected here are Sasha Weiss and Emily Eakin. Tremendous gratitude is also due to two great friends who have been my unofficial editors for a long time now, and without whom I would be lost: Bob Gottlieb and Chip McGrath. And above all, to Michael Shae, my editor at New York Review Books, who has now for the second time placed his discriminating eye and scalpel-sharp red pen at the service of shaping a collection of mine—this time during a period when I know he had very little time to spare.

Apropos of *The New York Review of Books*, which more than any other publication has been my home: no record of thanks would be complete without a word of deep appreciation to the editors, editorial assistants, and interns who have also been instrumental over the years in helping my pieces into existence, from ordering books to honing the prose to taking hair-raisingly complex galley corrections at one in the morning. Their names are too numerous to list here, but they know who they are. As they also know, I have tried to mark my gratitude in the sweetest way I know, but this time, I thought they deserved to be recognized in the medium with which they have helped me so greatly: print.

Finally, a word about the dedicatee of this volume. When I began writing thirty years ago—first for the Princeton student newspapers and magazines, and then for *QW* and *NYQ* and *The Nation* and *The Village Voice*, the beginning of what turned out to be my career—my first reader was always Lily, whose intellectual acuity, ethical rigor, and literary taste were instrumental in making both the pieces and the writer better. We have been partners in many ways since then, but whenever I think of those early days, I think of her and am grateful for everything that she's given me.